ALSO BY
JENNIFER KEISHIN ARMSTRONG

Seinfeldia

Mary and Lou and Rhoda and Ted

Sexy Feminism
(with Heather Wood Rudúlph)

Why? Because We Still Like You

SEX AND THE CITY

and Us

How Four Single Women Changed
the Way We Think, Live, and Love

. . . .

JENNIFER KEISHIN ARMSTRONG

Simon & Schuster

New York   London   Toronto   Sydney   New Delhi

Simon & Schuster
1230 Avenue of the Americas
New York, NY 10020

First Simon & Schuster hardcover edition June 2018

SIMON & SCHUSTER and colophon are registered trademarks
of Simon & Schuster, Inc.

For information about special discounts for bulk purchases,
please contact Simon & Schuster Special Sales at 1-866-506-1949
or business@simonandschuster.com.

The Simon & Schuster Speakers Bureau can bring authors to
your live event. For more information or to book an event, contact the
Simon & Schuster Speakers Bureau at 1-866-248-3049 or visit
our website at www.simonspeakers.com.

Interior design by Lewelin Polanco

Manufactured in the United States of America

1   3   5   7   9   10   8   6   4   2

Library of Congress Cataloging-in-Publication Data is available.

ISBN 978-1-5011-6482-8
ISBN 978-1-5011-6484-2 (ebook)

For my father, who definitely did not watch *Sex and the City*, but who would nonetheless have read every word here and gone to every book event he could and bought copies for everyone he knew.

Contents

NOTE ON REPORTING METHODS   xi

INTRODUCTION   xiii

1. The Real Carrie Bradshaw   1

2. A New Kind of TV Woman   23

3. Building *Sex and the City*'s New York   49

4. The Show Everyone Wants to Live In   75

5. A Very High Altitude   101

6. Shopping and Fucking   123

Contents

7. Van Talk, Real Talk   139

8. 9/11 Hits Home   155

9. Happy Endings   169

10. Ever Thine, Ever Mine, Ever Ours   191

ACKNOWLEDGMENTS   215

SOURCE NOTES   217

INTERVIEW LIST   231

Note on Reporting Methods

The following narrative scenes are re-created with the help of original interviews with those who were present, as well as accounts from newspapers, books, magazines, recorded interviews, and other research materials. I've indicated within the text, when necessary, who is doing the recounting. Scenes were checked by multiple sources when possible; dialogue comes from the accounts of those who were present. Full notes on specific sourcing are available at the end of the book.

Introduction

I left my fiancé for *Sex and the City*.

At the time, in the early 2000s, I was in my late twenties. I didn't know who I was, and it showed. One day I was wearing a striped sweater and beige slacks, purchased from a mall near where I lived in suburban New Jersey, to work at my magazine job in nearby New York City; the next day I was buying black spiky heels, a hot-pink miniskirt, and a black T-shirt from a thrift store in the city's punk-rock-steeped East Village neighborhood. I even recall a one-month hippie phase with faded jeans, fringed belts, and off-the-shoulder peasant shirts that I thought were particularly cool to wear to literary readings in dark downtown bars. Very Joan Didion.

I lead with the clothes because *Sex and the City* demonstrated how much they can mean. They indicated, for me, that so much was wrong, but that something right wanted to emerge. I was trying on selves. I was searching for an identity beyond what my upbringing in the Chicago suburbs, as the child of a dad who went to an office every day and a mom who stayed home with my younger brother and sister and me, presented as my ready-to-wear options: girlfriend, wife, or mother. I wanted a nameplate necklace like Carrie Bradshaw's and a distinct, authentic, messy identity to go with it. *Sex and the City* helped me find myself.

I fell for the show immediately when it premiered on HBO in the summer of 1998. As a TV nerd, I watched from the beginning; I read my *Entertainment Weekly* and other pop culture magazines dutifully, and the hype told me to pay attention to this one. The show followed four New York women through their simultaneously harrowing and glamorous dating lives. Carrie, who writes a sex-and-relationships column for a New York newspaper, narrates with excessive punning and digestible insight into modern single life. Charlotte longs for a traditionally romantic handsome prince, a type conspicuously absent from the Manhattan dating pool. Miranda prefers to focus on her career as a lawyer and make wisecracks rather than actively pursue the frustration of dating. And Samantha, the oldest of the four, has long since turned off her romantic longings in favor of sexual conquest.

Their stories started out simple: Carrie experiments with unattached sex. Miranda dates Carrie's younger beta-male friend, Skipper. Charlotte meets a guy she likes until he requests anal sex. Samantha hooks up with a serial "modelizer" who fetishizes fashion glamazons. As a woman still in her twenties who was living in the suburbs of Chicago and had slept with only one man total, I was entranced. On one level, I coveted the life they were depicting, and on another, I was happy not to be facing such a scary landscape: the sex part *and* the city part.

My fear would, however, eventually give way to a longing for a larger life like that depicted on the show—and this shift would mark the biggest turning point in my adult life. This impact of what many have derided as a featherweight TV show is what, nearly twenty years later, inspired me to find out how author Candace Bushnell, and then a group of writers and producers, turned their own life stories into a show that could so profoundly affect others' lives. In this book, I will share that story—all of those stories—with you.

But first, I want to give credit where it's due and tell you how *Sex and the City* helped to change my life. My college boyfriend and I moved to the New York City area together in 2001, from my hometown of Chicago. Our relationship thus far looked exactly the way I, as a white, suburban, Midwestern girl, was taught life should go. This was the third time I moved to accommodate his career, and I figured this time would pay off in an engagement, marriage, and happily-ever-after. I was an overachiever, and had always assumed those milestones came as part of the adult prize package I was working toward.

In New York City, I would pursue my professional dream, a job at a national magazine—and being close to the dreamy cityscape I'd seen depicted on the first three and a half seasons of *Sex and the City* wouldn't hurt. The show reached the heights of its powers in its fourth season that year, sending out a siren song to independent women throughout America: Come to New York, and your fantasy life will follow. I wasn't deluded about this; I didn't expect to instantly land a high-paying job as a sex columnist at a New York newspaper and find myself walking red carpets like Carrie. I just thought it would be fun to, say, walk past a cool new restaurant and see a glamorous party going on inside, or sip a cosmopolitan at a bar featured on the show, or enjoy a cupcake at Magnolia Bakery in the West Village like Carrie and Miranda did.

Mr. College and I bought a condo in Edgewater, New Jersey, just across the Hudson River from Manhattan. To be more precise, *he* bought us that condo. I didn't have a job yet. He got there a few weeks before I did. And between the time he moved there and I arrived, terrorists crashed two airplanes into the Twin Towers of Lower Manhattan, devastating all Americans' sense of security. But I went to the region anyway, fueled by love and the determination to work in national magazines, almost all of which were based in New York City. I knew I'd made the right decision when I saw the Manhattan skyline, the one I'd seen on *Sex and the City* and a million other TV shows, shimmering on the horizon as I approached on the New Jersey Turnpike. Smoke was still rising from the ruins of the Twin Towers. Ryan Adams sang, "Hell,

I still love you, New York," from the stereo in my Saturn. I already felt a connection to my ailing new city.

During my first few weeks there, the New York City region displayed its courage and its kindness, qualities always lurking beneath its tough exterior. The closer you were to the site of the attacks, the gentler people spoke, the more eager they were to help with the most basic questions from a New York City novice. "No, this subway is not headed uptown, it's headed to Brooklyn." "No, that's the East River, not the Hudson."

Two months and five interviews later, I got a job offer: I would be an editorial assistant at *Entertainment Weekly*, the publication I'd declared to be my dream job in college. I had hoped for such fortune, but I hadn't *expected* it. My perspective began to shift. Perhaps a life like Carrie's wasn't as far out of reach as I'd thought.

That fall, Mr. College arranged with my boss at *Entertainment Weekly* to get me the day off, then whisked me away on a surprise trip to Disney World, where, as fireworks exploded above the park's man-made lagoon, Mr. College got down on one knee and proposed. I don't remember much else, but I must have said yes, because I ended up with a one-carat-diamond-and-white-gold ring on my finger. The next week at work, my left hand shook with excitement as I showed it off and recounted the proposal to my new coworkers.

But in the months that followed, my infatuation with the ring cooled, while my passion for the city flourished. I met Heather, a tall blonde whose looks—and high-heeled sandals—announced from a distance that she was a Los Angeles transplant. Over sandwiches and iced tea, we discovered how much we had in common: blossoming feminist beliefs, an ambition to take over the world with our writing, and on-again, off-again long-term relationships that had dominated our young-adult lives. She was off again, and able to explore a new life in New York.

Surprised to find myself envious of her freedom, I dipped my toe into her life to see what it was like. We sipped white wine night after night at whatever downtown bar we decided was cool that week. Any place that appeared on *Sex and the City* shot to the top of our list. We lunched at Cafeteria, the slick Chelsea site of most of the show's brunch scenes. When her sort-of ex came into town for a visit, we double dated at Sushi Samba, the West Village hot spot where a reservation was portrayed as a status symbol on the show.

Sex and the City became my oracle. I had watched since the beginning, but now the show provided a guide to what I should or could do, wear, eat, and buy to fit into my new hometown—or at least the big city *across the river* from my new hometown. I honestly had no idea where to go or what to do in this overwhelming place, where walking down just one block looking for a restaurant for dinner could send a typical suburbanite into an existential crisis of indecision.

I spent many nights on Heather's fold-out sofa bed in her East Village studio apartment, giddy the next morning to take the subway to work instead of the New Jersey bus in through the Lincoln Tunnel. The city had more young men—so many of them sexy and smart—than I had ever seen in one place. And so many more of them were interested in me than I'd expected. Back home in the Midwest, twenty-eight put you well past marriage age. In New York, it seemed possible I was just getting started. *Sex and the City* showed me that not only was I still young, I was also under no obligation to get married *at all*.

As my doubts about my engagement grew, one scene from the show returned to me. In season 4, Carrie finds an engagement ring—meant for her—in her boyfriend Aidan's bag. She runs to the bathroom to vomit. Later, she recounts to her friends, "I saw the ring and I threw up. That's not normal."

Her friend Samantha replies, "That's *my* reaction to marriage."

I wondered if I had given up my own dreams of sex and the city too soon. I had had sex with one man, my fiancé. And now that I spent so much time in The City, I understood why it went with The Sex. Attractive, interesting people ornamented every street, every subway, every bar. Like so many new New Yorkers before me, I found myself enchanted by almost every second of my experience, like some manic Disney princess in a mystical kingdom. That man in the subway station who was painted silver and acted like a robot: Why did he do that? What was his life like? That woman who ranted in Times Square about the end of the world: Why did her words seem aimed right at me, as if she questioned whether I, specifically, was living my life to the fullest? And would that cute guy on the subway come over and talk to me? Should I walk over and talk to him instead? I didn't. I didn't have the guts yet. But I felt like I might have the guts eventually.

Everything, in short, conspired to make me feel like the Carrie Bradshaw of my own life, a heroine for whom the entire city was working to create a more interesting narrative. I had grown up in an average suburb of Chicago called Homer Glen, full of strip malls and cornfields that would soon become strip malls. I had idolized Belle in Disney's *Beauty and the Beast*. I loved all of the so-called Disney princesses—Cinderella, Snow White, *The Little Mermaid*'s Ariel—because I had grown up a *Sex and the City* Charlotte, sure my prince would come and grant me the happiness I had earned through working hard and being good. But I liked bookish Belle best of all, particularly the refrain of her movie's opening song: "There must be more than this provincial life."

I had found my "more" and had begun my transformation from a suburban Charlotte into a metropolitan Carrie.

• • •

What became clear to me right around this time, as I explored the possibilities of New York City, was that I had missed sign after sign that Mr. College and I didn't belong together. We ate dinner separately, each fixing our own little meal at different times, even if we were both home in the evening. He pushed me to wear revealing clothes that made me uncomfortable—short shorts, microminis—and accused me of not caring about his sexual needs when I refused. I was scared to voice even my most basic concerns, like wanting to go out on a Friday night instead of staying in to watch *Star Trek: The Next Generation* reruns with him, because I thought the confrontation would somehow lead us to break up. I had been attached to him my entire adult life and had no idea what would happen if I removed him from the equation, so I kept him in it.

Instead of facing my concerns, I spent even more time in the city. I met a twenty-three-year-old wunderkind male novelist with soulful hazel eyes who smelled like fresh laundry and was happy to encourage my own author dreams over too many watermelon margaritas. Now *this* was the kind of thing that happened on *Sex and the City*. Carrie had dated a few younger men, and it had gone badly, but no matter: Our meetings became regular, almost weekly, and stretched from happy hour until midnight. They looked and functioned a lot like dates, and they were hardly the right way for me to handle my fraying engagement, but I soaked up the attention Author Boy gave me.

These emotional cul-de-sacs are where you can end up if you see marriage as obligatory, as the only way to be an adult. My grandmother used to say, "If a man asks you to marry him, *you say yes*." My mom and I laughed at Grandma's throwback sexism without thinking about where it came from: My grandmother was a Russian immigrant who had been allowed to advance only to a fourth-grade-level education in America; for her, a good marriage meant survival. For my mother, it meant at least security. I hadn't thought a lot yet about what it meant to me, and yet I was following Grandma's order, just as my mother had. But *Sex and the City* mapped a way out for me with its vision of women in their thirties living carefree, successful lives without husbands or children.

Mr. College knew by now that I had doubts about our impending marriage. I had at least managed to voice some hesitation, spurred by his questions about Author Boy. Nearly every Sunday night, my fiancé and I sat out on our terrace, looked at the George Washington Bridge, and talked. I even declared my intention to leave, though I wasn't as decisive as I should have been. What I did was closer to asking if I could leave. I wanted his approval; I wanted it to be mutual and easy.

He would counter with logical arguments: We already had all this furniture together. We had known each other for so long. Did I even have enough money to live on my own?

One day, after months of these talks, I moved my ring from my finger to a silver chain around my neck. I explained this to Mr. College by citing the episode in which Carrie does the same with the engagement ring given to her by sexy furniture-maker Aidan. I even quoted her: "It's closer to my heart this way." We both pretended this was fine. We both pretended Aidan and Carrie hadn't long since broken up.

When others noticed—and they did—I said the same thing. My coworkers at *Entertainment Weekly* didn't miss a beat. They nodded solemnly. They didn't have to pretend not to get it. They covered entertainment for a living, after all. They knew their *Sex and the City*.

I had said during those Sunday night talks that one problem was that I wanted to live in the city. This was true. But I also didn't want him in my city life. I thought I was finally forcing a breakup. Instead, he bought a $600,000 condo on the Upper West Side.

You never know what that final blow will be. You never know why that moment is the moment and not some other moment. Mine came about three months after we moved into the new apartment, an eon later than would have been ideal. I looked around at our gleaming wood floors and the monstrous TV and the gorgeous Craftsman-style bookshelves filled with my books and felt crushed by the weight of it all. I was lucky by my grandmother's standards, but this was not what I wanted. What would come next in our attempt to construct what looked like a successful life as a couple? If I stayed with him now because of the condo, soon maybe we'd get a dog that would bind us together more. And he was already lobbying for kids.

Then a thought, the clearest one I'd had in months: *Even if we stayed together for all of that, we'd still get divorced in the end.* I knew this was true. In the future we could be divorced people fighting over condos and dogs and kids. Or we could deal with it and be broken-up people in the present.

Introduction

I packed enough to fit into one rolling suitcase and left the rest. I sat Mr. College down on our plush beige sofa on a Sunday night and told him this was a different kind of talk. I had to leave now. Time slowed down to about one-thousandth speed as I took the ring off and my hand moved toward the coffee table to place it there.

Sex and the City had ended the previous year. My *Sex and the City* had just begun.

• • •

I wasn't the only one who took this TV show so seriously that it changed my life. Women and men far beyond New York City took its lessons to heart. *Sex and the City* changed lives across the gender spectrum, across the sexual orientation spectrum, and around the world. It affected lives in ways both personal, like my story, and global. It changed the way we thought about women and sex, the way we talked about sex, the way we dated, married, or didn't. It did this for those who watched, of course, but even for those who didn't; it reshaped the cultural perception of single women, sex, dating, and marriage, spreading from viewers themselves to a large swath of America and beyond. It directed the way many women dressed, elevated drinking culture to a social obligation in some circles, and foisted brunch upon an unsuspecting nation. Most of all, it demonstrated that life-changing love comes in forms besides heterosexual marriage and nuclear family; it showed single people that friends could be at least as supportive as family, at least as important as a spouse.

It did all of this by telling stories. Specifically, by telling the stories of women—and a few gay men—on their own terms, in ways that had long been verboten in popular culture. *Sex and the City* began with Candace Bushnell's *New York Observer* column in 1994, in which she shared the secrets of her own love life and that of her party-happy, image-conscious Manhattan circles. The column became a book, and then the television show known across the world, all the while written by women and gay men whose stories came to us via the glamorous, emotional, bitter, and sweet adventures of sex columnist Carrie Bradshaw and her friends: romantic Charlotte, tough-minded Miranda, and sexually adventurous Samantha.

In *Sex and the City and Us*, I tell the stories behind those stories. While my own narrative demonstrates that I am a *Sex and the City* acolyte, throughout the rest of this book I draw on my experience as a television historian to trace the tale of how Bushnell's column became a book, a show, a pop culture phenomenon, a lifestyle, an economy, a commercial for the shiny new New York, and a love letter to post-9/11 New York. It was a deeply flawed work when it came to race and class issues, but it was a significant piece of television history—and its own debatable form of feminist manifesto.

Sex and the City and Us shows how a group of women and gay men—not one patriarchy-approved straight man among them—faced down dismissal, ridicule, and slut-shaming to make a show that helped to free people from traditional expectations. In the process, they also changed television, fashion, dating, feminism, female friendship—and, of course, sex and the city.

This is their—and our—story.

1

The Real Carrie Bradshaw

· · · · · · · · · · ·

Fifteen years in Manhattan, and Candace Bushnell was as broke as ever. She had arrived in New York City from Connecticut in 1978 at age nineteen, but after a decade and a half of trying to make it there, she barely had anything in her bank account to show for it.

She did, however, have several friends. And some of them *did* have money. One kept two apartments, using one as a home and the other as an office, the latter in a charming art deco building at 240 East 79th Street. When Bushnell needed a place to live, her friend stepped up and offered part of her "office" as living quarters for Bushnell. The friend kept her own office in the bedroom, while Bushnell slept on a fold-out sofa and worked in the other room. Bushnell liked having her friend nearby for moral support as she wrote articles for magazines such as *Mademoiselle* and *Esquire*, as well as the "People We're Talking About" column for *Vogue*.

Bushnell was still sleeping on the pull-out couch when she started freelance writing for the *New York Observer*, a publication distinguished by its pinkish paper and upscale readership.

Her boss, editor-in-chief Susan Morrison, who would go on to become articles editor at the *New Yorker*, called Bushnell the paper's "secret weapon," because Bushnell had a special aptitude for getting her subjects to speak candidly.

Morrison left the paper, but Bushnell stayed on as the top job was taken over by Peter Kaplan—a bespectacled journalist who would become the paper's defining editor. One fall afternoon in 1994, Kaplan said to Bushnell, "So many people are always talking about your stories. Why don't you write a column?" When Bushnell agreed, he asked, "What do you think it should be about?"

"I think it should be about being a single woman in New York City," she answered, "and all the crazy things that happen to her." She could focus on her life and her immediate circle: She was thirty-five and single, a status that was still shocking in certain segments of society, even in New York City in 1994. Several of her friends had also made it past thirty without getting married, and they would make great sources and characters.

Like many in the media, Bushnell lived an in-between-classes life: She scrounged for sustenance, attending book parties for the free food and drinks. But she also ran with the highest of the high class, big-name designers and authors, moguls who hired interior designers for their jets, and Upper East Side moms who pioneered "nanny cams" to spy on their expensive childcare providers. It was the model for the absurd lifestyle that her alter ego, Carrie Bradshaw, would make famous, balancing small paychecks with major access to glamour and wealth. That inside perspective on the high life would become a key part of the column's appeal.

• • •

Candace Bushnell knew nothing of private jets and nannies when she first arrived in Manhattan.

In fact, she lived in almost twelve different apartments during her first year in New York City, or at least it felt that way. Candy, as her family called her—honey-blond and Marcia Brady–pretty—had come to Manhattan to make it as an actress after she dropped out of Rice University. Then she found out she was a terrible actress, so she decided to make it as a writer instead.

Thus far, however, she'd only made it as a roommate, and even that wasn't going well.

In one apartment, on East 49th Street, which was something of a red-light district at the time, she lived with three other girls. All three wanted to be on Broadway, and, even worse, one of them was. All they did was sing when they were home; when they weren't home, they waitressed. Worse still, the women who lived above them on the third and fourth floors were hookers with a steady string of patrons clomping through.

Bushnell did her best to ignore the chaos and focus on her career. At a club one evening, she met the owner of a small publication called *Night*, where she landed her first entry-level gig. The magazine had just launched in 1978 to chronicle legendary nightclubs like Studio 54 and Danceteria. Other assistant-type work followed for Bushnell at *Ladies' Home Journal* (where the mix of stories in a given month might include career advice from Barbara Walters, an exposé on sexually abusive doctors, and "low-cal party" ideas) and *Good Housekeeping* (which favored more traditional topics such as a "Calorie Watchers Cookbook," White House table settings, and "How *Charlie's Angels* Stay So Slim"). Finally, Bushnell landed on staff as a writer at *Self* in an era when cover stories included "Are You Lying to Yourself about Sex?" and "12 Savvy Ways to Make More Money." This was at least a little closer to her speed.

Throughout the '80s, when Bushnell was in her twenties, she found ways to write about the subjects that interested her most: sex, relationships, society, clubbing, singlehood, careers, and New York City. At that point she still thought she'd like to get married and have kids. But her work reflected the times and spoke to the millions of young women who poured into big cities to seek career success and independence instead of matrimony and family life. To pursue her own big-city dreams, Bushnell braved New York at its lowest point, when the AIDS crisis ravaged lives, graffiti covered buildings and subway cars inside and out, beefy vigilantes called the Guardian Angels roamed the streets to discourage criminals, and Times Square was populated with prostitutes and peep shows.

• • •

It was the *Observer* column that would ultimately catapult her to the next level of her career. Bushnell and Kaplan got down to practicalities. She'd be paid $1,000 per column, which was $250 more than other columnists at the paper were paid. This, plus her *Vogue* checks and perks like flights to Los Angeles for assignments, added up to a decent New York lifestyle for the time, particularly given her frugal living quarters. Bushnell and Kaplan discussed the title of her new column and settled on "Sex and the City." A perfect newspaper column title: "pithy," as she'd later describe it. The column was headed by an illustration of a shoe, based on a strappy pair of Calvin Klein sandals Bushnell had purchased for herself on sale.

As Bushnell later wrote, she "practically skipped up Park Avenue with joy" leaving the office after Kaplan offered her the column.

But first things first: What to write about for her "Sex and the City" debut? Well, there was that sex club everyone was talking about.

• • •

One late night in 1994, Bushnell left a dinner party at the new Bowery Bar to head uptown to a sex club on 27th Street. She didn't know what would happen, but hoped it would be enough to fill her new column. As it turned out, Le Trapeze was, like most sexual escapades, neither as good nor as bad as imagined. It cost eighty-five dollars to enter, cash, no receipt. (Her expense reports were about to get interesting.) The presence of a hot-and-cold buffet took her aback. "You must have your lower torso covered to eat," said a sign above. Bushnell spied "a few blobby couples" having sex on a large air mattress in the center of the room. And, as Bushnell wrote, "many men . . . appeared to be having trouble keeping up their end of the bargain." A woman sat next to a Jacuzzi in a robe, smoking.

This experience became Bushnell's first "Sex and the City" column, published on November 28, 1994, with the headline "Swingin' Sex? I Don't Think So." Despite the come-on of the column's name, it contained a traditional and wholesome bottom line: "I had learned that when it comes to sex, there's no place like home." Over the next two years, Bushnell would chronicle the gulf between fantasy and reality, between what the hippest of the hip of New York City thought they should be doing and what they truly wanted in their souls. If they could find their souls.

As Bushnell wrote in that first piece: "Sex in New York is about as much like sex in America as other things in New York are. It can be annoying; it can be unsatisfying; most important, sex in New York is only rarely about sex. Most of the time it's about spectacle, Todd Oldham dresses, Knicks tickets, the Knick [*sic*] themselves, or the pure terror of Not Being Alone in New York."

Over the next two years, Bushnell would sit at her desk in her friend's apartment on the tenth floor of the 79th Street building, writing her column. She smoked and looked out on an air shaft from the dark three-bedroom apartment as she pondered the lives and loves of those she knew and tapped away on her Dell laptop keyboard. The words she wrote would turn her from a midlevel writer into a New York celebrity.

Her column gained such notoriety, in fact, that it affected her love life. High-powered men she met told her, "I thought about dating you, but now I won't because I don't want to end up in your column." She would think, *You aren't interesting enough to write about anyway.* Her on-again, off-again boyfriend, *Vogue* publisher Ron Galotti—a tanned man with slicked-back hair and a penchant for gray suits with pocket squares—did make the column regularly, referred to as "Mr. Big." When she'd finish writing a column and show it to him, he would read her copy and issue his version of a compliment: "Cute, baby, cute."

• • •

Bushnell never envisioned a mass audience for her work in the *Observer*. She never would have believed, at the time, that it would turn into a TV hit that all of America—much less the world—embraced. She only hoped to hook the select, in-the-know audience the *Observer* was known for, the upper echelons of high society. Bushnell's "Sex and the City" column emphasizes opportunistic women on the hunt for financial salvation in Manhattan's high-rolling men; her "Carrie Bradshaw"—a pseudonym for Bushnell herself—is unhinged and depressed; her friends have given up on the idea of love and connection. The result resembles a female version of *Bright Lights, Big City* and, in fact, the author of that book was her friend and frequent party mate Jay McInerney, whose wavy crest of dark hair, thick eyebrows, and natty style made him look more like a matinee idol than a novelist. Even McInerney, the chronicler of New York's party culture of the coke-fueled '80s, cracked that Bushnell "was doing advanced postgraduate work in the subject of going out on the town."

She went out nearly every night, interviewed people at her central downtown hangout, Bowery Bar, and found stories all across town. New York was, Bushnell says, a "tight place then. It was the day when restaurants were theater. Nobody cared about the food. You just saw who was coming in, who talked to who." If you wanted to know what was going on somewhere, you had to go there.

New York dating rituals still hearkened back to another era, "like in Edith Wharton's time," Bushnell says. "There were hierarchies. Society was important, the idea of wanting to be in society." Women still often felt as if they had to please men, like Wharton wrote in *The House of Mirth* of her character Lily Bart: "She had been bored all the afternoon by Percy Gryce—the mere thought seemed to waken an echo of his droning voice—but she could not ignore him on the morrow, she must follow up her success, must submit to more boredom, must be ready with fresh compliances and adaptabilities."

With the column, Bushnell had made herself into a professional dater. She got her material from dating, and she could use her profession to meet potential dates. This linked her to the city's earliest recognized wave of professional, single women: the shopgirls of the early 1900s. They made their living as retail clerks, but more important they were single girls whose jobs gave them access to wealthy men: "Shopgirls knew that dressing and speaking the right ways would help them get a job, and that the right job could help them get a man," Moira Weigel wrote in her history of courtship, *Labor of Love: The Invention of Dating*.

Bushnell and her friends had become the modern version of Edith Wharton heroines and those shopgirls, stuck between dependence on men and modern dating practices that lacked manners and rules. She envisioned herself writing for this select subculture, whispering their secrets to others like them, and perhaps even to the men who pursued them.

"SEX" BEYOND THE UPPER EAST SIDE

Before long, people began to buy the *Observer* just to read Bushnell's column, people outside the *Observer*'s standard readership. Readers loved to guess the real identities of Bushnell's pseudonymed characters. It was said that the writer "River Wilde" was probably Bret Easton Ellis, the *American Psycho* author. "Gregory Roque" was most likely Oliver Stone, the *Natural Born Killers* filmmaker. A Bushnell pseudonym became a status symbol of the time.

Soon everyone in town knew that Mr. Big was Galotti, the magazine publisher who drove a Ferrari and had dated supermodel Janice Dickinson. In the column, Bushnell, as a first-person narrator, introduces Mr. Big's paramour, Carrie Bradshaw, as her "friend." Eventually, detailed depictions of Carrie's life—her thoughts, her word-for-word conversations, her sexual escapades—overtake the column. That, plus their shared initials, made it hard to imagine Carrie wasn't Candace. In fact, Bushnell later revealed she'd created Carrie so her parents wouldn't know—at least for sure—that they were reading about their daughter's own sex life.

Readers took in every word. They read it on the subway and on the way out to the Hamptons. They delighted in Bushnell's dissections of city types such as "psycho moms," "bicycle boys," "international crazy girls," "modelizers," and "toxic bachelors," and they devoured the knowing insider commentary:

"It all started the way it always does: innocently enough."

"On a recent afternoon, seven women gathered in Manhattan over wine, cheese, and cigarettes, to animatedly discuss the one thing they had in common: a man."

"The pilgrimage to the newly suburbanized friend is one that most Manhattan women have made, and few truly enjoyed."

"On a recent afternoon, four women met at an Upper East Side restaurant to discuss what it's like to be an extremely beautiful young woman in New York City."

"There are worse things than being thirty-five, single, and female in New York. Like: Being twenty-five, single, and female in New York."

Bushnell's column contained seedlings of the fantasy life that would bloom in *Sex and the City* the television show. But "Sex and the City," as a column, was a bait and switch. The clothes command high prices and the parties attract big names; however, despite the column's name, there isn't much sexy sex and there's almost no romance. One character sums it up: "I have no sex and no romance. Who needs it? No fear of disease, psychopaths, or stalkers. Why not just be with your friends?" Bushnell puts it this way: "Relationships in New York are about detachment." The writer herself had soured on marriage, telling the *New York Times* it was an institution that favored men. She'd once been engaged, about four years before the launch of her column, and the experience had made her feel as if she were, she said, "drowning."

Despite the column's cynical soul, despite Bushnell's personal connection with novelist friends Jay McInerney and Bret Easton Ellis, she knew how her writing—because it was about women and feelings— was perceived.

"It's cute. It's light. . . . It's not Tolstoy," is how her friend Samantha describes Carrie's work in one of the columns. Carrie insists that she's not trying to be Tolstoy. Bushnell concludes, "But, of course, she was."

WRITING AND THE SINGLE GIRL

Bushnell's column fit into a long tradition of literary fascination with single women's lives. The title of the column, in fact, referenced the most famous of them all: Helen Gurley Brown's 1962 sensation *Sex and the Single Girl*. While women have never been published with the same frequency as their white male counterparts, they have proven throughout history that there was a surefire way to get attention: by explaining their exotic lives as single, independent creatures to the masses. How on earth did they survive without men? Was it as awful as it sounded? Was it as fun?

This phenomenon dated back at least as far as 1898, when Neith Boyce wrote a column for *Vogue* called "The Bachelor Girl." "The day it became evident that I was irretrievably committed to this alternative lifestyle was a solemn one in the family circle," Boyce wrote. "I was about to leave that domestic haven, heaven only knew for what port. I was going to New York to earn my own bread and butter and to live alone."

With "Sex and the City," Bushnell combined two historically popular column genres: the confessions of a single professional woman and the documentation of high society's charity events, fashion, fancy homes, and gossip. She offered a juicier version of the age-old society pages.

Given this winning combination, the book publishing world inevitably pursued Bushnell. Atlantic Monthly Press released a collection of Bushnell's columns in hardcover in August 1996. As she toured college campuses to promote the book, she noticed something unexpected: The column resonated far beyond Manhattan, far beyond its outer boroughs . . . and far beyond even the Tri-State Area. Women in Chicago, Los Angeles, and other cities throughout the nation saw their own lives in *Sex and the City*. They had their own Mr. Bigs; they were their own Carrie Bradshaws. "We thought people could only be this terrible in New York," Bushnell says. "But this phenomenon of thirty-something women dating was much more universal than we thought." She wasn't just reporting on high society for in-the-know Manhattanites; she had become the new Holly Golightly, the glamorous single woman her college fans hoped to be someday.

The book represented an unquestionable pinnacle for Bushnell's career. She had chased exactly this kind of fantasy from the Connecticut suburbs to New York City in 1978 with no connections, no Ivy League degree, and no money, then worked her way up the media ladder.

Reviews for the book, however, ran lukewarm. The *Washington Post* called it "mildly amusing," then used most of the review to take aim at the *Observer*, "a singularly peculiar weekly newspaper that is printed on colored paper and edited with only two circulation areas in mind: chic Manhattan and drop-dead Hamptons." The book, the review said, did nothing more than collate several of Bushnell's columns, "presumably for the convenience of those who do not have their copies of the *Observer* bound by Madison Avenue leather crafters."

Some reviewers mustered up more respect, like Sandra Tsing Loh in the *Los Angeles Times*, who compared Bushnell's view of New York City to those of some of Bushnell's friends, influential members of the '80s "literary Brat Pack" such as Jay McInerney and Tama Janowitz. A *Publishers Weekly* review noted the "opulent debasement that suffuses this collection" and called it "brain candy"—emphasis on the "brain" as much as the "candy."

The "candy," however, took over as the main public perception of *Sex and the City* as a book. *Sex and the City*'s publication coincided with the introduction of another memorable thirtysomething singleton into the literary landscape: British columnist Helen Fielding's hapless Bridget Jones. Comparisons flourished, and did nothing to boost *Sex and the City*'s respectability. Alex Kuczynski in the *New York Times* described Bridget's obsession with men as "perfectly normal behavior, if you're a 13-year-old girl," then acknowledged that Bridget "makes some women laugh in sad recognition."

In the *Village Voice* Meghan Daum wrote that *Bridget Jones* "concerns itself almost entirely with the neurotic fallout of popular women's culture. . . . Bridget's constant failure to follow through on even the most basic lifestyle tips offered up by her mentor, *Cosmo* culture, will undoubtedly provoke the disapproval of those who remain devoted to that culture's major tenet, that self-improvement and positive thinking are synonymous with substance."

With the exception of that last one, these reviews seemed oblivious to Bridget's satirical nature, the fact that she and her creator were in on the joke. But Bridget and Carrie did not belong together in any sense, even though they kept getting stuck together in trend pieces. Kuczynski's *New York Times* piece quotes Bushnell criticizing Bridget as "ten years out of date." Bridget struggled with her weight and suffered from low self-esteem, but also seemed to like her life, her friends, her family, and her middle-class status. Carrie, on the other hand, knew how attractive and thin she was, dated and drank with the upper echelons of Manhattan society, and was still moody and cynical. Where Bridget was sweet and well-adjusted underneath her snark and borderline alcoholism, Carrie suffered mood swings and self-sabotaging behavior. In short, they sat at opposite ends of the single-woman character spectrum: Bridget an updated version of the single woman who knows her place, and thus is quite likable; Carrie an unsympathetic character, a true antiheroine at a time when unlikable lead female characters were rare. "I don't write books because I want everyone to like the characters," Bushnell says. "These are women who make some choices that maybe aren't the best choices in terms of morality."

With Carrie, Bushnell was going more for a Dorothy Parker type or Edith Wharton heroine than the lead of a romantic comedy, but she and Fielding were linked in the cultural ether and credited with—or blamed for—the advent of a new, much-derided book category equivalent of the rom-com: chick lit.

• • •

Whatever the perception of "Sex and the City," it was popular. So popular, in fact, that starting about three months into the column's run, enamored New Yorkers in the media business began faxing copies of it to their friends in the movie business in Los Angeles. Even before the collection of columns came out in book form, Bushnell began to get calls from producers eager to buy the rights for film.

TV network ABC also pursued her, particularly executive Jamie Tarses after she became president of ABC Entertainment in 1996. During her previous job at NBC, Tarses had developed *Caroline in the City*, *Mad About You*, and *Friends*—all New York–centric hits about young, beautiful white people. It made sense that she'd be interested in *Sex and the City*, which she saw as a more sophisticated, forward-thinking version of those shows. The thirty-two-year-old had just become the youngest person to run a network entertainment division at the time; she was also the first female network president ever. Industry observers were waiting for her to fail. Her new network lagged in third place of the Big Three. She needed a standout hit, and she thought a "Sex and the City" adaptation could be it.

Tarses's thick, curly, Sarah Jessica Parker–like hair, blue eyes, and power suits would have made her look right at home on *Sex and the City*. Like many of the female characters, she was in her early thirties and trying to balance dating with a high-powered career. She had become a fan of Bushnell's column and its perspective on modern relationships because she related to it. The column felt like it could become the basis of the show she had always been looking for, a voice and point of view that wasn't already represented on television. The popularity of the column and subsequent book gave the title a recognizability that made it perfect for TV. And it appealed to the female audience ABC most wanted at the time. Tarses just had to figure out how much of the "sex" a broadcast network could allow.

As Bushnell's star rose, the writer ran into Tarses and her boyfriend, David Letterman's executive producer Robert Morton, in the Hamptons. Bushnell was Rollerblading when the couple pulled up next to her, as she remembers it, in a cherry-red Mercedes convertible. "Jamie wants to buy 'Sex and the City,'" Morton told Bushnell. "ABC's really interested." The pursuit was on.

But others were wooing Bushnell for the "Sex and the City" rights as well. One of Galotti's friends, Richard Plepler—senior vice president of communications at HBO—also thought the column would be a perfect fit for his pay-cable network. Bushnell and Plepler often saw each other at the stretch of shoreline called Media Beach in the Hamptons, and every time, he'd urge her to come to a meeting at HBO.

• • •

Cable seemed like a better fit for *Sex and the City*, given its similarities to another book that started as a newspaper column, then became a critically acclaimed series for PBS and, later, cable network Showtime: Armistead Maupin's *Tales of the City*. In fact, that *Publishers Weekly* review that called *Sex and the City* "brain candy" also referred to Maupin's 1978 collection of *San Francisco Chronicle* columns that followed young, single people of various sexual orientations in the liberated city: "The effect is that of an Armistead Maupin–like canvas tinged with a liberal smattering of Judith Krantz," the reviewer wrote.

Tales of the City had become a television miniseries around the same time "Sex and the City" debuted as a column; it premiered in the UK in 1993 and in the United States on PBS in 1994. The series took on issues well ahead of its time for TV, with extramarital affairs, sex, several gay love affairs, and a major transgender character. But like *Sex and the City* after it, *Tales'* true message came down to the importance of friendship in a major metropolitan area. It also highlighted a different kind of love affair that *Sex and the City* would also emphasize: the relationship between a city and its denizens.

Tales couldn't afford to be a glitzy production, however, when it came to television. Such a risky proposition meant a miniscule budget, with costumes even for its wealthiest characters coming from secondhand shops. "It was a total shoestring," says Barbara Garrick, who played heiress DeDe Halcyon Day (and would later guest-star on *Sex and the City* as a spagoer who gets a happy ending from her massage therapist). "They'd hand you a dress they just bought at Goodwill."

Tales' frank approach to modern sexuality won it plenty of attention, both good and bad. It became the highest-rated broadcast to date on PBS at the time, but also sparked controversy as one of the few US programs to show kissing between male lovers. Attempts to produce a follow-up based on Maupin's book series had so far failed because of the US government's threats to pull PBS funding if it remained involved with *Tales*. "I did have my top off once [during the miniseries], and that went to Congress, like a pirate tape with black bars across my chest," Garrick says. "It had all the scenes of the pot smoking and the guys kissing and the nudity." Later, HBO rival Showtime would pick the show up for a second season.

This was the landscape into which any *Sex and the City* television show would take its first steps.

WHEN CANDACE MET DARREN

Just before the birth of the "Sex and the City" column, Bushnell had gone on an assignment that would change her life—and, even more, the life of her column. In fact, without this one routine assignment, the *Sex and the City* we know would never have come to pass.

Vogue had asked Bushnell to write a profile of Darren Star, a TV producer who had worked with Aaron Spelling to create *Beverly Hills, 90210* and *Melrose Place*. Star had a new show on CBS, *Central Park West*, that transplanted his flashy, soapy approach to New York City, with Mariel Hemingway as a glamorous magazine editor and Lauren Hutton as her boss's suspicious wife. Star was branching out on his own without Spelling, and the critics would be watching to see if Star was the real deal.

In the September 1995 piece, Bushnell follows Star—dressed "California-style" in a black Armani jacket and jeans—on a late-night visit to an S&M club called Vault, which he's scouting for *Central Park West*. Star couldn't have known at the time that it was the effect of this profile, not the show he was producing, that would resonate decades later.

Soon after the two met for the piece, Star moved to Manhattan, and Bushnell swept him into her orbit to show him around the area—for *Central Park West* research, of course. He had never met anyone more fun. She personified all the clichés: "A force of nature," he says. "She opened a lot of doors." She took him to clubs, and of course to Bowery Bar. They commemorated their friendship in ultimate Hollywood fashion: Bushnell would take the first half of her column pseudonym from Star's nightlife columnist character on *Central Park West*, Carrie Fairchild, played by Mädchen Amick.

Star—a handsome gay man with brown, spiky hair—connected with Bushnell as a fellow suburban kid made good. He spent his childhood in Potomac, Maryland, a middle- to upper-class DC suburb full of politicians, ambassadors, and their families. Young Darren took film classes in high school and hoped to work in the movie industry as a writer and director. He used his bar mitzvah money to get himself a subscription to the show business trade publication *Variety*. While other kids partied or played sports, he made his own movies with his Super 8 camera. After graduating high school, he moved to California to study writing and film at UCLA, from which he graduated in 1983. Degree in hand, he took the classic first step toward a Hollywood career: He became a waiter.

He soon, however, got his first industry job. Star was working as a publicist for Showtime when he sold his first screenplay to Warner Bros. at age twenty-four. *Doin' Time on Planet Earth*, a comedy about a teenager in Arizona who comes to believe he's an alien prince, premiered in 1988, directed by Charles Matthau. It made little critical or commercial impact, but it helped launch Star's career. He could now quit his job to write screenplays full-time. His next project would be *If Looks Could Kill*, with *21 Jump Street*'s Richard Grieco as a high school French student who's pulled into an international spy ring on a class trip.

As Star awaited that film's release, he fulfilled a lifelong dream by moving from Los Angeles to New York City, a place whose glamour he had long admired from afar. But soon after, he got a call from Paul Stupin, a movie executive who'd just taken a job as head of drama at the new Fox television network. Stupin asked if Star would write a high school show, given his teen-oriented script experience. Stupin hoped to pair him with the much older producer Aaron Spelling (a golden TV touch who'd created 1970s hits *The Love Boat* and *Charlie's Angels*) to create a high school series. Star thought he'd be crazy to turn down the chance to work with such a legend, which seemed like the perfect way to kill time while he waited for *If Looks Could Kill* to come out. So at age twenty-eight, he moved right back to Los Angeles to make a show with Spelling.

The gamble paid off. Together, Spelling and Star created a series called *Beverly Hills, 90210*, which followed the melodramatic lives of a group of wealthy Los Angeles teenagers. With the money Star made on the pilot, he paid cash for a Porsche. The show premiered in October 1990 to unimpressive ratings, but Fox executives decided to air the second season in the summer, when there was minimal competition for audiences. The strategy worked. Teenagers home from school for the season fell for it by the millions in July 1991. But good fortune brought with it a heavy burden: *90210*'s second season would be unusually long, twenty-eight episodes instead of a standard twenty-two. Not about to fix what wasn't broken, Fox ordered thirty the following year and thirty-two each for the next five years. This made for an insane production schedule; the *90210* staff had almost no hiatuses to break up long seasons of twelve-hour workdays.

Amid all of this, Star's movie, *If Looks Could Kill*, came out in March 1991 to disappointing box office returns and reviews. In a typical review for the film, the *Washington Post* called it "insipid, tiresome, and full of gross kids." But by now Star had little time to notice.

90210 became what remains the most iconic series of the teen drama genre by dealing with timely issues (date rape, drug abuse, suicide, and many others) as well as teen sex and angst-filled relationships. But Star wasn't content to stop there. For the 1992 television season, Star created another show for Fox, the young-adult drama *Melrose Place*, which featured even more unapologetic sex and sensational plot lines about twentysomethings. Fox once again followed its supersized *90210* strategy and ordered thirty-two episodes of *Melrose* each of its first three years.

In short, Star spent the early 1990s becoming rich and successful, and working too hard to notice. The ratings numbers told him millions watched, but he rarely got the chance to see his shows' popularity on the outside, beyond the Fox lot. Because he was in his early thirties, this streak hit at the perfect time in his life; he had energy and ambition to burn, with few other responsibilities to distract him. He'd look back on it later in life and wonder how he did it.

Bolstered by his success, he moved again to New York, this time to make a show about the city: *Central Park West*. He and his golden retriever, Judy Jetson, settled into a three-floor apartment owned by model-turned-restaurateur Eric Petterson. Finally living in his dream city, Star took lunches and breakfasts at 44, a restaurant known for its publishing-industry clientele, so he could get a better feel for the magazine world he planned to depict on his new series. He went to charity benefits and book parties for further research.

After meeting Candace Bushnell for that 1995 article, he had more material than he ever dreamed possible. As he hung out with Bushnell, he got to know her friends, including her paramour, Ron Galotti—a.k.a. Mr. Big. He loved to read about them in Bushnell's new column. He admired how she mixed journalism and her own personal stories. He respected the way she exposed herself, writing about her "crazy experiences," as he says, for the world to see.

He told Bushnell that he wanted to be the one to option the column. He thought it might make a great follow-up project to *Central Park West* someday.

This seemed like the answer to Bushnell's quandary as well. She couldn't decide whom to give it to—ABC, HBO, or a movie company. A broadcast network like ABC seemed so sanitary. HBO seemed so niche and male-centric, with its signature boxing matches and standup comedy specials. She had no idea what a movie company might do with her work.

But Star was her buddy. Star had witnessed the column's happenings and met the people featured in it. With Star involved, she'd be able to follow how the project was proceeding.

After all of the mid-Rollerblading courtship and Media Beach cajoling she had been through, she decided this was the answer.

Reports put the price at a mere $60,000; she'll only say it was "a little bit more." "I wasn't in a position [to negotiate much]," she says. "It was my first thing."

Mediaweek reported the acquisition, quoting Star as saying Bushnell had "a unique voice that is ready to be captured and put on film." He described her as "irreverent, vulgar, funny . . . a '90s Dorothy Parker." He didn't know yet how he'd adapt the "Sex and the City" columns, which he thought were "great social satire, but too rarefied" for television. He later told the *New York Times*, "Only 500 people in New York know or care about that world. I needed to make it more accessible."

But that was for later. For now, he took pride in the work he was doing for CBS on *Central Park West*. He had long wanted to make a glamorous show set in New York City. At the time, TV's main vision of New York came via the grit of *Law & Order*. Star aimed to bring the posh world of New York media, of glossy magazines like *Vanity Fair*, to television audiences. He wanted viewers to have a taste of the life he'd discovered there: producing *Central Park West* by day, clubbing and dining with Bushnell at night.

New York City itself had entered a time of transition with the election of Rudy Giuliani as mayor in 1994. It was no longer the crime-ridden New York of the 1980s, not yet the theme park New York of the 2000s. Shifts in public life foretold the city's future: A smoking ban in restaurants. An Old Navy discount chain store in the hip gay haven of Chelsea.

Neighborhoods were transforming faster than many residents could stand. Bowery Bar, Bushnell's preferred hangout, battled neighborhood residents who wanted the establishment to operate under a restrictive special permit. They worried Bowery Bar would set a precedent for similar clubs, which, according to reports, "could change NoHo from a refuge for artists and light manufacturing to a trendy neighborhood flooded with late-night revelers." The Meatpacking District was shaking off its slaughterhouse past to become a nightlife hot spot as well. A waiter at the neighborhood's fashionable new restaurant Florent told the *New York Times* its customers ran the gamut, from old New Yorkers to young hipsters: "Everyone and everything, butchers, drag queens, club kids, weddings." Many longtime New Yorkers rolled their eyes at these developments—signs, they said, that New York was *over*.

But the changes also indicated a shift toward a Manhattan that was more inviting to the rest of the country—that is, the majority of television viewers.

CREATED BY DARREN STAR

Darren Star invited columnist Candace Bushnell, author Bret Easton Ellis, and publisher Ron Galotti to his apartment on the evening of September 13, 1995, to watch a little television. The first episode of Star's *Central Park West* was airing on CBS, and they would witness it as a group at Star's posh rental near Union Square. They watched as a sultry Latin beat and crooning saxophones played over the opening credits. Mariel Hemingway, Lauren Hutton, and Michael Michele looked seductive in black-and-white images while "Created by Darren Star" flashed across the screen, signifying his first solo TV effort without Spelling.

By the time the end credits rolled, Bushnell wasn't blown away by *Central Park West*, though she saw its potential. Like all of Star's work, it was fun and glamorous. But, she says, it "missed the New Yorkiness."

He had her to help him get a better feel for true New Yorkiness, but, as it turned out, not in time to save this series. CBS had just gotten a new president, Les Moonves, who would take the network from last place to first in the ratings—unfortunately for Star, Moonves did this by focusing on CBS's core audience, older viewers. They were hardly the target for *Central Park West*, nor Star's specialty. *Central Park West* lasted thirteen episodes before the network stopped production, tried to retool it, and then dumped the remaining episodes onto the schedule the following summer. *Central Park West* closed down for good.

Star was disappointed that his first show about New York City, and his first show without Aaron Spelling, had failed. The experience had also tried Star's patience with big network shows that were subject to intense scrutiny, meddlesome executives, and constant pressure to produce bigger ratings. So that summer, as the remaining episodes of *Central Park West* aired, he started to think about how, specifically, to adapt Bushnell's columns as an independent film. Done correctly, he thought, they could make for a great, honest movie about sex and relationships from a female perspective, with a New York sensibility. Perhaps this, instead, could be his ticket to a respectable solo career.

He liked the idea of returning to film. Though he had tried to push boundaries on *90210* and *Melrose*, TV overall remained, as he says, "this anachronistic space" where characters spoke in euphemisms, sex was vaguely alluded to, gay characters were rare and chaste, and nobody used dirty language. He wanted nothing to do with it anymore. *Central Park West* had broken him. *Sex and the City* could show the world he could make it without Spelling, and do so in the more prestigious world of film.

Forces began to align toward *Sex and the City*'s Hollywood moment with Star's entry into the equation. But momentum pushed him back in the television direction. ABC's Tarses and HBO both remained the show's most enthusiastic suitors, and they could still give Star's version of the series a TV home. Plus, Star's name had more pull in the world of TV.

Over the summer of 1996, as Bushnell and Star Hamptons-hopped, they debated where they'd like the series to end up. Star wondered if a show could even be called *Sex and the City* on a major broadcast network like ABC. He didn't know what Tarses wanted or why she wanted it, but taming the material for broadcast rules made him nervous. He didn't want another *Central Park West* experience. HBO, on the other hand, seemed so New York; it was based there and would be more likely to produce the show there. Star loved his place in Manhattan and didn't want to give it up. He also admired the one show he knew from HBO, *The Larry Sanders Show*.

In his meetings with HBO, Star explained to vice president of original programming Carolyn Strauss that he saw *Sex and the City* as a modern, R-rated version of *The Mary Tyler Moore Show*—a series about sex and relationships from a female point of view. This intrigued Strauss. She'd read Bushnell's columns and was interested based on those alone—she thought Bushnell's world would be, as she says, "a fun place to hang out" for television viewers. Strauss liked the female-centric approach, too, even though, as a gay woman, she didn't relate to Bushnell and her man-crazy friends.

In Star's meetings with ABC, Tarses tried to argue that her network *could* realize Star's vision for the series—and, yes, the network would call the show *Sex and the City*. But she understood HBO's advantage when it came to unfiltered content.

In the end, Star gave it to HBO. Its reach couldn't match ABC's, but at this point in his career, he longed for freedom more than commercial success. In fact, he specifically *did not want* commercial success. He wanted to make something special that he could be proud of.

Tarses had lost, and she understood why. Her tenure at ABC would last two more years, with a few middling new hits like *Dharma & Greg*, the critically adored and barely watched *Sports Night*, and a fizzled *Fantasy Island* remake. From there, she went into the production side of television, where she could create the shows she liked best; her credits would include acclaimed singles-focused comedies *My Boys* and *Happy Endings*. She wouldn't have to spend any more time in uphill battles to compete with permissive cable networks for great shows.

Bushnell was happy with Star's choice of HBO, which would, in fact, keep the production entirely local—with less chance of screwing up *Sex and the City*'s inherent New Yorkiness.

As HBO's victory over ABC in the battle for *Sex and the City* demonstrated, the cable channel's new philosophy, while it more aggressively pursued original programming, was impossible for broadcast networks to counter: HBO executives would search for series that met their own quality standards, thus ensuring that artistic merits came first. In evaluating a show, they asked whether it was good and whether it would get attention—not whether everyone in America would watch. Broadcast networks, which run on advertising dollars, had never cared about quality as much as they cared about ratings. They couldn't, if they wanted to survive. Their business model had to prioritize commerce over art. HBO, as a channel viewers paid a premium for, didn't have to worry as long as viewers paid. This resulted in the channel buying not only *Sex and the City* but also *The Sopranos* and *Six Feet Under*, and later *Game of Thrones* and *Westworld*—playing a leading role in what we would eventually call the Golden Age of Television.

Cable channels were homing in on broadcast vulnerabilities in other ways as well. TV had taken the summers off for as long as it had existed. Cable networks had noticed the weakness and scheduled new movies, series, and specials at a time when the traditional channels ran traditional reruns. By the summer of 1997, the major networks hit a new low when they attracted less than 50 percent of available viewers during the Fourth of July week. Broadcast channels scrambled to mix up their traditional slate of reruns with unseen episodes of canceled series. But HBO planned to take advantage of this network weakness by scheduling new episodes of its prison drama *Oz*, as well as the sports dramedy *Arli$$*, during the summer.

The question remained whether *Sex and the City* could benefit from this same strategy, even as that one pop of bright pink in the middle of HBO's gritty, dark, predominantly male lineup.

2

A New Kind of TV Woman

· · · · · · · · · · ·

As Darren Star began to write his first *Sex and the City* TV script in late 1996, it occurred to him that it was a little strange for him to write a show that was so female-centric, for a man to be molding Carrie and her friends Miranda, Charlotte, and Samantha. He figured it was because he had the juice to get this show made, while few women in the business did. But he took the responsibility seriously and set out to create characters who were smart and independent as well as vulnerable, vulgar, and sexual. He would not allow these female characters to be defined by men and their relationships.

Star didn't talk much to his friends in the business about his *Sex and the City* script. In Hollywood, when people talked about television deals, they talked about shows bought by major broadcast networks. Doing a show at HBO looked roughly equivalent to writing an indie script that would never get made, just a step above scribbling in your

23

diary. He consulted here and there with Bushnell as he wrote, but mostly kept to himself as he developed his own approach to Bushnell's source material.

He pushed aside the thought that this script could make or break the rest of his career. His movies hadn't made much of an impression, and *Central Park West* had failed without Aaron Spelling's help. Whether or not anyone watched *Sex and the City* on HBO, Star hoped it would prove his artistry.

He enjoyed tackling the script's challenges in relative obscurity. The column did not lend itself easily to a TV show. It told the stories of all kinds of New Yorkers, with few consistent characters aside from Bushnell as "Carrie." At first, Star thought he could make it into an anthology series, like the 1970s hit *Love, American Style*. Columnist "Carrie" would narrate other people's love stories, focusing on new characters each week—an approach that would most accurately reflect Bushnell's work. But Star had made his name with his soap operas, which hinged on serialized stories about a core group of characters. Besides, ABC was considering remaking *Love, American Style* that fall, and Star needed his show to be distinct. (Ultimately *Love, American Style* didn't make it onto ABC's schedule.)

Star decided to focus on Carrie—after all, the real-life version of her, Candace Bushnell, was one of his best friends. While Bushnell wrote Carrie as a brittle, neurotic New Yorker, Star had a more sympathetic view of Bushnell that he injected into his vision of *Sex and the City*'s main character. For instance, he remembered listening to Bushnell call her mother for a recipe to make for dinner. He viewed Bushnell, and thus Carrie, as hard on the outside but soft on the inside. He would turn Carrie from the pulsing red version Bushnell had created to a softer pink version. Hot pink, but pink.

With Carrie beginning to gel in his mind, he moved on to thinking about how the show would be structured. He decided to focus on her love life as well as that of a few of her friends—based on some women mentioned in the columns and some female friends of Bushnell's whom Star had met. He needed characters who would have distinct points of view about the subjects Carrie would tackle in her columns. He decided on the foursome concept that had worked so well throughout pop culture, from boy bands and girl groups to *The Golden Girls* and *Designing Women*. He wanted the characters to have frank conversations about relationship questions that resonated with women. The first topic posed by the pilot script: Can women have sex like men?

He wrote without any consideration of what would sell, what would succeed in the television marketplace he had mastered over the previous six years. He wrote something he himself would want to watch. He wrote, at long last, frank adult talk about sex, R-rated stuff he could never have gone near in *90210*, *Melrose*, or *Central Park West*.

He finished a draft in the fall, rewrote over another few months, and completed a final version in December.

A month later, he turned to casting. Everything depended on the casting of Carrie Bradshaw. The right actor would, in the short term, bolster HBO's faith in the show's future and, in the long term, determine if enough people wanted to allow Carrie into their living rooms every week. By the time he finished the pilot script, he had one actor in mind for the role of Carrie Bradshaw: Sarah Jessica Parker. She had an unusual combination of physical characteristics that deepened her impact: A taut figure and cascading curls allowed her to play bombshells, sparkly blue eyes and a warm smile allowed her to play sweet, and a Barbra Streisand–like profile allowed her to play sophisticated or quirky. Like Bushnell, Parker had an eye for high fashion, favoring tiny dresses and stilettos that showed off her sculpted shoulders and legs, and appearing at events such as the VH1/Vogue Fashion Awards or a Cartier book release party.

Star didn't know Parker personally, but her movie work projected the humor, intelligence, and likability that he wanted Carrie to have. Star understood Carrie was a complicated character whose combination of sexual freedom and unapologetic foibles had rarely, if ever, been attempted in a leading lady on television. He couldn't imagine anyone except Parker pulling it off.

As HBO's Carolyn Strauss says, "Putting a face and a voice with a main character makes all the difference" in a young series's life. And this series would pioneer a new kind of single woman on television: over thirty, successful, independent, and at least as interested in sex as in romance. To get there, Star had to woo Sarah Jessica Parker. Hard.

• • •

Parker knew Candace Bushnell's book and the column in the *Observer*. She remembered one specific installment of the column, which was about what Bushnell dubbed "bicycle boys." Parker's fiancé at the time, actor Matthew Broderick, had been born and raised in New York and had spent his whole life as a "bicycle boy" in the city. He had a tricked-out bike, the kind that messengers would ride, self-built with no brakes. She had shown him that column to tease him a bit about his prized possession.

But Parker didn't see herself in Carrie Bradshaw or any of Carrie's friends.

Bushnell and Star, of course, did. They knew Parker had come to New York City from Cincinnati—where she was raised as one of eight children from two different marriages—as a child actress. She starred in a Broadway revival of *The Innocents* at eleven and as the lead in *Annie* at thirteen. Parker spent her teens in auditions, pursuing what would be a lifelong career in show business, just as Bushnell had come to the city at nineteen to pursue acting and writing. "She gets the city and the grittiness of the city," Bushnell says. "She wasn't someone who had been living in LA. She feels very New York. She was one of the few actresses people knew lived in New York." Star loved that Parker knew the city, was a terrific actress, was just the right age (thirty-two), and was known for her movie work—perfect for HBO.

Parker had made a long career of being almost famous, first on the 1982 high school show *Square Pegs* and then in films such as *Footloose* (as Kevin Bacon's sidekick's love interest) and *Girls Just Wanna Have Fun*. In 1991, Steve Martin's magical-realist fairy tale *L.A. Story* brought her a little more fame, thanks to the scene-stealer role of the flighty clothing store clerk/aspiring spokesmodel SanDeE*. The part helped to prompt a *New York Times* profile (headline: "Bimbo? Sarah Jessica Parker Begs to Differ") and follow-up roles in *Honeymoon in Vegas* with Nicolas Cage and *Striking Distance* with Bruce Willis.

"Everything that has happened to me is because of Steve," she told the *Times* in that 1992 piece. "Everything. I don't know how to thank him. He just stood there and let me be extremely large in that movie. I went way over the top, and he could have just stopped it with a word. Most men would have. I wanted to write him a note, but I thought that would be kind of dorky."

Parker's love life had made her somewhat famous, too, much to her regret. She had a short but well-documented fling with John F. Kennedy Jr. that she'd later call "the Kennedy fiasco" for its overblown nature, as well as a tabloid-friendly relationship with Robert Downey Jr., whom she dated for seven years during his publicly known drug use.

By the time the *Sex and the City* script arrived in her life, she was about to marry Broderick—the *Ferris Bueller's Day Off* actor, whom she called "lethally charming"—after a quiet courtship. But with decades of experience in the business, she had yet to find the breakout role that would make her a star for the ages.

Star admired Parker's "open quality." And Bushnell loved the idea of Parker in a role that was, essentially, Bushnell herself: "She's funny," Bushnell says. "I always thought that was kind of my thing, so it was thrilling to have somebody who was just funny."

• • •

Parker wasn't sure she wanted to commit to a TV series. But she agreed to meet with Star in March 1997 at E.A.T., a restaurant on the Upper East Side owned by Eli Zabar. Its bagels, sandwiches, and matzo ball soup are legendary. As Parker and Star lunched, he told her that when he wrote the script, he heard Carrie in Parker's voice. She didn't hear it herself, but she was flattered and delighted. She did find the script compelling—seductive, even. She had never read anything like it. And her agent loved it.

She had conditions, however, for considering the role. She didn't want Carrie to throw around the word "fuck" just because the show was on cable. She hoped Carrie would be thoughtful about language, given her profession as a writer. No problem, Star told her.

Parker did like the idea of playing a character so different from herself. And she felt comfortable with Star once she met him. She was still wavering about whether she wanted to do a television show and how it would fit into her schedule. But Star reeled her in when he said, "You should produce the show."

"I've never produced television," she said. "I don't know anything about it."

"You'll learn." This hit her in a sweet spot: Parker was intrigued by the promise of learning a new part of the business she'd been in her whole life.

She had one more concern: the sex part of *Sex and the City*. "I just don't see that it's important," she said of doing nudity. "But we should have that conversation."

Star assured her neither he nor HBO would require her to do anything she didn't want to. "If you want to wear a bra and roll around in bed with somebody, and that's what makes you comfortable, then that's what you shall do," Parker recalls Star saying. "And if one day you decide you don't want to wear the bra, then that's what you shall do."

After the lunch with Star, Parker discussed the project with Broderick, as well as with her oldest brother and her agent. They all reacted the same: "You have to do this." She worried if she did TV, she wouldn't be able to do plays and movies—her career had allowed her a variety of challenges up until that point. But everyone she consulted insisted *Sex and the City* was the right path.

And Parker *liked* Carrie Bradshaw. She had never seen anyone like Carrie in a script before. She had never heard a female protagonist talk like that—or a male protagonist for that matter. The tone felt new to Parker.

Then again, movies provided decent paychecks without interfering with her lifelong love of theater. She aimed to perform in a play at least once a year. Two years earlier, she had played the title role in *Sylvia* (the role of a dog) the same year she also starred in *Miami Rhapsody*, a major-studio romantic comedy. A TV role, large on commitment and short on flexibility, with no definitive end date, could wreak havoc on her current life, which was just settling down with her marriage to Broderick.

On the other hand, this television show would air on HBO, home of movies that had burned out at the box office and occasional boxing matches. What were the chances of that lasting beyond one season?

Finally, Parker relented. But she was starring on Broadway as Princess Winnifred in *Once Upon a Mattress* and was about to get married. She and Broderick would need time to have their wedding, and then she wanted to finish the final two weeks of the play before filming began.

The *Sex and the City* pilot started shooting early in the morning on Tuesday, June 2, 1997—two days after the last performance of Parker's play.

Before then, Star would have to find his Miranda, Charlotte, and Samantha.

MAKING MIRANDA

Casting the part of Miranda Hobbes, one of Carrie's three friends, proved tricky in other ways. Star swiped the character's name from one of the many cynical women featured in Bushnell's columns, but he elaborated from there, making her a career-focused lawyer who appears to have given up on love. But Miranda's characterization as the "smart one" meant, in Hollywood code, the "not-pretty one," which, in Hollywood, didn't appeal to every candidate for the part.

Respected actor Cynthia Nixon, however, didn't harbor such vanity. Nixon, thirty-one at the time, had her share of conventional beauty— strawberry blond hair, translucent pale skin, gray-blue eyes. But of the Miranda role, she said, "I was excited about playing somebody who

29

was so angry, bitter, and cynical because, having been a child actor with long blonde hair, I was always playing sweet, waiflike, hippie characters. It was nice to grow out of that."

Nixon shared at least one major qualification for the show with Parker: She was a New Yorker. She was born in the city, grew up there, and came of age on the stage and screen. In fact, she and Parker had become friends when they were preteens who sometimes auditioned for the same roles.

Nixon made her film debut in 1980 at the age of fourteen in *Little Darlings*, a dramatic comedy about teen girls at summer camp who bet on which of them will lose her virginity first—a shock for the time, a kind of *Sex and the City* for the teen years. The same year, she debuted on Broadway as Blythe Danner's younger sister in a revival of Philip Barry's *The Philadelphia Story*, for which she earned a Theatre World Award. She then had roles in the thriller *Tattoo*, starring Bruce Dern, and Sidney Lumet's crime drama *Prince of the City*. The *New York Times* profiled Nixon when she was a ninth grader at Hunter College High School, describing her as "a formidably self-possessed and articulate young woman whose manner is thoroughly adult." The precocious Nixon described acting as "challenging . . . and part of the educational process." She didn't want to leave high school to be tutored on set like many child actors: "I think the most important thing is to go to a good school with good people and grow up normally."

She'd go on to attend Barnard College. In 1984, while a freshman, she appeared in two Broadway plays at the same time, *Hurlyburly* and *The Real Thing*, a likely Broadway first. After graduation from Barnard in 1988 (along with future *Gilmore Girls* actress Lauren Graham), she returned to Broadway in Wendy Wasserstein's *The Heidi Chronicles* and Tony Kushner's *Angels in America: Millennium Approaches* and *Angels in America: Perestroika*. She scored her first Tony nomination as part of the original cast of Jean Cocteau's *Indiscretions* in 1995. A theater nerd, she said she wanted her own funeral to feature Judy Garland's "I Happen to Like New York." In the two decades previous to *Sex and the City*, she appeared in twenty-five plays on and off Broadway.

With this weighty résumé behind her, Nixon—who liked the idea of being on a cable show so everyone on the street wouldn't recognize her—showed up to read a scene for HBO executives in which Miranda tells off a guy named Skipper in a bar. She was, as HBO vice president Carolyn Strauss recalls, "the sublime actress she is." Strauss had worked with Nixon on Robert Altman's political mockumentary *Tanner '88*, in which Nixon played a candidate's daughter, so Strauss knew Nixon would nail the part. But Nixon also surprised Strauss with her comedic skill; Strauss laughed as Nixon delivered a kiss-off after feeling Skipper's hand on her leg: "Let's just keep 'em where I can see 'em. All right?"

While Nixon had never done sex scenes before, she didn't mind nudity. Her previous roles hadn't required it, but, as she later explained, she breastfed her newborn daughter on the subway; she didn't see on-screen nudity any differently.

She was perfect for the part except for one thing: She was blond. As Carrie, Parker would be blond, or at least blondish. For another of Carrie's friends, Samantha, Star was hoping to get Kim Cattrall, who was also blond. Three blondes seemed like . . . a lot of blondes. Star thought of the lawyer who had helped to inspire the Miranda character; she had bright red hair.

Nixon agreed to dye her hair red. Miranda Hobbes had arrived.

CHOOSING CHARLOTTE

Actress Kristin Davis, meanwhile, had been awaiting The One in Los Angeles. Davis had classic actress features: long, brown, wavy hair; pale, luminous skin; huge brown eyes; and a face in a perpetual state of animation. She had gotten her early break on the soap opera *General Hospital* in 1991, then took her soap skills to Star's nighttime drama *Melrose Place*, her first major prime-time job. She'd appeared in memorable guest roles on *Seinfeld* and *The Larry Sanders Show*. But she was still looking for the right role to challenge her and grant her career some stability. She believed that Carrie's second friend, the optimistic-in-love art dealer Charlotte York, could be it.

Davis was intrigued when she heard Star was adapting *Sex and the City* for television. The HBO part of the equation confused her: She'd been on *Larry Sanders*, but that was the only show she knew at the network. That plus all the boxing matches they broadcast made them seem like a guy network to her. Everyone in town was now talking about Star's HBO deal, but not because they wanted in. They just wanted to know *why*.

Davis, however, did want in. At that point, women didn't have many interesting TV roles to choose from. Sitcoms ran fairly standard—*Just Shoot Me!* and *Dharma & Greg*, for instance—and dramas were mainly law shows like *The Practice*. Nothing particularly juicy was available in the medium in which she was known.

Star, meanwhile, knew Davis from *Melrose* and perceived an innocence and "old-fashioned quality" beneath her glossy surface. Before he had ever conceived of the character of Charlotte, he thought of Davis as "the *Rules* girl." He could see her as the quintessential traditional woman, and he could see the humor in offending her. He'd also watched her on *Seinfeld* as Jerry's girlfriend who unknowingly uses a toothbrush that's been dropped in the toilet—so Star knew she could do comedy. She had a sense of humor as well as a sense of propriety, and her expressive face showcased even the tiniest tick of outrage. As Star says, "There's just something about throwing a pie in the face of a beautiful girl."

This lined up with Davis's goals: She wanted to transition to comedy. After *Melrose*, she had gotten several offers for soapy roles, but she didn't want to get stuck in the melodrama genre. She had spent a year in auditions for *Seinfeld* for just that reason. She wanted one of the coveted guest spots that went to Jerry's endless string of gorgeous girlfriends. Those parts usually lasted only one episode, but forty million viewers watched every week, and a startling percentage of the actresses who got them went on to stardom soon afterward—Lauren Graham, Jane Leeves, Courteney Cox, Teri Hatcher, Debra Messing, and Davis's

Melrose costar Marcia Cross among them. Davis auditioned for *Seinfeld* ten times or so before she landed the toilet-toothbrush role.

Because Parker was still indecisive about signing on at the time, when Davis received a copy of the *Sex and the City* pilot script, it came with a cover letter from Star that asked her to consider reading for the role of Carrie. But Davis shut down when she read Star's description of Carrie as having "the body of Heather Locklear and the mind of Dorothy Parker." All Davis could think was, *I am never in a hundred million years going to have the body of Heather Locklear.* The character also smoked and swore a fair amount—before Parker shifted the character a bit—which felt quite outside Davis's boundaries. She thought, *Carrie's fantastic, but I'm Charlotte.*

That made sense. Star's Charlotte neatly matched his perception of Davis: She is sweet, easily shocked, and traditional. She believes in Prince Charming and happily-ever-after. A character named Charlotte also shows up in Bushnell's work, but she's an English journalist who is intrigued by the public spectacle of sex clubs and breaks up with an eligible man because his penis is too small—nothing like the Charlotte whom Star had invented for the show.

When Davis told her agents she was more interested in the secondary role, they tried to talk her out of it. But then Parker committed to the Carrie part anyway, so Davis went in to read for Charlotte.

Even though Charlotte's part in the *Sex and the City* pilot was small, Davis felt this was her big break. She believed Charlotte's voice was distinct and necessary in the series and could grow with time. She gave her agent the go-ahead to negotiate her deal, as was required before she could test for the pilot. She had no problem committing to the standard seven-year contract. She just needed to sign the documents on her testing day, and she was in if HBO wanted her.

At her screen test at the HBO building in the Century City section of Los Angeles, she encountered a good omen: actor Willie Garson, a friend of hers, was there to test for the part of Carrie's friend Stanford. Garson—who had the reputation of knowing everyone in

Hollywood—soothed Davis's nerves as she headed into the small theater where she'd try to prove that she was Charlotte York to HBO's president of original programming, Chris Albrecht, and vice president Carolyn Strauss.

But just after she saw Garson, an HBO employee informed her that the printer had broken. No documents to sign. No documents meant no testing.

For two and a half hours, she sat in the office waiting for the pages and pages of contract that would (or would not) determine the next several years of her life. At least Garson was there to keep her company. They talked and talked, which made time fly. She saw other actresses there to read for the part of Carrie's third friend, Samantha, and there was a guy reading for the part of Carrie's love interest, Mr. Big.

Finally, the printer came back online. Davis signed. She went in and did her thing for the producers and executives. Her scene was set on the steps of the Metropolitan Museum of Art. In it, Charlotte tries to turn down an end-of-date invitation to notorious bachelor Capote Duncan's place. He tempts her with a mention of a famous painting he owns. "Maybe just for a minute," she agrees.

Albrecht stood up when she was done. "Can you do it again and kind of hit the jokes?" he asked. Davis thought, *What jokes?* But she tried again.

Then she returned to the waiting area. They might want to bring her back in; they might not. She didn't know which she wished for. But she couldn't leave.

Star emerged after who knows how long. Davis had, at this point, spent the entire day at the studio. She had grown nervous and calmed herself ten times over.

"You need to be funnier," he said. "You need to be bigger. You need to be funnier and bigger." She knew Star well enough to know it was not good that he was waving his hands around. He did that when *he* was nervous.

"Okay, Darren," she said, hoping to placate him, but still unsure

34

what any of these instructions meant. To Davis, Charlotte didn't seem like the big, funny one. She also knew, however, that often producers and executives weren't sure what they wanted during the audition phase. They just wanted to see all of their options. She wished she could say, "Charlotte doesn't have jokes," but she kept her mouth shut.

Davis returned to the audition room and did her best to be bigger and funnier. Strauss didn't know Davis's work, but she responded to the actor's combination of "daffiness with that traditional sensibility."

Davis left, thinking, *Oh, God, I hope I got that, because I'm really right for it.*

By contract, HBO had a one-week hold on her following the audition. Days went by with no news. On the last day, Davis decided to catch a movie at noon. She doesn't remember what movie because she didn't pay attention. She was distracted, thinking about how she must not have gotten the part.

When she returned home, the call finally came: "You got it. But they might want to make Charlotte a recurring character, not a regular character." That is, she might appear only in some, but not all, episodes.

She thought, *Ew, but okay.* She figured she would do everything possible to stay on the show, and at least she had gotten a shot. She would go to Manhattan to shoot the pilot of *Sex and the City* with three other women, and it would, she believed, change her life. She would show the producers she deserved to stick around for every episode.

SEDUCING SAMANTHA

That left Samantha, a difficult role to cast—the unapologetically sexual character was over-the-top, but too much could make her into a Jessica Rabbit–like cartoon.

When actor Kim Cattrall first got the pilot script from her agent asking her to read for Samantha, she passed on it. She didn't mind that the show was set to air on HBO; she had done an episode of the network's early-'90s comedy *Dream On* and loved it. But this series came with too many unknowns for her: Like Parker, she resisted commitment to a series. She didn't know where this character could go. She felt self-conscious about playing a sexy role at forty-one. She'd read a little more than half of Bushnell's book, but couldn't stomach any more than that, so overwhelming was its cynical mood. She was single when she read it, and its dim view of relationships depressed her. She'd never liked the idea of people who were interested only in the latest drinks, the latest restaurants, and the latest designers. And she felt her actor-boyfriend didn't like the idea of her playing libertine Samantha Jones either.

In short, the role had little to recommend itself to Kim Cattrall. She'd had a long Hollywood career playing sex objects in movies such as *Mannequin* and *Police Academy*, and now she was looking for a role that would catapult her beyond that. She did not believe this was it.

When Cattrall declined, Star cast Lou Thornton, a Phoebe Cates–like actress who'd appeared in a guest spot on *Friends* and as a cast member on Jenny McCarthy's MTV sketch show. Star liked Thornton and thought she was brash and funny. But he couldn't shake the feeling that she wasn't Samantha. He had envisioned Samantha as older than the other characters, and Thornton was closer to the age of Davis, Nixon, and Parker, who had all been born within a year of each other. Still, he had chosen the best he could among his options when he thought, *Okay, let's just get it cast. We'll tweak the character to make it work.*

Star showed Thornton's tape to his partner, Dennis Erdman, a former casting director and current television director. He watched Erdman, hoping for a sign of approval.

Instead, Erdman said, "Oh, no, you can't. You just can't." Star explained that he'd found no one better, but his panic rose. He knew Erdman was right. Erdman didn't hesitate to add, "It's Kim Cattrall. It's got to be Kim Cattrall." Star reiterated that Cattrall had declined. But Erdman insisted: "I know her. Let me call her and see if she'll have lunch with you."

Erdman called Cattrall on a Sunday morning a few weeks before shooting was set to begin. "I think this is your role," he said. "Nobody is going to play it the way you're going to play it." He asked her why she'd said no.

"I don't know, Dennis," she later recalled telling him. "I feel like I'm over the hill to play this kind of role."

"You're wrong," he said. He begged her to have lunch with Star the next day, and she agreed.

• • •

Soon Star sat face-to-face with Cattrall at Lantana, an airy studio and office complex in Santa Monica distinguished by its white floors and ceilings, huge windows, greenery-packed courtyards, and modern art. He was finally lunching with the bombshell who indeed looked like someone who had once been cast as a mannequin. At forty-one, she was nearly a decade older than the rest of the cast. And she was as perfect as Star knew she'd be.

Cattrall was born in Liverpool, England, and raised on Vancouver Island in British Columbia, Canada. Like Bushnell, she moved to New York City as a teenager; she did so to attend the American Academy of Dramatic Arts. Cattrall's film debut came at age nineteen in Otto Preminger's film *Rosebud*. She did theater and commercials for the next few years, and because she was a beautiful blonde, she ended up mostly in sexpot roles in movies such as *Police Academy*, *Porky's*, *Mannequin*, *Masquerade*, *Big Trouble in Little China*, and *The Bonfire of the Vanities*.

When she heard Parker was committed to *Sex and the City*, that helped to bolster her confidence in the job, and her meeting with Star further assuaged some of her fears. In fact, she shared many of the same reservations that Parker had expressed about the project: She was scared to sign on when she didn't know what the show would be. She felt better once she met Star in person and talked it over. They discussed the character, the possibilities, and why Star thought she was perfect for it.

Still, Cattrall didn't identify with the character he was asking her to play. Her sex life had not, overall, set the world on fire like Samantha's; in fact, for most of her life, she later wrote, her sexual experiences had been "unfulfilling." She took longer to get over an intimate relationship than Samantha did. But Cattrall also had faith Samantha could change and grow, should the series continue long enough.

And Cattrall could see Samantha's strengths. "Samantha is street-smart," she said. She imagined that Samantha had come up as an assistant to a powerful publicist like Peggy Siegal, who was known for running A-list actors through brutal Oscar campaigns.

Star told Cattrall at lunch that he couldn't guarantee anything except that she'd have a say in her character's trajectory. He told her he genuinely believed the show could be "something special." His honesty got to her. Later that day, she told HBO she was in. And she soon left the boyfriend whom she felt didn't like her playing Samantha.

With Cattrall's commitment, the *Sex and the City* core foursome was completed: Parker, Nixon, Davis, and Cattrall would become known as "the girls," as everyone on set began calling them. It was often followed by an apology, and a correction: "I mean, women." But "the girls" were who they would be, forevermore.

MEETING THE MEN

The women handled, Darren Star and HBO could turn their attention to the men in the pilot. The first episode included the show's first male recurring characters who stood out from the blur of suitors: Carrie's best gay friend, Stanford Blatch, played by Willie Garson, and Mr. Big, played by Chris Noth.

Everyone in Los Angeles knew Garson as the "mayor of Hollywood" because he had appeared in so many shows and films—with more than 250 TV credits alone, including on *NYPD Blue*, *Party of Five*, and *The X-Files*. He knew nearly every actor working.

Garson grew up in New Jersey and had met Parker two decades

earlier when they were set up on a date. (Though straight, he would become most famous as one of *Sex and the City*'s standout gay characters.)

Noth played the suave, ungettable man we would know as "Mr. Big" until the series's end. The women give him the nickname in the first episode and stick to it thereafter, just like Bushnell and her Mr. Big in the column and book. When casting the role, the producers looked for someone sexy, of course—described as "an early Alec Baldwin type." Noth, who was forty-three, portrayed the character as a Cary Grant–like mirage, always shimmering just beyond Carrie's reach. At six foot one, with a flop of dark hair and brown eyes with just the right hint of wrinkles at the corners, he filled Big's suit nicely.

Noth knew the terrain depicted in *Sex and the City*. As a handsome, single, New York City–based actor, he embraced his bachelorhood: "I've had a lot of intense, crazy love affairs," he said in an interview at the time. "I think that as you get older and you're comfortable in your own skin, you're not afraid of being alone. But it's not as easy to fall in love." He claimed to be as ungettable in real life as Mr. Big was on-screen: "I don't know if I'm a very good catch. I love women and that gets me into trouble."

Born in Wisconsin and raised in Connecticut, Noth loved to perform from an early age and attended the Barlow School, a high school for the arts in upstate New York, where he also engaged in his share of skinny dipping, smoking "herb," and sex. In his youth, he has said, he made a lot of trouble and drove his mother, a New York City TV reporter, nuts. He got his master of fine arts degree from Yale School of Drama in 1985 and appeared in films such as *Baby Boom* and *Naked in New York*, but was best known for his role as Detective Mike Logan on *Law & Order* from 1990 to '95.

Though he related to the dating scene *Sex and the City* portrayed, he found his character hard to pin down. The other male characters' dysfunctions made them fun to play, but Big didn't have any. Noth would complain to Star, "All you have me doing is opening up another good bottle of wine and being remote." In other words, Big did not match the rambunctious Noth in personality.

DESPERATELY SEEKING *SEX*

The parade of men passing through *Sex and the City* wouldn't stop until the final season, but male characters would mostly remain accessories to the female stories at the show's center. To highlight that fact from the beginning, Star approached a female director, Susan Seidelman, to handle the pilot episode. She had directed *Desperately Seeking Susan*, which topped Star's list of favorite movies because of its New York sensibility.

Seidelman made her name directing the 1985 hit about a bored housewife who assumes the identity of a New York City bohemian played by Madonna, in all of her '80s Madonna glory. Seidelman had also directed the Roseanne Barr–Meryl Streep movie *She-Devil* as well as *Smithereens*, her 1982 full-length debut about a young female runaway set in New York's punk scene. (By coincidence, *Smithereens* had also featured Noth in one of his first roles ever, as a cross-dressing hooker in the back of a van.) She hadn't done much television, and that was the point: Star was looking to bring a filmic sensibility and unique visual style to the series.

Star had sent the script to Seidelman before auditions began. Going into it cold, she was pleasantly surprised. She loved it, and she never loved TV scripts. They were usually so generic. This felt fresh. She herself would watch this show. She agreed to direct the pilot. Star told her that above all, he hoped she'd make the pilot look as far from standard TV comedy as possible.

Seidelman brought with her a film-caliber staff. The director of photography, Stuart Dryburgh, had worked on films such as Jane Campion's *The Portrait of a Lady* and *The Piano*. Production designer Mark Friedberg had helped set the visual tone on stylized films such as Ang Lee's *The Ice Storm* and Mira Nair's *Kama Sutra: A Tale of Love*.

Because of the staff, as well as the luxurious timeline for the shoot—nine days to make a half-hour show, plus several weeks of prep time—Seidelman felt as if she were making a short indie film rather than a television series. (Later episodes would be shot two at a time over ten days, and many traditional half-hour sitcoms at the time shot one per week.) She'd be able to invent the look and feel from scratch.

She was also shooting in downtown Manhattan neighborhoods where she'd lived for decades. She loved being able to explore SoHo's hidden clubs and streets. She filmed one scene at the East Village restaurant Lucky Cheng's, known for its drag queen waiters. She couldn't believe she got to put that in a television show; this was not *Friends* New York or *Seinfeld* New York. Audiences rarely got to see this New York on-screen, and HBO placed no limits or demands on what should be shown. The network trusted the creative team to do as it pleased.

• • •

Seidelman was perfect for the job for reasons beyond her résumé: The Third Wave of feminism—the movement that picked up where 1970s Women's Lib left off—would find its way into the heart of mainstream culture with *Sex and the City*. And the woman who made Madonna a movie star was the perfect person to lead it there.

The Third Wave movement had gained steam throughout the 1990s with help from the pop star, among many other cultural forces. It was named in succession with the Second Wave, the movement of the 1970s and what many of us think of as classic "Women's Lib": Betty Friedan arguing for women's right to leave the domestic sphere in *The Feminine Mystique*, Gloria Steinem fighting for legalized abortion and women's workplace rights, protests against the Miss America pageant, marches for the Equal Rights Amendment, consciousness-raising circles, and the push to recognize domestic violence and rape. Pop culturally, the Second Wave was Helen Reddy's "I Am Woman," Steinem's *Ms.* magazine, and *The Mary Tyler Moore Show*. (The First Wave had focused on women's suffrage, which succeeded in the United States in 1919 with the Nineteenth Amendment to the Constitution.)

The Third Wave accelerated with Susan Faludi's book *Backlash* in 1991, which called on feminists to wake up and smell the regression of the 1980s, a time during which conservative values reigned and, accordingly, the only real feminist television shows were *Roseanne* and *Murphy Brown*. Most other shows of the era—*Growing Pains, Who's the Boss?, The Cosby Show*—centered on traditional family structures with slight tweaks for the times, working moms and male nannies often played like wacky anomalies.

When the Third Wave arrived, it sought to reconcile femininity, sexual power, and equality—exactly what *Sex and the City* grappled with. Third Wavers emphasized female sexual pleasure as a form of liberation, something the Second Wavers of the 1960s and '70s had been loath to do, for fear of seeming selfish in relation to survivors of sexual assault. The Second Wave had taught women to protect themselves from the dangers of sex at the expense of exploring its pleasures. In contrast, the 1984 anthology *Pleasure and Danger: Exploring Female Sexuality* argued for the approach that rose to prominence during the Third Wave: "The overemphasis on danger runs the risk of making speech about sexual pleasure taboo. Feminists are easily intimidated by the charge that their own pleasure is selfish, as in political rhetoric that suggests no woman is entitled to talk about sexual pleasure while any woman remains in danger—that is, never."

Still, the Second Wave had raised the consciousness of millions and offered a path toward more progressive views of marriage—and singlehood. This, in turn, made it possible for Third Wavers to focus on such luxuries as sexual pleasure and career advancement.

The most provocative female artist to hit the mainstream, Madonna, made the erotic a mass-market concept with her coffee table book of photographs, *Sex*, in 1992. Madonna declared that her brand of feminism was pro-porn: "I don't see how a guy looking at a naked girl in a magazine is degrading to women," she wrote in the book. "Everyone has their sexuality. It's how you treat people in everyday life that counts, not what turns you on in your fantasy. If all a person ever did was get off on porno movies I would say they are probably dysfunctional sexually, but I don't think it's unhealthy to be interested in that or get off on that." Photos in the book included nudes of Madonna and other celebrities, such as Vanilla Ice and Naomi Campbell; Madonna shaving a man's pubic hair; and Madonna frolicking suggestively with a dog. *Sex* incited a boycott led by the Vatican. It was also a bestseller, moving 150,000 copies in the United States on its release day.

Third Wave feminism's underground musical offshoot, the '90s Riot Grrrl punk movement, also espoused viewpoints that would go mainstream in *Sex and the City*. Riot Grrrl leaders such as Kathleen Hanna wore revealing outfits and reclaimed derogatory terms like "slut" and "bitch." (Hanna wrote "SLUT" on her bare midriff for performances.) Poppier iterations of Riot Grrrl ideas—and precursors to *Sex and the City* themes—came through in indie rocker Liz Phair's 1993 album, *Exile in Guyville* (sample lyric: "Every time I see your face I get all wet between my legs"), and Alanis Morissette's 1995 breakthrough, *Jagged Little Pill* (sample lyric: "Is she perverted like me? Would she go down on you in a theater?"). *Sex and the City* would similarly embrace epithets aimed at sexually expressive women (one episode was called "Are We Sluts?"), objectify men, and advocate for women's guilt-free enjoyment of a variety of sexual pleasures. Morissette would later call *Sex and the City*'s producers to ask for a guest role; she'd play a bisexual woman who kisses Carrie during a game of spin the bottle.

The message was clear: The marriage plot was no longer the only one that interested women. They were just as interested in the sex plot, and many of them saw the pursuit of their own as a feminist act.

Sex and the City embodied those Third Wave ideas, spreading them throughout the United States and around the world. Single women, it taught us, deserved material success on their own and great sex of their choice. The young women carrying the rekindled feminist torch built a movement that fit their modern needs, with overarching themes of career success, financial independence, sexual freedom, and pop cultural power.

And if *Sex and the City* was the first show with truly feminist themes to arrive on television in a while, it was appearing just in time: The same month it debuted, in June 1998, *Time* magazine's cover asked, "Is Feminism Dead?" It pictured a succession of images—Susan B. Anthony, Betty Friedan, Gloria Steinem, and TV character Ally McBeal, implicated as the movement's death knell, presumably because she was a bit of a nervous flibbertigibbet who was obsessed with love and babies. She was also, it must be repeated, fictional.

Darren Star's confident, independent characters would face at least as much backlash as the bumbling Ms. McBeal once the show started to air. Women couldn't win on television. But *Sex and the City* would eventually prove that they could make progress.

GETTING TO "ACTION!"

Candace Bushnell had just finished shooting an episode of her 1997 VH1 talk show, *Sex, Lies, and Video Clips*, at the network's studios on the Hudson River in Manhattan. She was still living her life of contradictions—wearing Dolce & Gabbana and hosting her own show while sleeping on a fold-out sofa. She walked a few blocks downtown along the city's west side on that June day, turned a corner, and there it was: Cranes reached up to the sky; TV crew members huddled among camera equipment. They were shooting scenes for the pilot episode of the adaptation of her book *Sex and the City*. The crew was filming on location at an apartment meant to belong to "toxic bachelor" Capote Duncan, who goes out on a romantic date with Charlotte, then sleeps with Samantha.

Bushnell was seeing her work come to life. Pure magic.

Parker, meanwhile, was beginning to dig into playing the show's version of Bushnell, a character Parker was excited to figure out. She was particularly enamored of the final moment in the pilot episode. It was some of the best writing she had ever read. In the scene, the independent—but romantically inclined—relationship columnist gets out of a Town Car she's shared with the dreamy Mr. Big after running into him repeatedly throughout the episode. She asks him if he's ever

44

been in love, and he says, "Abso-fucking-lutely." The episode ends with a freeze frame on her face. Her face would have to convey something. *Everything.* The potential ending of the series, whenever it might come, felt like it began with that look. She might already be in love. She didn't want to be in love. She desperately wanted to be in love.

Upon reading that scene in the script, Parker saw the promise of the show to come. *It's all potential*, she thought. It was like the city, as Parker later recalled: "Every time you walk out the door, you don't know what you'll bump into, who you'll bump into, what experience you'll have." You might step in dog poop. Or you might meet your destiny.

No big deal: Just the city she called home, the center of the universe, in one scene. Just the entirety of the show she was staking her future on in one look.

Now she understood what her husband and her agent saw in this script for her. This exhilarated her.

Seidelman loved working with the show's four stars on the pilot. Parker, she says, "is such a professional. There are actors you need to direct, and then there are actors who create their character and they're just there to tell the story." Seidelman knew Nixon's work from the stage: "She's a great New York actress," Seidelman says, the ultimate compliment from a New York director. "It was wonderful to be able to work with somebody who's so good at what she does." Davis, she recalls, seemed to be "the good girl," not unlike her character. Cattrall, she remembers, "was fun, up for anything. She was excited to be pushing the boundaries," the most important quality for any *Sex and the City* cast or crew member.

THE FIRST TIME

Amid the green hills, palm-tree-dotted beaches, and turquoise waters of Nevis, the first cut of *Sex and the City* made its debut.

A few months after the pilot shoot, friends Bushnell and Star took another one of their trips together, this time to a small Caribbean island, where Bushnell was researching a *Travel + Leisure* article. As

Star unpacked his bags in their room, he produced a VHS tape. "I've got a surprise," he told her, brandishing the finished pilot episode. She sat down right there and watched the entire thing, ignoring the waves lapping outside.

Star was apprehensive. What if she didn't like it? What would happen to the show? And their friendship? He had spent so much time thinking about this pilot, he had no idea what it would look like to someone else. He had no idea if it was good.

When it ended, Bushnell turned to look at him. He saw, with great relief, pure admiration. "Darren," she gushed, "they're going to be watching this in film school." He thought, *Okay, Candace, you are too close to your own material.* But he was chuffed.

• • •

After that auspicious private premiere in late 1997, however, the show's progress stalled in the corporate morass. After any pilot episode is shot for television, its network must then decide whether it warrants being made into a series. For broadcast networks, a typical timeline was in place, with pilots shot in the early spring, then picked up or rejected by summer, but HBO, which had made fewer shows and didn't adhere to the traditional fall TV season, had no such system in place. Months went by with no word from HBO. No one knew if the pilot would turn into a series or sit on a shelf at the network forever.

During that time, Parker ran into Meryl Poster, the copresident of production at Miramax Films, on the street in Manhattan. Miramax, the movie studio founded by Bob and Harvey Weinstein, was at the height of its power, riding the indie film renaissance with hits like *Chasing Amy* and *Good Will Hunting*. When Poster saw Parker on the street, she recognized her; she had worked with Broderick on the 1993 romantic comedy *The Night We Never Met*.

"I just saw your show," Parker remembers Poster saying. "It's so great!"

Parker, a veteran of television and movies, had learned to shoot and then move on with her life, not giving projects another thought until someone called to tell her it was time to go out and promote or shoot more. And since HBO didn't work on a traditional broadcast timetable, she had no idea when such a call might come. Seeing Parker's confusion, Poster added, "Didn't you do a pilot? *Sex and the City?*" Parker hadn't seen it yet; she didn't even know there was a finished version of it. But she was happy to hear good buzz, especially from someone with taste like Poster.

Mostly happy, anyway. Parker *still* didn't know if she wanted to do a TV show. But she'd worry about that when the call came.

• • •

A few more months went by. Kristin Davis returned to her regular life in her rented house in Los Angeles. One day as she walked her dog, Davis was surprised to run into Parker on her small side street in the Brentwood neighborhood. This quiet part of LA rarely hosted such run-ins. It turned out Parker and Broderick had rented a house nearby while Broderick shot the *Inspector Gadget* movie. Thanks to Parker and Broderick's full work schedules, they were apparently ubiquitous on the streets of both New York and Los Angeles.

Davis asked if Parker had heard anything about *Sex and the City*. "No," Parker said. "I don't know what's going on." Davis thought Parker seemed like she hoped it wouldn't be picked up, though perhaps Davis was reading too much into the interaction. In actuality, Parker had simply put the project out of her mind, but Davis prayed every day for her phone to ring with good news.

• • •

The call did come, though not until nine months after they had shot the pilot. *Sex and the City* had been picked up for a full season. Parker's first thought, now that it was real, was clear: *I have to get out of it. I can't be tied down to a television series.*

She had starred on the CBS teen comedy *Square Pegs* from 1982 to '83, the NBC family drama *A Year in the Life* from 1987 to '88, and the

ABC legal drama *Equal Justice* from 1990 to '91. None had lasted longer than twenty-seven episodes, and still the experiences had given her a sense of foreboding about television. Everything became so routine on a series: every day, driving onto a studio lot and saying hello to the same people and parking in the same space.

And worse, that routine could last far more than twenty-seven episodes, keeping her tied down when she could be going off to different places all over the world to shoot movies or perform in plays.

She told her agent she wanted out again. As Parker remembers it, she and her agent put together an alternate proposal, an offer for Parker to work for HBO for free in other, shorter-term projects in exchange for springing her from this one. She could back out without scuttling *Sex and the City*'s future entirely. Star had taken Parker's reservations so seriously that he had a backup Carrie just in case Parker skipped out: Lisa Edelstein, whose credits included the *Superman* TV show, *Sports Night*, *Frasier*, and *Just Shoot Me!*

But HBO didn't want to let Parker go.

Vice president Carolyn Strauss and her boss, Chris Albrecht, knew how important their leading lady was, and they wanted Parker. Faced with Parker's proposal to leave, they asked for a meeting to discuss her concerns. They explained to her that they weren't a broadcast network that would demand twenty-two-episode seasons on a tight schedule. They could time things in a way that made sense and maintained quality. They could pull the plug if it was a miserable failure.

She recalls them telling her she could hire a producer of her choice if that made her feel more comfortable. (It did. She chose Barry Jossen, with whom she'd worked on *Miami Rhapsody*.) She still worried: What if she wanted to go to Los Angeles with Broderick for a shoot? What if she got a movie role in London or Paris or Bangladesh? But HBO's persistence, patience, and kindness won her over. She told herself they would take care of her, pushed away the feeling of doom, and hoped for the best.

3

Building *Sex and the City*'s New York
· · · · · · · · · · ·

It was Carrie's vulnerability that drew comedian and writer Michael Patrick King to *Sex and the City*.

In early 1998, King, who was based in Los Angeles, watched the pilot, sent by an executive friend of his at HBO, Carolyn Strauss. King had met Strauss when she scouted the comedy circuit for talent years earlier. Now, Strauss thought King would be "the perfect fit" as a writer-producer for the show: "He would add that zing."

As King watched, he wasn't sure if it was for him—the self-conscious analysis of whether women could have sex "like men"; the faux interviews with random male characters on the street; the main character, played by Sarah Jessica Parker, talking directly to the camera.

Then he saw something that got his attention: the last moment of the episode, which freeze-frames on Parker looking like she's been punched in the stomach. She's just gotten a ride home from the dapper

Mr. Big in his Town Car and asked him if he's ever been in love. His response before he drives away: "Abso-fucking-lutely." Just like Parker, King was intrigued by that freeze-framed expression: the pain of starting to fall in love.

King's thought: What else might there be here? She's in pain. She's thrown. Why? In that moment, Carrie Bradshaw was cocky, but she was rattled. The potential of that story and that last moment of Sarah Jessica Parker's performance intrigued him so much that he wanted to give that character more. He didn't know what else this show might become over a season, but he wanted to be there when it happened. He told Strauss he was in.

Creator Darren Star couldn't keep *Sex and the City* to himself any longer now that he faced making eleven episodes in three months, so King was hired as co–executive producer and the two began to write the show. A former stand-up comic and Emmy-nominated TV writer for his work on *Murphy Brown*, King provided the perfect comedic counterpoint to Star's extensive drama experience. Together, they would write most of the first season.

While building his writing career in New York City years earlier, King played the stand-up comedy clubs before moving to Los Angeles to do his first TV job as staff writer on the CBS comedy *Good Sports*, which starred real-life couple Farrah Fawcett and Ryan O'Neal as a fictional couple of sportscasters. He joined the hit *Murphy Brown* at the start of its fifth season, the one infamous for upsetting Vice President Dan Quayle with Murphy's single motherhood, and he stayed there from 1991 to 1993. Then, after taking over the reins of another CBS comedy, *Good Advice*, he made the dicey decision to join the Cybill Shepherd sitcom *Cybill* in 1996 as an executive producer. It was a tumultuous seven episodes before he and the show parted ways. Asked about the experience later, he said, "Never take a job just for the money."

He took a break afterward to travel in Europe and was now back in the States ready to write again. HBO asked King to help Star make the show funny, to lighten up Bushnell's dark take on Manhattan women.

King and Star started to write the first season in Los Angeles, where King was now living and Star kept a place. Their process was simple: They sat in a room, went through the script, and tried to make each other laugh. At one point, Star gave King the ultimate compliment: King offered a joke for the script they were writing, and Star—suffering from the flu—snotted down his face with laughter. They worked together to translate what had made them laugh (or snot) into what they thought would entertain the actresses and, hopefully, the audience.

It did not escape King nor Star that they were two men writing a show about women. But as gay men raised in that particular time, they could relate to the pressure from society to conform to traditional values—much like the way single women were expected to conform and play traditional roles as well. King and Star also both felt unusually connected to the women in their lives. King had three sisters, so he always saw girls as his friends and equals; plus he already had experience writing the voice of a very strong female character like Murphy Brown. Star, on the other hand, had written two hit shows with largely female audiences, and had come to *Sex and the City* thanks to his close friendship with author Candace Bushnell. In Los Angeles, King and Star also had some help from two female script consultants: Andrea King, a writer friend of Star's, and Terri Minsky, who'd been on staff at *Central Park West*.

• • •

As the writing burden for the show grew, help came in other forms.

Amy B. Harris, Star's assistant, proved to be an asset to the writing team as well; she was always the first to question a story line that didn't fit Carrie's reality. She had been Star's assistant since the *Central Park West* days. Both she and Star grew up near Washington, DC. Harris had gone to nursery school with Star's brother. She and Star crossed paths again while both were visiting their parents' vacation homes in Bethany Beach, Delaware. Harris had moved to New York in 1993 after graduating from Duke University. She had meant to take just a year off and then go to law school, but she loved the city so much that she stayed.

When Star heard that Harris was an assistant at *Vanity Fair* magazine, he asked if he could meet with her to chat about her experience for research on *Central Park West*. Afterward, she told him she'd love a job on the show if he was shooting in New York. He hired her as his assistant.

Harris lived a *Sex and the City* life. A sunny blonde with long, wavy hair, she actually resembled Candace Bushnell. From her time at *Vanity Fair*, she knew how to get into trendy restaurants and clubs. Even though she was an assistant, she blew a few paychecks on Manolo Blahniks. She knew how to make her money go a long way: Flirting with the right people and going to the right events could get you food and drinks. She knew whom to ask to get designer clothes.

On *Sex and the City*, Star made her a producer, tasking her with helping out at Parker's voice-over recording sessions. King often took her out for dinner so he could bounce plot lines off her. As a Manhattan woman in her midtwenties, she was the show's target audience. "I see your face," he told her, "and I know whether the stories are working." From there, he encouraged her to try writing a few scripts. Soon he and Star moved her onto the writing staff.

As production revved up, they shifted to the East Coast to set up an official writers' room in New York City. There, they hired an inexperienced young writer named Michael Green and added Jenny Bicks, who'd worked on the Téa Leoni comedy *The Naked Truth*.

Michael Green joined the *Sex and the City* writing team having never written a television show. As a twenty-five-year-old man, he ranked among the least likely people for a job writing about thirty- and fortysomething women. He had just signed as a screenwriter with a new talent agency called Endeavor. When he told his new representatives that he'd be interested in TV as well as movies, they suggested he try for a job at a new HBO show, *Sex and the City*, which needed help and didn't exactly have prestigious writers lining up to beg for work.

When Star called Green in for an interview, it was Green's first meeting ever in the television business. It didn't occur to Green to ask to see a tape of the pilot before the meeting or to find out much about the show at all. He had no idea what to wear to the interview. He pulled his long hair back into a ponytail and settled on a suit with no tie. He was wrong. "Are you going somewhere after this?" Star asked him. Once Green started work on the show, he saw the uniform: T-shirts and jeans.

Green was so young that he had written a dating column for his college paper just a few years before, "mostly about how I couldn't get laid," as he says. Star asked to see some copies. After the meeting, Green made photocopies of his clips and dropped them off with Star's doorman.

The next week Green got a call at his parents' house in Westchester County, New York, where he was staying. He had finally watched a tape of the pilot, so he was excited; he thought this would be a good show. He tried to sound cool as he complimented Star on the first episode, but he was so nervous, he wrapped himself up in the spiral phone cord in his parents' kitchen as he talked.

Star offered him the job. "Sure, that sounds fun," Green said, attempting nonchalance while all but doing a happy dance. He was becoming a television writer!

He told friends and family he was going to work on a cable show with the word "sex" in the title. "You should really go into real estate with your dad," many replied.

He had no idea how he would do this job, and he wasn't sure he was suited for *Sex and the City*. "It's so specific in voice and humor. Everything about it that makes it a show I couldn't write is what makes it worth watching," he says. "It isn't a show any writer could come and crack and tune into the voice."

• • •

Green's first day on set was a location shoot around the block from where he now lived with his brother, at 82nd Street and Madison Avenue, just blocks from Central Park. He spent his first day eating French fries and watching the crew shoot some people-on-the-street interview sequences. He pitched a joke, someone laughed, someone else faxed the joke to the production office, and before Green knew it, one of the actors said his line. It was the highlight of his twenty-five years of life thus far.

Green was charged with writing the eleventh episode of the first season, "The Drought," in which Carrie is mortified after she farts in bed with Mr. Big. He knew it broke new ground—women did not fart on television, much less discuss it in the context of a sexual relationship. He hadn't come up with the story line, but he got to write the script.

Green learned everything about the business from King and Star, who he says were outrageously patient with his inexperience. He found out what "breaking story" meant: the process of brainstorming to figure out the outline of a script before it's assigned to a writer.

He also understood for the first time what it meant to be truly funny—and he learned he might not be funny enough for television comedy. King's humor instincts, in particular, felt like a supernatural force to him, one he would never possess himself. He knew he could never match a comedic mind like King, and began to think about how he could lean into his own gifts, perhaps more dramatically oriented.

Green remembers when King and Star returned to the set from an interview with the *New York Times*. "What do you think they would say if they knew the show about women was being written by two queens and a twenty-year-old?" joked King.

It wasn't totally accurate. But it was a damn good joke.

• • •

Jenny Bicks came to write for *Sex and the City* with far more experience than Green, both as a woman and as a TV writer. King called her out of the blue, four years after he worked with her on a CBS comedy called *The 5 Mrs. Buchanans*: "Look, I'm writing on this show," he said. "We're just starting it and I thought of you because I thought you'd have fun writing it. Do you want to come and have fun with us?"

Star had read the script Bicks wrote for *Larry Sanders* and loved it. She joined for the eighth episode of the first season. In "Three's a Crowd," Charlotte's new beau requests a threesome and Carrie feels like she's in an emotional threesome with Big and his ex-wife.

Bicks identified with the show's main character. "She's smart," Bicks says. "Where others might shut down at certain things, she was always open and nonjudgmental. And I think that's what made her so likable to an audience." Bicks also loved to write for Samantha. The character, she says, "had no boundaries in a great way. She was all about fun, not being intimidated and being confident." Like King, Bicks enjoyed the character's combination of sexual freedom, self-respect, and loyal friendship.

The character of Charlotte allowed Bicks to tap into a different part of her own life. She had grown up on the Upper East Side, so she felt like she knew Charlottes. She knew what traditional Upper East Side culture, full of business titans and debutantes, expected of women. Bicks was perfectly suited to write about Charlotte's ingrained longing for a husband who was a paragon of masculinity, handsome and wealthy and proper and Protestant.

Bicks had never had a job quite like *Sex and the City* before. Though it was a television show, she considered it the first time she had done film work. She had to be on set every day, from the earliest call time to wrap. There wasn't just one showtime with a live audience like she was used to from sitcoms. Plus, much of the shooting happened on location throughout New York City, which complicated matters. The first season of shooting, before the show aired on HBO, she recalls that the owners of many locations the scripts called for didn't want to shut down business for a day just to let some show they'd never heard of tear the place apart. The *Sex and the City* team was shooed away from restaurants and street corners, met with a common New York response:

"Get the fuck out of here. You're making too much noise." They didn't give a shit who Carrie Bradshaw was.

Being the only woman on staff in the early days of a show about women's sex lives presented its share of unique experiences. Once, she had to draw a detailed diagram of women's sex organs on a dry-erase board to explain some basic mechanics to King and Star. As much as they knew their way around a TV script, they did not know their way around a vulva and clitoris.

• • •

The New York writers' room, as well as the interior sets for the show, took up residence at Silvercup Studios in Queens, just across the East River from Midtown Manhattan. Most of the writers, actors, and crew came in over the Queensboro Bridge, whose entrance and exit ramp curl around the building, a converted bread factory. The bridge's yellow metal frame consists of triangles upon triangles that stretch straight out across the water along the golden-brown brick building's north side and send traffic right past the grand red Silvercup sign.

The regular writing schedule began that fall, and, as King describes it, "We just started going: 'Can we say that? Can we say that? Can we say this? Can we do that? Can we do this?'"

Almost every plot line they tackled was being shown for the first time on television—"and for the first time in this generation," as Star says. "I was inspired by movies of the '70s, like *Shampoo*. When I went to the movies as a kid, I went to the movies to learn about sex. You were always trying to sneak into R-rated movies because you didn't get it anywhere else. That was a different era. This show, for me, was what those R-rated movies were when I was a kid."

After he joined the show, King had another moment—just as clear as when he'd seen Carrie's look at the end of the pilot—in which he knew *Sex and the City* would be special. It was the moment he met Sarah Jessica Parker for the first time in a design meeting with her and Star. King doesn't remember the subject of the meeting—because he wasn't paying any attention. He was too busy leaning back on the couch and laughing with Sarah Jessica. It was an instant connection. King felt like they'd known each other forever. Making her laugh was intoxicating. He knew, in that first meeting, that Parker was the perfect muse for him. She would continue to be for at least the next twelve years.

The real-life Carrie, Candace Bushnell, provided extra inspiration. Every time she talked, King's head exploded. She had an Oscar Wilde–like penchant for making sweeping statements that were neither true nor terribly sensical. Baffling things like, "Every woman in New York knows everything about every man's penis in New York." He would think, *Okay, that's not true at all, but I love the grandiosity.* All King needed to do when he was stumped for a line was to think of her.

Bushnell continued to read scripts as the writers churned them out, and she provided notes like, "No one shops there anymore," when a certain Manhattan department store was mentioned as a location. "Now it's Gucci, Gucci, Gucci." She sometimes visited the set, perusing the crew for handsome men who weren't wearing wedding rings.

A relationship columnist, after all, is never really off duty.

GETTING COMFORTABLE

Shooting began on the rest of the first season. Parker walked to the set at the beginning of production, just a few blocks from where she lived in the West Village. They were filming near the Banana Republic store on Bleecker Street and Sixth Avenue. Suddenly, she knew: no more feelings of doom. She didn't wish she were somewhere else. There was no lot to drive onto, no parking space to suffocate her with its sameness. She loved her new job. She'd made the right decision in the end.

Her character had even moved to Parker's own neighborhood, in a sense. Though Carrie lived on the Upper East Side—where the pilot episode had been shot on location—the crew had chosen a brownstone on Perry Street, just blocks from Parker's home, to serve as the exterior of Carrie's apartment.

Routines and relationships began to develop among the cast and crew hired for the series beyond the pilot. The crew would shoot the episodes in sets of two, which allowed for more location-shoot coordination. (Restaurants, clubs, and other locations for both episodes could be clustered near each other for efficiency.) The two directors of photography for the show could alternate two-episode blocks, and directors were usually assigned both episodes in the pair. Writers had to have two scripts at a time ready to be scouted, cast, and costumed.

As filming continued, the cast and crew began to notice a strange feeling, one they couldn't immediately identify. Then it dawned on them: While many of them had worked in television before, they hadn't done it this way. They hadn't ever shot an entire first season without airing one episode. But this was how HBO decided to shoot the first season, allowing the producers to hone the season with a definitive arc.

But that meant that on *Sex and the City*, the cast and crew didn't have the compass a viewing public provided: *This* worked. People loved *that*. *This* didn't go over so hot. *That* was a surprise hit. They had only each other. In yet another way, they were shooting the show like a movie. No viewer would see a second of it until after they had wrapped the entire first season. It was both freeing and dread-inducing.

They were reminded of this vacuum in which they worked whenever they went out to do the people-on-the-street interview sequences. HBO was known for boxing, yes, but also for a series called *Real Sex*, which became the bane of *Sex and the City* in its early days. *Real Sex* documented ordinary people's fetishes, fantasies, and other sex-related activities in naked detail. In a standard episode, you might get an eyeful of a guy with a girdle fetish, sex-doll enthusiasts, a sex club in a Holland farmhouse, or a suburban sex-technique party. King describes *Real Sex* as "that sleazy show where they were always dipping somebody's penis in polyurethane to preserve it." (It is not clear that this ever indeed happened on *Real Sex*.)

When *Sex and the City* producers fanned out across New York City to film the people-on-the-street interviews, they finally got a reaction from the public, though it wasn't quite what they were longing for. They were filming the interviews with actors who were cast as people on the street, but New Yorkers who walked by would often ask what they were shooting. When they said, "It's *Sex and the City* for HBO," the passersby would respond with something along the lines of "Ewww."

• • •

While *Sex and the City* was often confused with *Real Sex* in those early days, *Real Sex* did play a role in readying the world for *Sex and the City*, with its explorations of striptease classes and sex toy parties. It was part of a wider culture clash happening in America over sex: On the one hand, sexual misconduct allegations dogged President Bill Clinton and were about to explode with the revelation of his affair with White House intern Monica Lewinsky, which made salacious sex a national conversation. On the other hand, abstinence-only education swept the nation as part of a welfare reform bill passed in 1996, closing off school as a source for practical sex information. The Internet and cable television became key to disseminating the information about sex young people craved. *Real Sex* played a part in that, and *Sex and the City* would as well.

Parker felt her character balanced both sides of American sexual discourse, weighing her interest in sex against traditional romantic values: "She's actually old-fashioned," Parker said of Carrie. "If she weren't old-fashioned, she wouldn't be on this endless search. Carrie is a very honest person. You can say a lot of things about her, but she has a moral compass."

That said, *Sex and the City* also began to push the conversation forward, as King saw it: "Sex, up until *Sex and the City*, was sort of dipped in black and it was dark and dirty and oily. After us, sex was seen differently. We made it pink. And fizzy. We took it into the light and made it something empowering, but also funny."

They were making a show about sex with a lot of sex scenes, but for the first time such a show was aimed at women. This represented a clear step forward in television. *Sex and the City*'s sex wasn't salacious; it was there to illustrate a point. It wasn't there to turn people on. It was there to make them laugh. If you can make people laugh at sex, King thought, that was more revolutionary than shoving sex in viewers' faces just to be edgy. "For me, an Irish Catholic, to tap into my well of sexual shame, it's a gold mine for comedy," King says. The laughter allowed for real conversation instead of reinforcement of taboos. "Our sexual story lines were funny and sometimes very shocking but always in the show to illustrate how we evolve as people through our sexual experiences." King saw humor as a sneaky and effective way to break taboos and make sex, in all its variations, a little more acceptable.

One of the show's most shocking early moments—what would become known around the set as the "up-the-butt cab-ride scene"—became evident at the first table read for its script. As the four women discussed the relative merits and demerits of Charlotte's new beau's request for anal sex, the actors flushed. King felt certain no one had ever committed the sentence "Who ever heard of Mrs. Up the Butt?" to film. "If he goes up there, there's going to be a shift in power," Miranda says. This was a discussion heretofore unknown in the annals of female-driven television shows.

Suddenly TV had a space for a line like, "His dick was the size of one of those miniature golf pencils. I didn't know if he was trying to fuck me or erase me."

The writers had to learn to navigate what was just right and what was too much. As they progressed, they learned to balance the show's more shocking elements with its sweeter, more emotional side: While it was not particularly interested in the heroines having sappy romances with men, it concerned itself deeply with the friendships among the four women. The show's focus on supportive female friendships became the second prong in its revolutionary attack. It softened the impact of the sex talk, but it also had its own progressive power. As Nixon once said in an interview: "*Sex and the City* is about how important friendships are when you're not married and don't have a family. It's a gay thing, and a single-person thing, where your friends are your family." The women of *Sex and the City* were looking for love and children, but didn't need either; all they needed were good sex, the ambition to succeed without a man, and good friends.

There was a moment when Star realized friendship was the show's crux: a scene at the end of the third episode in which the four women meet at a movie theater, then walk in with their arms around each other. Seeing that on film in the editing room choked him up. He got it: *These women love each other, and that is our show.* That magical transition comes with any good show, the time when it becomes something beyond what the creator initially knew it could be. Star suddenly became an audience member, invested in the emotions that showed up on-screen. For the first time with *Sex and the City*, he thought, *I'm there.* He could see that these characters had made each other their family, and he could imagine viewers wanting to join it.

• • •

Kristin Davis could finally breathe easy.

Even though she'd left the split-level home she'd bought just two weeks before in Los Angeles to film *Sex and the City* in New York in early 1998, she was happy to be working. She wanted *Sex and the City* at least as much as anything she'd ever wanted in her career. Now that the show was a sure thing, Davis was thrilled. As the least established of the four main actresses, Davis had a lot to prove. She would give her all to Charlotte.

Davis now had to find a local place to live for several months. She had spent a few tough years in New York City while she was, as she says, "actress-waitressing" just after she graduated from Rutgers University. Then Los Angeles' sunshine and hiking trails and yoga studios had stolen her heart after those difficult years, and now she didn't want to go back to New York life permanently.

For the first season of production, she found a building that rented rooms to actors. It had terrible furniture, but it would allow her to bring her dog. She could handle it for the three months it would take to shoot the eleven episodes.

Soon, all four women's days and nights were spent navigating the West Village's spiderweb of picturesque streets in high-heeled stilettos. As they loitered on Perry Street, where the brownstone stand-in for Carrie's apartment building was located, it began to feel like a kind of home for all of them.

Each episode would have a theme, with each of the four main characters experiencing some variation on it. A typical script contained at least one relationship conflict, a sexual issue, and a friendship issue. The producers could tell early what worked for the show: The coffee shop scenes, in which the four women gather to discuss the theme of the week, were gold. The New York–specific jokes were on point. For instance, Miranda: "There are no available men in their thirties in New York. Giuliani had them removed along with the homeless."

Yet the coffee shop scenes, one of the show's earliest trademarks, proved daunting to shoot. The dialogue had to move at rapid-fire pace, which meant the actors had to know their cues inside out. They had to watch each other for exact timing. Those scenes sitting around talking and eating often exhausted the actors as much as running down the street in stilettos.

In early episodes, the story lines hew closely to Bushnell's columns, and the themed questions pulled directly from them. One focuses on "modelizers," Bushnell's word for men who date only models; another examines "secret sex," clandestine hookups with partners not deemed worthy of introduction to family and friends. Carrie plays the part of journalist Bushnell, often seen out on the town for "research" and interviewing New Yorkers about their dating habits. Though Carrie is not shown scribbling the way Bushnell did—she had pads that fit in her purses and often ran to the bathroom in the middle of a night out to scrawl some notes—the character does engage in a TV form of note-taking by sharing her thoughts directly with the camera as well as in voice-over. First-season episodes also feature those interstitial people-on-the-street interviews about sex and love—techniques later abandoned once the show found its footing.

Carrie's voice-overs brought their own challenges. During Carrie's sequences, camera shots had to be timed to a monologue that hadn't been recorded yet. So Parker would rehearse her voice-over for an assistant director, who would then read it as similarly as possible for the director and camera operators to time out shots. Parker would later record the official versions of her voice-overs in one swoop at the end of the season in a recording studio. It was Parker's least favorite part of the job—so monotonous and lonely. She had grown up surrounded by so many siblings that she never even brushed her teeth alone.

By contrast, she loved to shoot her solo sequences in which Carrie types her columns and muses, often beginning with her signature phrase: "I couldn't help but wonder . . ." To maximize efficiency, the producers would finish with all the other actors for the week, then film a day or two straight of what they called "Carrie smokes and types." (Parker did smoke on and off in real life, though she sometimes smoked fake cigarettes for the show.) That was all it would say on the production's call sheet for the day. She would be the only actor on set with the crew for eighteen hours or so as she ran back and forth to wardrobe and hair and makeup to change up how she looked for each scene. For the directors, it was a little challenging to figure out new, slightly different locations in the apartment for her to smoke and type and slightly different angles to shoot. But most of the crew on set were relaxed, their only job to film her, yell "Run and change!" and then film her again.

Parker liked being with the crew for a relatively easy and fun day or two, something of a treat at the end of a long series of days spent running around the city.

. . .

Director Alison Maclean took on the show's first two post-pilot episodes. The female perspective and the unique take for television had attracted her to the job. When she saw the pilot, she liked Star's vision of a little indie movie every week. She even liked the bits where Carrie talked to the camera. She loved the directness, the intimacy.

It's a good thing she liked intimacy: She had to spend her first day on the set shooting snippets for what would be depicted as a male artist character's collection of sex tapes. For hours, she shot sex scene after sex scene with actor Gabriel Macht and a succession of women. Maclean had to choose among the extras willing to do nudity, then get to work. She picked about four women who were styled to look different enough from scene to scene that they played about ten women. She tried to mix things up with different lighting and positions.

After that first day, everything else seemed easy.

Like pilot director Susan Seidelman, Maclean came to the show with hip cred. Maclean had directed an episode of the Nickelodeon show *The Adventures of Pete & Pete*, by far the coolest kids' show ever created—its innovative, surreal comedy attracted guest stars such as Steve Buscemi and Iggy Pop. She was responsible for the memorable music video for Natalie Imbruglia's "Torn" and the 1992 film *Crush*, starring Marcia Gay Harden. Her debut came via a short film called *Kitchen Sink* in New Zealand; also known for its surrealism, it premiered at the Cannes Film Festival and won eight international film awards. Despite the solid résumé, Maclean was surprised to be hired for *Sex and the City*: "I'd made my first feature and I'd just done this little bit of television. I'm not quite sure of the thought process, to be honest."

Maclean's sex-tape assembly line was for the first post-pilot episode, "Models and Mortals," in which *Sex and the City* introduces the handy term "modelizer." The main modelizer, an artist friend of Carrie's played by Macht, makes secret sex tapes with models, then assembles his installations from those tapes, displayed via several monitors, à la Nam June Paik. Maclean loved overseeing the fictional exhibit, an art project in itself.

In the second episode Maclean directed, "Valley of the Twenty-Something Guys," Timothy Olyphant plays a younger man whom

Carrie dates, and his character lives in one of the show's first *extra-*authentic locations. When Carrie sleeps over, she awakens to realize how disgusting this apartment full of young men is—which meant Maclean and her crew had to scout out some "mind-bogglingly gross apartments," as she recalls. They ended up at one in NoHo, somewhere between Bleecker and Houston Streets. It smelled of cat pee and looked exactly as Maclean had envisioned the scene; the set dressers barely did a thing. No one wanted to touch anything in the kitchen or the bathroom. It was perfectly disgusting.

FASHION AS THE "FIFTH LADY"

Starting with that second episode, the punk rock icon Patricia Field joined the production as its costume designer, thus casting fashion as the show's "fifth character," as Parker says (though she's also called New York City "the fifth lady," so you can decide the order of importance for yourself). Field would be the woman responsible for the naked dress, the tutu as streetwear, and the heels that turned Carrie into fashion roadkill, among many iconic looks.

Field, fifty-five at the time, is distinguished by her "Pillar Box Red" dyed hair, as she herself describes it, and her Warhol Factory–honed fashion sense. She has a classic New York accent underlined by a smoker's rasp, and she is considered an institution of New York's downtown punk scene. She spent her childhood in a one-bedroom apartment on the Upper East Side. Her parents owned a dry cleaning business at Third Avenue and 74th Street, where Field first learned her way around fabric. The family moved to Queens in 1950, and while she attended Flushing High School, she spent evenings at jazz clubs such as the Five Spot and the Blue Note, where she saw Sarah Vaughan and Dinah Washington perform. In the 1960s, she attended New York University, where she studied government and philosophy.

A $4,000 trust fund left to her by her father helped her and her girlfriend at the time, Jo-Ann Salvucci, open a store called Pants Pub near

NYU in 1966. They sold bell-bottoms, tailored pants for women, and go-go boots.

That store became the Patricia Field boutique, a name change Salvucci suggested, and moved from Washington Place to 8th Street. Field's deconstructed aesthetic attracted stars such as Patti Smith, who bought her stage clothes there, as well as drag performers and designers like John Galliano.

In the years just before *Sex and the City*, Field had dabbled in costume design for films—including *Miami Rhapsody*, which starred Parker. Field was attracted to the chance to bring a more interesting aesthetic to pop culture. Actresses who worked with Field described her as the best costume designer they'd ever had. She sat in fittings herself instead of sending staffers. And she focused on making an actress look fabulous—she never implied the actress needed to lose weight to wear the right clothing.

Field turned out to be the magical consequence of Parker's reticence to sign on to the show. When Parker wavered that final time before production got the go-ahead from HBO, she negotiated to hire *Miami Rhapsody* producer Barry Jossen, who in turn suggested Field for the costume design job. Field brought a fresh perspective to the job, scouring thrift stores—not just to save money, but also to evoke the eclectic downtown aesthetic she'd perfected.

The thrifty part of thrifting *did* work particularly well in the first season, when the clothing budget was minuscule and designers weren't interested in lending anything to a show they'd never heard of. Field would often travel to her second home in Miami to take advantage of its lower prices in relation to New York City. She hired two young men who "come from our school of fashion," she later told the *New York Times*, to travel the country in search of clothes and accessories. She frequented designer consignment shop INA on Thompson Street, where she got a fur coat for Carrie for about thirty dollars, among many other items.

She also gave Carrie a signature piece of jewelry from her own store: a nameplate necklace that had become popular among the young people in the East Village. Field and Parker agreed it fit with the show's themes: "Every woman has a name," Field later said. "You could be any age, any color, any weight, and you still have a name." The show followed Carrie's quest to find and express her own identity apart from societal expectations. Her "Carrie" necklace was her talisman on that journey.

Even Bushnell, for all of her "Gucci, Gucci, Gucci" script notes, approved of Field. She remembered going into Field's shop on 8th Street at about age twenty and being intimidated because it was so cool. Whoever was there would look you up and down to assess your qualifications for being there. At the time, budding fashion plate Bushnell didn't feel she measured up.

Field brought a radical change to TV costume design when she joined *Sex and the City*. The professional women on this show would not be limited to off-the-rack business suits and pumps. Her East Village aesthetic infused the characters' looks, putting them in outfits to wow fellow fashionistas, not pander to the male gaze. The outfits were meant to inspire viewers to express themselves just as independently and creatively through fashion in their own lives.

Field's involvement turned Carrie Bradshaw into a fashion aficionado, the kind of woman who had a vision for every outfit, from vintage to ready-to-wear—similar to Parker in reality. Field loved to dress the *Sex and the City* women as what would later become known as streetstyle stars, she said, because "they weren't teenagers. They were individuals." Field made Carrie Bradshaw an icon.

Parker often worked with Field to choose Carrie's clothes and trusted Field so much that she would "put anything on for Pat. I will never say no to Pat. I don't care how ridiculous or hideous or foolish, or how much of a mockery will be made of me." Parker felt as strongly about Field's vision as she did about the writers'. She wouldn't tell the writers how to write a scene, so she wouldn't tell Field how to dress her character. "You've *got* to be ridiculous," Parker says of some of Carrie's looks. (She didn't say which, but I'm reminded of the belt across her bare midriff and the Heidi-like dress.) "You can't be pretty all the time."

But the transition didn't go smoothly for all of the actresses. Davis did not care much for fashion. She liked to look at designer clothing on other people; she just thought it wasn't for her. She would peruse fashion magazines, but all she could think was, *Wow, those girls are thin. No hips allowed.* And now on *Sex and the City*, she could tell she drove Field crazy with her resistance, but the idea of trying to fit into clothing like that was stressful for her. She wasn't shy about expressing her discomfort: "That's too tight." "Those shoes are too high."

Several weeks into production, Star invited Davis out for dinner. Davis knew: *Oh, I'm in trouble.*

As they ate, Davis wondered what kind of bomb he would drop on her. Was she not doing a good job? Finally, as they walked home, he said, "You know, I just think you need to let Pat have her way and not disagree so much."

"Darren, she wants to dress me in skintight stuff," Davis recalls saying. "It's *weird*. I'm just uncomfortable."

"You just need to listen," he said. "She knows more than you do."

Davis vowed to try. Then, at end of that first season, Field hit on a description of Charlotte's look: "sexy secretary." At last, Davis got it. That, she knew, she could do.

• • •

To go with its stylish look, the show would also need stylish music and, most important, a theme song. Though themes were fading from the prominence they enjoyed in the 1980s—when every minute of a show had to be watched live without fast-forward, including the opening credits—the right song would set the tone for this aesthetically obsessed series. Besides, HBO was reinventing television, bringing it to the commercial-free, premium-cable space at the time. Broadcast theme songs had shrunk down to as short as three to ten seconds, while *Sex and the City*, in the end, would get a relatively luxurious thirty-seven seconds. (HBO's other soon-to-be hit, *The Sopranos*, featured Tony Soprano driving to Alabama 3's "Woke Up This Morning" for an unheard-of minute and thirty-seven seconds.)

Composer Douglas Cuomo was working on the music for NBC's brutal police drama *Homicide: Life on the Street*, of all things, when he got a call from the producers of *Sex and the City*. Cuomo had written the score for a pilot the previous year, and one of the producers of that pilot ended up at *Sex and the City*. They wanted him to do the music, no questions asked, no other candidates for the job.

He would always remember watching an early cut of the pilot with his wife to get a feel for it. He figured he'd take the job, but he wanted to know what he was signing up for. When it ended, he turned to his wife next to him in bed and said, "I don't know who's going to watch this show."

"People will watch this show," she said significantly.

After he scored the pilot, the producers asked him to try his hand at a theme song before they asked anyone else. (The pilot, which would originally have been seen only by executives, hadn't needed a theme song, since HBO was ordering the show to a full first season that would be shot in its entirety before airing.)

Star told Cuomo, "I don't know what the music should be, but I know what I want it to do. It has to have three elements: It has to be sexy, it has to be sophisticated. And it also has to let the audience know it's okay to laugh." Cuomo didn't know what he would do yet, but he loved Star's specific, yet not controlling, direction.

For inspiration, Cuomo headed to the Virgin Megastore in New York's Union Square, a 57,000-square-foot, two-level wonderland lined with row upon row of CDs. He wandered around as he waited for something to strike him. Finally, he found a section called "Space Age Bachelor Pad," full of 1950s-'60s instrumental music with Latin-tinged elements made to sound great in that era's new high-fidelity stereos. Sexy, check. Sophisticated, check. Funny, check.

With this inspiration in mind, Cuomo looked over Star's rough storyboards for the opening sequence, which showed cartoon versions of the four women in various New York City shops and restaurants. From there, Cuomo came up with the theme that would become millions of fans' future smartphone ringtones: the string of almost entirely ascending marimba notes that tumble down at the end, the maraca-driven beat. If you listen to it now, you can hear how Cuomo shifted the music notably every few measures, meant to allow for a new storyboard scene in the planned sequence.

However, Star hadn't firmly committed to that concept for the visual yet. About halfway through filming the first season, Star realized what he actually wanted—not the series of vignettes featuring the four women that Cuomo had seen storyboarded, but something focused more on Carrie and shot on film.

Star thought about the openings to iconic single-woman shows *The Mary Tyler Moore Show* and *That Girl*, and realized that each told a little story about its main character. At first, Star envisioned *Sex and the City* starting with Carrie strutting down the street in New York, then tripping, à la Dick Van Dyke's tumble over his living room ottoman in *The Dick Van Dyke Show*'s title sequence. This would help with Star's mission to make sure audiences understood that *Sex and the City* was a comedy, was okay to laugh at.

The show was preparing to shoot an episode called "Secret Sex," which included a city bus with an ad for Carrie's column on it, when it occurred to Star: The bus with Carrie's sexy photo plastered across its side, a sign of Carrie's glamour and clout in the city, should be the distraction that causes her to trip. Or it could hit a puddle and splash her as it passed her by—a classic moment of New York City humiliation. He saw it as a metaphor for "how life was always going to be giving her big expectations, then smacking her in the face."

• • •

The day arrived for the bus shoot on Fifth Avenue near 58th Street, amid landmarks such as Tiffany & Co. and the Plaza Hotel, in the heart of the city's famed Midtown shopping district. Star wanted Parker to wear a blue, businesslike sheath dress for the credit sequence. But, in a moment that foretold countless on-set discussions to come, Parker and Field instead presented him with a tutu-like tulle skirt Field had gotten for five dollars in a wholesale showroom. "Why a tutu?" Star asked. "I don't understand."

"She'll stand out," Field explained.

Like many times to come, Star deferred to Field. "I don't get it, but if you guys love it, then it's got to be good."

The crew shot two versions that day: One in the blue dress with the trip, and one in the pink tank top, Jimmy Choo shoes, and white tulle skirt with the splash. They didn't have time to do multiple takes for the splash, but they got it. Star didn't see Field's point until he saw it on tape: In the tutu, Parker popped among the dark-clad, business-suited New York extras around her. She had the grace of a ballerina and the guts to look different from everyone else. It was perfect.

In the final cut, Carrie's strappy Jimmy Choo sandals never make it into the frame, but Parker wore those shoes over and over throughout the series.

ON THE SET

Behind the scenes, *Sex and the City*'s cast and crew settled into comfortable routines and found their own parts to play in the process.

Parker bobbed and chattered among the crew in between takes, staying on set instead of rushing back to her trailer—a marked difference from the behavior of most actors. She'd sit on a camera box and chat with crew members, share snacks, or smoke cigarettes. Even when she had just finished a serious, dramatic scene, she would "bounce off the set to chat and play with the crew like she was at a beach party," as director Dennis Erdman says. Then she'd drop right back into the serious scene for another take. Many who worked with her appreciated her penchant for acting like part of the team.

Nixon contributed to the process in her own distinctive way: She had detailed thoughts about every character decision, nuance, prop use, and wardrobe or styling consideration. She didn't concern herself with the grander fashion decisions, which she left to Field, but she could get wrapped up in the most minute implications of a haircut or engage in serious debate with King over whether Miranda would wear socks with her pajamas while at home. In that case, she decided Miranda would not. But then when King saw the dirty soles of her feet on camera, she agreed to put the socks on; Miranda was even less likely to have dirty feet than she was to wear socks with pajamas.

Night shoots had become standard, given the characters' active nightlife. The cast and crew often saw the sunrise together near the end of a shoot. Parker stayed to the bitter end, out with the crew even when she didn't need to be, grabbing a beer from the camera truck and watching from the sidelines. She led them in sing-alongs at 4 a.m.— anything to stay awake and keep everyone's energy up. Cattrall would join in, as would Nixon, who seemed to know every word to every show tune ever. Davis would cheer them on, not feeling like enough of a singer to belt anything out. Despite these displays, King ruled out the possibility of a musical episode; they would need to keep their singing off camera.

Thus far, the little bit of press the show got came via disgruntled reports of the crew blocking city thoroughfares. The *New York Times* chronicled the production's obstruction of a sidewalk on Fifth Avenue between 80th and 81st Streets. As Parker paraded down the street in a tan coat, the paper reported, pedestrians grew irritated with the interruption. "I'm a doctor," one woman said. "I have patients waiting."

The results of this difficult location work, however, would distinguish the show among a decade's worth of supposed New York shows that were shot on Los Angeles sets, like *Friends* and *Seinfeld*. Finally, *Sex and the City* would bring real New York to the small screen. If fashion was *Sex and the City*'s fifth character, let's call the city its sixth.

HBO's permissive boundaries and schedules allowed for all of the show's unique aspects—the location shoots, the authentic New York feel, the fashion, the sex.

The network's other new series, *The Sopranos*, was also shooting at Silvercup Studios and taking the same filmic approach as *Sex and the City*. HBO, long known for showing movies after their theatrical run had expired, was now co-opting the cinematic process to build its television brand. If you liked mobster films, you would love *The Sopranos*. If you liked romantic comedies, you would love *Sex and the City*—and come back for more every week.

The neighboring productions made for some surreal scenes, however. At 4 p.m. on a typical day at Silvercup, you might spot *Sopranos* actor James Gandolfini in his boxer shorts, T-shirt, and robe ready to shoot a family breakfast scene and then round the corner to find the *Sex and the City* girls glammed up in designer dresses and heels ready for a night on the town.

• • •

The first season of *Sex and the City* wrapped in early 1998, having not yet aired one episode. In fact, another six months would pass before it premiered. Staffers didn't know what to do. They were offered jobs on other shows. How could they turn those down when they had no idea what HBO would do with *Sex and the City* or whether anyone would watch it? Writer Michael Green was offered a writing gig on an ABC dramedy called *Cupid*, which starred Jeremy Piven. He didn't know: Should he take it, should he not take it? He took it and moved on.

Writer Jenny Bicks got a consulting job on teen drama *Dawson's Creek*, which would allow her to practice her single-camera TV writing and storytelling skill while she waited to hear if *Sex and the City* would make it to a second season.

King, too, took a consulting producer gig at new NBC comedy *Will & Grace*, which he described as "new millennium Noël Coward . . . the pedigree of an intellectual show, but ridiculously funny and silly." King said he enjoyed "the opportunity to form this new show where there are gay characters and straight characters living in the same world, and no one is a villain." When he returned to *Sex and the City* afterward, he would bring these ideas back with him, making them central tenets of his writing on the show.

Everyone involved with *Sex and the City* hedged their bets. But when the show premiered on HBO in June 1998, it would do more than become a hit television show. No one, least of all its own cast and crew, saw it coming.

Kristin Davis, Kim Cattrall, Cynthia Nixon, and Sarah Jessica Parker (and background extras) on location shooting baseball game scenes for the second-season premiere "Take Me Out to the Ball Game." *Courtesy of HBO®*

Writer Elisa Zuritsky, actor Kyle MacLachlan, and writer Julie Rottenberg at the Golden Globe awards. *Courtesy of Julie Rottenberg*

Adam Peck (writer Jenny Bicks's boyfriend), writers Zuritsky, Jenny Bicks, Judy Toll, Rottenberg, and Toll's husband, Rick Trank, celebrate the show's Golden Globe win with writer Amy B. Harris balancing the award on her head and executive producer Michael Patrick King kneeling. January 21, 2001. *Courtesy of Julie Rottenberg*

Parker preparing to shoot a scene on a New York street with onlookers and cameras behind her. *Courtesy of HBO®*

Magnolia Bakery's official "Carrie" cupcake, named for the character who famously ate one in a *Sex and the City* scene. The West Village bakery itself is in the background. *Courtesy of Magnolia Bakery*

Celebrating a recent Golden Globe win with a fancy lunch sent to the writers' offices by HBO. Co–executive producers John Melfi and King under the watchful eye of a Carrie Bradshaw poster. *Courtesy of Julie Rottenberg*

Melfi, Rottenberg, King, and Davis at a Los Angeles dinner during the writers' pre-season West Coast brainstorming session for an upcoming season. *Courtesy of Julie Rottenberg*

King hamming it up at the computer for Zuritsky. *Courtesy of Julie Rottenberg*

King and Bicks simulating sex in the writers' room to choreograph a scene. *Courtesy of Julie Rottenberg*

Writer Liz Tuccillo and actor David Eigenberg enjoying the Atlantic City board-walk while there to shoot the fifth-season episode "Luck Be an Old Lady." *Courtesy of Julie Rottenberg*

Writers Tuccillo and Cindy Chupack, King, and writers Zuritsky, Rottenberg, and Harris at dinner in Margate, New Jersey, on location to shoot in nearby Atlantic City. *Courtesy of Julie Rottenberg*

That's the thing about Manhattan
Some things look prettier
from the outside...
As for me,
I was back here in Aidan's
arms, and I was hoping
① that would hold me.

_____

② And sometimes the
couple that is arguing the loudest is
the one ins ide each of us.

_____

③ And sometimes it's
inside of each of us that
the real battles take place

④ Sometimes Sometimes you yourself
people lose themselves
in a relationship and sometimes you
people have to sacrifice lose
the relationship to save
themselves. yourself.

· · · · · · · · · ·

Chupack's notes working out options for Carrie's voice-overs in the fourth-season
episode "All That Glitters." *Courtesy of Cindy Chupack*

Toll and King celebrating Toll's birthday in January 2002 before her death four months later from cancer at age forty-four. *Courtesy of Julie Rottenberg*

Nixon, Parker, Davis, and Cattrall on location at a Meatpacking District restaurant to shoot the sixth-season episode "To Market, To Market." *Courtesy of HBO®*

4

The Show Everyone Wants to Live In

. . . .

Cindy Chupack fell in love with *Sex and the City* just like every other fan: When she started watching, she saw a little bit of herself in each of the characters, and found herself not only enjoying but also relating deeply to the stories the show was telling.

At the time, *Sex and the City* was airing its first season, and Chupack had one of the best jobs in TV writing. She was on staff at the critically praised, hugely rated CBS sitcom *Everybody Loves Raymond*. A strawberry blonde with brown eyes and a ready smile, Chupack had been a TV writer for years, waiting for her chance to be on a hit show like *Everybody Loves Raymond*.

But in 1999, *Sex and the City* came to tempt her away from her cushy job.

Chupack, who was single at the time and also wrote a relationship column for *Glamour*, had kept a journal full of story ideas and notions that she thought might one day be fodder for a television episode, a movie, or her column. Although nothing in her journal seemed quite right for *Everybody Loves Raymond* (a sitcom about a sports columnist, played by comedian Ray Romano, and his extended family), Chupack hoped someday she might get the chance to create her own show that would be the right vehicle for these ideas.

Then she watched HBO's new series *Sex and the City* and thought: *Well, there's the show I wish I had created.* All of the stories in her journal seemed like they would make perfect episodes.

Chupack had grown up in Oklahoma and was thrilled just to work in television, which might as well have been Mars compared with her upbringing. After college, she had taken a night class in TV writing at UCLA that Ellen Sandler was teaching. Sandler had just broken up with her former writing partner and asked Chupack to be her partner; thus Chupack's television career was born.

Sandler's former writing partner was her husband, which made the partnership with Chupack emotionally loaded. When they started out together, they had a schtick of sorts: Sandler's getting divorced, and Chupack's newly married! Things began to go south two years later when Chupack's husband realized he was gay. She and Sandler, as Chupack puts it, "were then just two sad, divorced women."

Over the years Chupack and Sandler had written for sitcoms about motherhood or family life, neither of which matched Chupack's own experiences. Then came the stint on *Everybody Loves Raymond*, a huge, mainstream network hit. Now seven years into their career together, they had finally gotten some traction and respect—they were even nominated for an Emmy—but Chupack was ready to strike out on her own. In addition to writing a produced script for *Raymond* to show what she could do as a solo writer, she wanted to write a spec—a sample script—of another show that might more accurately reflect her life. *Sex and the City* seemed like the perfect show to try to write.

She knew *Sex and the City*'s creator, Darren Star, from TV writing circles, and she was also good friends with *Sex and the City* writer

Jenny Bicks. Jenny encouraged Cindy to forget the spec and instead come in to pitch a freelance episode. She did, and at the meeting Cindy impressed Star and his co–executive producer, Michael Patrick King, with her comedic sensibility as well as her perspective on being a single woman. She had stories to tell, stories *Sex and the City* could use.

This led to her first *Sex and the City* episode, "The Chicken Dance," about a love interest of Miranda's who marries someone else—the seventh episode of the second season. Chupack had taken the assignment as a freelancer, but after the table read and filming (which she was able to attend in New York), the producers asked her to join the staff.

The problem was that nobody left *Everybody Loves Raymond*. Chupack felt strange even considering ditching a job that had been so good to her after such a long slog through the trenches of bad sitcoms. But she had never seen a show that was as good a fit for her as *Sex and the City* was. The show might as well have been about her own life.

She took the job, even though leaving *Raymond* meant moving to New York and taking a substantial pay cut.

Chupack filled a void of sorts on the staff: Despite years of bad dates and her failed marriage, she still considered herself optimistic when it came to love. She was a self-identified Charlotte at heart. "There are times when you're not sure if your hopefulness is helping or if you need to be more pessimistic," she says. "I thought it was interesting to write her and struggle with that." Chupack admits she wanted to write a happy ending for Carrie, too: "I thought, as a writer, if I can't make something good happen for someone, even someone fictional, what hope do any of us have?"

Because she had worked on shows less inspiring to her, Chupack understood how special it was to work on *Sex and the City*. She had worked on shows that didn't match her voice. She had worked on shows that were mostly staffed by men and about men. Finally, in this writers' room, she could talk openly and honestly about issues from her own life.

"The Chicken Dance" documented several moments from Chupack's firsthand experience. She had been asked to write a poem for a friend's wedding (a friend who got engaged while house-sitting for Chupack), and like Carrie, she teared up while she read it, not because she was touched by the couple's happiness, but because in the time it had taken them to meet, get engaged, and get married, the only milestone she'd reached with her own boyfriend was when he gave her a pink electric toothbrush head to use at his place. Carrie's equivalent: getting choked up because she sees Big leave to take a business call during her reading.

Chupack also wrote an episode called "Evolution," in which Carrie asks the question: "Are New Yorkers evolving past relationships?" It included a cathartic story line for Chupack with Charlotte trying to determine if her new love interest, a pastry chef played by Dan Futterman, is gay. Chupack also loved writing the story line in the same episode about Carrie trying to solidify her relationship with Big by leaving some of her stuff at his apartment, while he keeps returning it—another experience straight from Chupack's own life. "What is it about Big's apartment?" Carrie asks. "Nothing ever sticks. It's like Teflon for women."

• • •

Despite Chupack's enthusiasm, *Sex and the City* wasn't universally loved when it first aired. It debuted for the public on HBO on June 6, 1998, while Bushnell and Star watched together from Bushnell's place; neither of their parents called afterward. Like many parents of those involved with *Sex and the City*, they chose not to watch. This attitude made Parker nervous. She wondered if people would, as she said, "find it saucy and smart or say, 'Well, this is just completely inappropriate.'"

The critics leaned toward the latter. Reviews often took on a harsh, personal, and sexist tone. Tom Shales of the *Washington Post* wrote in his June 6, 1998, review, the day the show premiered: "Sarah Jessica Parker has an in-your-face face. . . . Parker, with her scraggly hair and jutty jaw, is certainly not the worst thing about this smirky-jerky sexcom, but she usually seems so light and funny that it's dismaying to see her in bad form, looking like a walking flea market and coming across about as subtly as a tsunami. It took some sort of perverse talent to make her unattractive, although the producers were clever enough to insert a shot of her in a wet clinging top during the opening credits." One could argue it also took some sort of perverse talent to see the splash sequence as a wet T-shirt contest.

Shales went on to call Star a "one-time wonderboy." "On HBO," Shales wrote, "he has the freedom to spice up the comedy with smatterings of nudity and dirty words, but they don't help." Shales paused to praise Nixon's "cheering, luminous presence that helps save many a scene" before he backed up to run over Mr. Big: "[Chris] Noth is just the same old sleaze he always plays." Shales concluded that the show was "total immersion in self-absorption," in which the characters "indulge in what might be called White Whine." Credit where it's due: Excellent line, sir.

At about this time, HBO vice president Carolyn Strauss and others involved with the show realized it would be an "uphill climb" with critics, as Strauss says. Shales's words stung, both because of their focus on Parker's looks and because he was, as Strauss describes him, "the dean of TV criticism at the time"—he had won a Pulitzer for his criticism a decade before. To sell subscriptions, HBO had to convince people that its shows could not be missed, so it relied even more heavily on reviews than broadcast networks. This one hurt.

Sweeping judgments about single women, lack of empathy for their lives, and a deep concern for the fragile feelings of men who watched the show snaked through many of the early reviews. And male reviewers weren't the only culprits. Ellen Gray wrote for Knight Ridder, "While this show is probably too depressing for single women in their 30s to watch for very long—the women it features make *Ally McBeal* look emotionally healthy—it can be satisfying viewing for those of us whom Helen Fielding's *Bridget Jones's Diary* describes as 'Smug Marrieds.' At least for the female half of those couples. Watching my husband wince during an onscreen discussion of men who weren't particularly well-endowed—okay, the word 'gherkin' was used—I realized that listening to this was probably as much fun for your average guy as listening to (or watching) Howard Stern pick apart a naked fat girl would be for most women."

Newsday's Steve Parks called the series "so self-consciously arch in its attempt to be hip about relationships that it comes across as far more sophomoric than sophisticated. It's not enough anymore to have women sitting around talking about doing it. Where's the novelty in that as we approach the end of the millennium?" Despite his implication that women who are all talk and no action aren't enough excitement for him, Parks went on to describe Samantha as "excuse the expression—a slut." He concluded, "Even voyeurs who regularly tune into HBO's soft-porn features and movies will be disappointed in this half-hour comedy for 'mature' audiences with immature tastes."

And the *Daily News*' Eric Mink sighed, "Maybe I'm too old, too married, and too male to appreciate *Sex and the City*. Maybe I'm too naïve. I know I'm too tired." His quibble appeared to be with what he viewed as an unrealistic fictional schedule for our heroines. He complained that the show "asks viewers to accept the notion that its main characters are vital, competitive, successful, professional females who spend night after night drinking, dancing, flirting and, whenever possible, having sex with strangers until the sun comes up."

Even producer-writer Michael Patrick King's own mother—the rare *Sex and the City* parent who tuned in—had complaints. After the fifth episode aired in July 1998, his mom called him. In "The Power of Female Sex," the otherwise demure Charlotte poses for a famous painter whose work depicts women's vaginas. "That was disgusting," King's mother scolded. "I got embarrassed in front of the dog. And she's a girl."

Some critics did see the show's merits. The *Chicago Tribune*'s Michael Kilian wrote, "From the Greeks through Shakespeare and French farce to the modern TV sitcom, sex and comedy have had an enduring, if not always endearing, relationship in popular culture. But seldom have the two come together as bitingly and cynically as in the new HBO adult comedy *Sex and the City*."

Despite this mixed critical reaction, the show proved to be a modest hit out of the gate. It landed at No. 10 on the cable Nielsen ratings chart for its first week, with 3.8 million viewers—a respectable showing for a pay-cable network without a strong record in original programming. *Sex and the City* officially began HBO's assault on traditional broadcast television. In seven months, the channel would premiere its other revolutionary show, *The Sopranos*.

• • •

These conflicting feedback signals from the public affected the way *Sex and the City*'s producers envisioned their second season. Critics skewed unnecessarily harsh, but they weren't entirely wrong. First up: dropping Carrie's direct camera address. King reasoned, "I want to believe this. I believe her. I think she's the real thing. But whenever she turns to the camera, I no longer believe this. Can we stop that?" Parker had always hated doing it: As she says, it takes a special actor—like her husband, Matthew Broderick, in *Ferris Bueller's Day Off*—to do it naturally. Like King, she trusted the audience to get the story without her help.

Second, they ceased the people-on-the-street interviews, though that technique lingered for part of the second season before disappearing. The scenes not only jarred viewers from the stories at hand, but also took up valuable time that could go to the four main characters' plot lines.

Costume designer Patricia Field experimented with how far she could push the show's fashion in the second season, as evidenced in particular by what became known on the set as "the Heidi dress." In the fourteenth episode of the second season, Carrie wears a dirndl, laced bodice and all, her hair in pigtails, for a picnic lunch in the park with her friends. Parker exaggerated the look further by having the makeup artist dust her face with freckles. Many crew members objected that it was just too ridiculous, and viewers didn't necessarily disagree when it aired. But Parker wanted to see how much she could get away with when it came to her character's look, seeing the extreme British series *Absolutely Fabulous* as an aesthetic inspiration.

Field, of course, agreed: "The straight types just don't get the irony," she later said.

Downtown fashion designer Rebecca Danenberg, in an interview, backed up Field's vision: "The reason the show works for me is that it looks like it came from an intelligent planet. It doesn't look like Hollywood. It looks like Barneys." *Sex and the City* would take more fashion chances from then on.

Fashion also began to drive some story lines rather than just accessorizing them. The season 2 episode "The Cheating Curve" has Charlotte hanging out with a new crowd, the "power lesbians," who first invite her into their circle after admiring her Prada loafers. The relationship continues, defined by fashion and lifestyle choices: drinking at a bar called G-Spot, eating at a French fusion restaurant called Luxe with a lesbian chef, and dancing at a club called Love Tunnel.

One could almost forget lesbianism is a sexual orientation, not a trendy new lifestyle. Charlotte concludes, "While sexually I feel that I am straight, there's a very powerful part of me that connects to the female spirit." Alas, she's forced to stop connecting to that particular part of the female spirit—and going to dinner at Luxe—when she's outed as a straight woman. As one of Charlotte's new companions bottom-lines it to her: "If you're not going to eat pussy, you're not a dyke." Prada loafers or not.

SEX GROWS UP

With the second season, it was also time for *Sex and the City* to meet what now was a known quantity of demand. Production needed to be ratcheted up in several ways. From the first season's twelve episodes, the second season grew to eighteen. Some of the original crew got promotions, the beginning of a trend that would establish the show's reputation for treating staffers well, mentoring young crew members, and promoting from within. Director of photography Michael Spiller, who had turned down a chance to work on the now-successful *Sopranos*, got the opportunity to direct in the second season while also DP-ing. It was scary, he says, "like walking on a tightrope with a blindfold on." But "the entire cast and crew is down below with their hands up, saying, 'We got you, Mike.'"

Shoots stretched even longer than they had for season 1. The cast and crew once spent twelve hours on Fifth Avenue, from noon to midnight. For Chupack's episode "The Chicken Dance," they spent a "hysterical twenty-four-hour day in the Plaza [Hotel]," Davis says. Crew members grabbed patches of sleep along the edges of the ballroom where the wedding sequence was shot. The actors had rooms where they'd sleep for a while, then be woken up and pulled back downstairs by a producer to shoot. The actors kept thinking, *They've gotta pull the plug*. They never pulled the plug, at least until a full day had passed and all scenes had been shot.

Shoots also became more elaborate as the producers' and directors' confidence grew. However, they could control only so much before location problems or weather interfered.

Once, as a lightning storm threatened, Spiller set up a massive crane shot, which allows for cameras to rise up to ninety feet in the air. He had never used such a big piece of equipment. The crew lit up five blocks surrounding Fifth Avenue at 65th Street, the lush trees of Central Park lining one side of the avenue and green and beige and gray apartment-entrance awnings dotting the other side.

It was 2 a.m. on a Friday as they stood ready to get their first take of the night, which featured Carrie and Mr. Big as they walked down the street and talked. Spiller and his crew had to get just this one shot from this particular setup, and they would be set.

Then one of the crew jinxed the entire operation. "We got lucky with this rain, huh?" he joked of the so-far dry shoot.

"Are you insane?" Spiller snapped back. "Don't talk about that until the wrap party, man." Just then, lightning and thunder struck, and the rain began to pour down. The crew lowered the crane and the lights as fast as they could. Ultimately the shot focused just on Carrie and Big under an awning instead.

Now that the first season had begun airing in June 1998, the production was no longer some show no one had heard of. Occasional paparazzi lingered around the edges of location shoots to snap a few photos of the actors. The click-click-click of their cameras distracted everyone and caused sound problems, an issue that would grow worse in later seasons. Passersby began to stop and watch the shoots, recognizing the actors, as opposed to simply being annoyed at the nuisance. Restaurants and clubs welcomed the crew. Businessman Donald Trump, playing himself in a cameo, ad-libbed a line to promote his building: "Think about it," he said to Samantha's older tycoon date. "I'll be at my office in Trump Tower." He knew good product placement when he saw it.

• • •

Davis knew for sure that *Sex and the City* was onto something when she ran into George Clooney, with whom she'd worked on an episode during the first season of *ER*. As the first season of *Sex and the City* was airing in 1998, Davis attended the premiere of Clooney's steamy crime drama costarring Jennifer Lopez, *Out of Sight*. At the premiere, Clooney ran up to Davis and said, "Congratulations!"

"On what?"

"The show. It's so great!"

She hadn't realized how much *Sex and the City* was on people's radar, much less men's, much less George Clooney's. *If George is aware*, she thought, *that's good*.

Buzz was beginning to build. Those same elite New Yorkers who had complained about the disruptive shoots were now driving home from their shares in the Hamptons to catch Sunday night TV on HBO.

Sarah Jessica Parker was nominated in the winter of 1998 for a Golden Globe for her performance in the first season, and the announcement caused many more non-HBO viewers around the country to say, "Wait, for *which* show?" They wouldn't be asking that for much longer.

. . .

To solidify the directorial vision for the second season, HBO brought in Allen Coulter, a producer on the first season of *The Sopranos*. The crime drama debuted on the network on January 10, 1999, and was instantly regarded as a tour de force from auteur David Chase. From the beginning, critics waxed apoplectic about its television-changing, filmlike aesthetic and complicated storytelling. The two series, now HBO's signature shows, were strikingly different-looking. *The Sopranos* favored the classic and controlled, like a Martin Scorsese film. But Coulter took the job on *Sex and the City* precisely because he relished the idea of being able to do whatever he wanted, to create his own vision.

HBO charged Coulter with unifying *Sex and the City*'s visual style, and to do so he would direct the first several episodes of the second season. Because each director in the first season had her or his own approach, *Sex and the City* didn't look as cohesive as *The Sopranos*. Coulter started by looking for ways to highlight each episode's theme with visual motifs. For example, in the fifth episode of the season, "Four Women and a Funeral," in which Charlotte meets a recent widower at a cemetery, he highlighted the death theme by lingering on diaphanous curtains blowing in the wind like ghosts.

He also loosened up the cameras, allowing them to move more with the actors: more cinematic, less like a sitcom.

Coulter's arrival on the set illustrated how much the network cared about the show. *The Sopranos* had made a huge critical splash from the start, so Coulter's presence demonstrated that HBO wanted the same for *Sex and the City*. Coulter felt the cast's enthusiasm about the show's prospects, and he was impressed by how open they were to direction during rehearsal.

What Coulter perceived was a shared positive attitude that reflected the creative satisfaction of those behind the scenes. Star felt as if he was flourishing on *Sex in the City* in a way he hadn't on his previous shows. For the first time, he was writing in his own, pure voice rather than mimicking what someone else wanted from him. And he'd gotten to do it while he told the story of his friend Candace Bushnell. He could use all the frank, dirty talks they'd had as material.

King felt the same. Finally, he got to pour himself into his scripts. While he couldn't identify with womanhood, he did identify with the feeling of "I'm single and I feel like a leper." Being gay made him even more of an outsider. He knew what it was like to be at a party on New Year's Eve with no one to kiss. He could not marry a man in the United States. With *Sex and the City*, he could say to the world, "It's okay to be single."

This vision of singlehood also emphasized the idea of friends as true family, especially for urbanites in their thirties. This take on family happened partly by mistake, at least at first. In the second-season episode "Shortcomings," Samantha sleeps with Charlotte's visiting brother, Wesley. But the producers struggled with casting Wesley, feeling he was far more important than a typical suitor of the week. No one could agree on what Charlotte's brother should be like. After that, writer Amy B. Harris says, they knew: "We have to be really judicious about using their families."

They were so judicious, in fact, that family members were rarely depicted again, and when they did show up, they stayed in the background. This went even for weddings and other major events, which were more likely to feature the male partner's family members than the main female characters'. Over time, this effect became deliberate, highlighting the fact that the women were each other's true family.

• • •

With this new approach to singlehood on television, *Sex and the City*'s froth and gloss served a subversive purpose. It thrust two marginalized groups—unmarried white women and gay men—into the mainstream by making them appear more glamorous than the accepted norms of suburban sitcom family life. Perhaps the shoes and clothes and bars and parties looked extravagant, but that was the point: *Sex and the City* transformed singledom from a drab *Cathy* comic strip into something enviable.

Feminist writer Rebecca Traister, in her book *All the Single Ladies*, details her own long-running grudge against *Sex and the City*, which premiered just a year after she moved to New York. She felt that the billboards picturing Carrie Bradshaw in her tutu, and the implied expensive and glamorous life to go with it, were taunting her: She couldn't afford to live in Manhattan, so she ended up in a hovel in pregentrification Brooklyn. She could afford neither the clothes nor the shoes nor even a subscription to HBO to watch the show. She didn't hate *Sex and the City* on its artistic merits—she'd never seen it. She simply resented that friends and family in other parts of the country started telling her that her life was "just like *Sex and the City*." It was, in fact, the exact opposite.

New Yorker TV critic Emily Nussbaum had an experience more akin to my own with the show. She was also single during its run, and noted the switch from people comparing her life to *Cathy* to the glitz of *Sex and the City*. She loved that *Sex and the City* scared people. "Better that one's life should be viewed as glamorously threatening," she wrote, "than as sad and lonely."

Traister eventually came around on *Sex and the City*, too, once her city life got a little more comfortable, with a better job and a decent apartment of her own. "If *Sex and the City* used shoes and closets and cocktails as material emblems of larger freedoms," she wrote, "I reveled in my own pricey symbolism: 450 square feet of unrenovated rental apartment." She later chastised herself for judging the *Sex and the City* women on their indulgent purchases in a way she never would have critiqued a sitcom mom: "I might have reared back from the scene of Carrie Bradshaw dropping hundreds of dollars on a pair of shoes," she wrote, "but would I have batted an eye at Carol Brady writing out a check for drapes?"

Even some young women in the suburban Midwest were starting to identify with the show. Writer Andrea Bartz, who was in high school outside Milwaukee at the time, would hit the city with her friends and declare, "You guys, we're just like *Sex and the City!*" They often joked that their version, however, would be called *Third Base and the Suburbs*. As she grew older, the trope remained: Anytime she went out with three other women, they were "just like *Sex and the City!*" As she says, "Mid-college summer internships in New York: You bet, as we pregamed before heading to gross bars that we knew didn't card. Grad school nights in Chicago: Yes, always, especially when somebody ordered a cocktail."

Editor Tia Williams had a slightly different experience: She watched those early seasons in her midtwenties, having just moved to New York City for a magazine job after graduating from the University of Virginia. She could relate to hanging out with other young, professional women, wearing clothing that stretched her budget, and dating men who tried her patience. But as a black woman who loved the show, she still felt left out of it, even though she and her black friends existed in the real-life circles of New York City it depicted: high-fashion media professionals.

"I watched *Sex and the City* and recognized their world as the same one we were navigating, but we were nowhere to be found on the show," she later wrote on Essence.com. "The problem wasn't even the absence of a black main character—this was a show about four White friends, I got that—but their *environment* was totally white-washed. It's unrealistic to paint a portrait of New York, especially the fashion, art, media, and entertainment industries, and completely leave out black faces. We absolutely exist in this world!"

She continued to watch, enduring her frustration, just as audiences of color enjoyed *Friends* or *Seinfeld* despite those shows' lack of diversity: "[O]ver the years, I've learned to look at Carrie and her glittering circle of friends as raceless archetypes of certain women we all know.

That way, I won't have to ask the question that's always gnawing at my brain—where are the fabulous black women?!"

Veronica Chambers, who wrote about the show's rise to cultural prominence for *Newsweek* in 1999, felt the same way. Chambers, a black Latina, ordered HBO just to get the show and connected it with her own group of girlfriends. "The fact that me and my girlfriends were of color didn't seem to matter as much as the fact that the characters' inner journeys mirrored our own," she says. "It took awhile to bother me that there were so few women of color on the show. There were so many fabulous women of color on the fashion and art scene in the '90s, from Dawn Brown at Isaac Mizrahi to models like Veronica Webb to people like my friend Thelma Golden, whose wardrobe, even back then, was like a temple of style. When you opened Thel's closet doors, angels sang. I thought, *There are so many real-life inspirations who could interact with these girls.*"

It was a criticism that would follow *Sex and the City*—and rightfully so—throughout its otherwise remarkable TV run.

MEN GET THEIR MAN

The show had, as so many early reviews noted, objectified men as part of its fantasy vision of single women's lives. But King and Star soon decided to let up on straight men, at least a bit. To that end, they hired Greg Behrendt for the enviable job of straight male script consultant. Their only previous token straight guy on the writing staff had been Michael Green during the first season, but he had been too inexperienced to truly fill the role and had since moved on to the ABC show *Cupid*.

King had known Behrendt as part of a group of comedians who performed at the UnCabaret in Los Angeles, an alternative comedy hub of the early 1990s that host Beth Lapides describes rather grandly as "the revolution that reclaimed comedy as an art form, allowing for depth, meaning, even transcendence." Janeane Garofalo, Kathy Griffin, and Patton Oswalt, among others, headlined. When King met Behrendt there, King told him: "You're who I used to pretend I was when I was pretending to be straight." Eventually, King directed Behrendt's stand-up special for HBO, *Mantastic*.

After a few seasons of *Sex and the City*, King thought the writing room had a hole Behrendt might help fill. So King offered Behrendt a job by saying, rhetorically, "We need somebody to come over and tell us what pussy tastes like." (This, from a guy who grew up in an Irish Catholic home and was taught by nuns.) Even though the writers still loved creating the "one and done" male characters like Mr. Pussy, King felt it was time to add real, long-term relationships to the mix, so they'd need to create more rounded, believable male characters who could go the distance.

A straight male voice could also help balance the show's perspective, which was tipped toward the gay male—so much, in fact, that many critics had suggested *Sex and the City* was really about four gay men who were played by four straight women for convention's sake. Not that there was anything wrong with that: As TV historian Ron Simon wrote, "The creative dialogue between the gay sensibilities of the male executive producers and the writing team gave the series its unique voice."

Still, Behrendt hit every qualification for the job: a funny straight guy who was a feminist and had lived in a house full of female comedians, including Garofalo, Margaret Cho, and Laura Milligan. Now, for *Sex and the City*, Behrendt got $500 a week and his name in the credits of an up-and-coming TV series just to show up for the first few weeks of writing for the season, which took place in Los Angeles. (White male privilege strikes again!) He came in every day for the LA portion—during which the writers mapped out the season—to talk to Bicks, Chupack, King, and Star about dating and sex rituals. He'd tell them if the straight male characters were way off—usually they erred on the side of too insensitive, he felt. He'd weigh in on the female writers' personal problems as well, since they often came up in the writing process.

The talks among them all in the writers' room became group therapy. Suddenly, being single had transformed from a liability to an asset. Every bad date turned into good story fodder. Unfortunate romantic liaisons no longer disheartened the writers; they couldn't wait to get to the office the next morning to talk them out.

As they talked, they found ways to show that being single and female was not merely okay—it was something special, an independent phase worth preserving unless the perfect partner came along. Bicks, for one, had grown tired of people making assumptions about what she could and couldn't do as a single woman. If she wanted to buy an expensive pair of shoes and she could afford them, she would. And furthermore, why was everyone else rewarded for settling down? As Bicks says, "Where's the china pattern for going on vacation alone? As single women, we went through a lot, and there's no reward for that." No reward, that is, except for the liberty that *Sex and the City* celebrated.

• • •

The series was now, as production on the second season progressed, veering far from its source material.

As the focus tightened on the four main characters, the writers cooked up longer-term schemes and challenges for the women. They gave some of them real relationships to contend with, someone more than just a bachelor with a sexual predilection of the week. They debated the ultimate fate of Carrie and Big: Should they end up together? So far, most of the writers said yes. But they'd have to stall on that one to keep the fun going.

When it came to life-changing relationships, they started in some ways with the toughest case: Miranda, the clever, defensive lawyer. King describes her as "the absolute sarcastic voice of smart women." Most viewers at the time didn't name her as their *Sex and the City* personal archetype; it was more fun to imagine dressing up like Carrie or letting loose like Samantha. But King saw Miranda as the character most representative of regular *Sex and the City* viewers—smart, funny, professional, cynical, and fed up with dating. And that was a good thing: "What I loved about Miranda was she was the bullshit detector," King says. "She would call bullshit on it all. Bullshit on society, bullshit on men, bullshit on tradition, bullshit on feeling bad, and bullshit on herself."

Nixon's brilliant and brittle portrayal of Miranda made the character ripe for breaking wide open with the introduction of the perfect love interest. King told the writers, "We have to bring in the antidote. What's the opposite of Miranda? Just soft and loving and easygoing."

Character actor David Eigenberg, who'd appeared on *Homicide: Life on the Street* and *The Practice*, had auditioned several times to play *Sex and the City* suitors of the week. But King remembered the thirty-four-year-old as someone "real. Sexy but also disarming. Strong but not threatening." Handsome, but not model-actor handsome, Eigenberg comes off as a guy any of us might know, with dark brown hair, striking blue eyes, a killer smile, and a working-class accent that melds that of his birthplace, Long Island, and the place he grew up, the Chicago suburbs.

Eigenberg hadn't worked out for any of the onetime roles, in part because King was saving him for something special.

When it was time for Miranda to fall in love, the choice was Eigenberg. The writers had already started their Steve scripts, so they hoped Eigenberg and Nixon would have chemistry.

Though Eigenberg had appeared on several television shows, he didn't own a television, so he'd never seen *Sex and the City*. He had heard about it via Willie Garson, who played Stanford Blatch. He respected Garson, though he had the same reaction as many others when Garson first told him about the show. Upon hearing Garson was doing some sex show on cable, Eigenberg thought of the pornographic *Red Shoe Diaries* on Showtime. He thought, *Oh, man, I'm sorry. That sounds like a load of junk.*

But now that he'd auditioned about nine times for the show, Eigenberg had a good feeling about the people running it. The producers always seemed happy and interested in him during auditions—not to mention just plain nice, an unusual trait in show business. King, he thought, had a "phenomenally huge heart" and was one of the funniest men Eigenberg had ever met. "As soon as you're trying to get out a punch line, he's already got three out that are five times funnier than what you were thinking," Eigenberg says. Eigenberg made the perfect straight man—in all senses—to King's setups.

When Eigenberg got the offer to play bartender Steve—who meets Miranda in the bar where he works while she waits there for Carrie—he assumed he'd be around for two or three episodes, maybe four, tops. His contract designated him as a day player, so it was never clear. His career had scraped by for quite some time, so this was nothing new for him. He lived in New York on the Upper West Side in a bedsit while he took whatever small parts he could score. He wasn't picky.

Even after he was cast on *Sex and the City*, he neither got a TV nor watched the show. He knew it only by the table reads he attended. He loved to watch the four main actresses at work.

He had no idea what had happened to Miranda before his character arrived on the show. He took her for someone who had been hurt before and had her defenses up, but was worth loving. Steve was the guy who says, "Hey, I'm here." He understood that Steve was not Miranda's typical lover, that he wore his heart on his sleeve in a way Miranda couldn't comprehend. Steve's first word to Miranda is "please," which shows his caring side; but it's also a chide to her to remember her manners.

One of Eigenberg's most memorable scenes with Nixon was in his first episode, the eighth episode in season 2. In it, Steve meets Miranda's friends, but Miranda is still a bit embarrassed to be dating a bartender. He leaves in a huff, but when she follows him outside into the rain, they kiss, in grand romantic comedy style. Making it rain on location was expensive—decadent, even, as King described it. But, he said, "we had to melt her with the rain."

Despite the connection Eigenberg and Nixon displayed on camera, their relationship didn't go beyond the set. They had a respectful interaction, not a sour note between them, but they never palled around outside of work. Nixon, as one of the show's stars, set the tone for the work relationship, and that tone, as Eigenberg read it, was strictly professional. It was always, "How are you? Did you have a good weekend?" And then straight to work. Not that they would have had time to grab dinners together anyway, with the hours they worked. "We had a very fictional relationship," Eigenberg says, "and it was intense."

Eigenberg calls Nixon "one of America's great actresses." He was, if not intimidated, at least impressed when he heard he'd be acting opposite the woman who had been doing two plays on Broadway at the same time when he moved to New York City. That was iconic! Once he began to work with her, he appreciated her warmth and patience in their scenes together, and her ability to always look at the bigger picture of the narrative and the overall production.

One day, for instance, he came to work having not shaved in several days. When Eigenberg saw Nixon on set, he asked, "Do you think I should shave for this episode?"

After looking at his scruffy face for a few seconds, she launched into a dissertation about why he should or should not have a beard for this particular moment in Steve's life. Eigenberg had no opinion on whether Steve should have a beard. In fact, he can't remember what the right answer was in this case. They came to acting from opposite approaches: He was a "point-and-shoot" actor; she was a cerebral actor. Or, as Nixon said, "David's a real guy. He's very suspicious of actors and actor-speak. He's a doer, not a talker." Their styles complemented each other. *If you want to be a better tennis player*, he thought, *play with somebody who's better than you.*

Eigenberg soon found himself recognized for his role on the streets of Manhattan, and not by whom you might think. As an everyguy who played an everyguy, he attracted the attention of real everyguys: A cement-truck driver on Ninth Avenue in the up-and-coming Meatpacking District saw him and yelled, "Hey, Steve!" Eigenberg thought,

Wow, that was cool. He began to get a distinct feeling: This might just be a career highlight. No one had ever known his character's name on the street before.

From there, it got even stranger: People would come up to him with opinions on "his" relationship with Miranda. "You're too good for her," they'd say. "You shouldn't let her treat you that way." He hated that, because he liked Miranda. Sure, she was tough, but she had a huge heart. He figured some people didn't like the feeling that Steve was "emasculated" by Miranda's success and her resistance to settling down with a man. He didn't give a shit about those people, but it still bugged him a little. He felt defensive of his on-screen love.

SEX GETS GRAPHIC

The show ventured into more emotional territory, but it was still distinguished by its graphic sex scenes—it was on cable, after all—and, even more, by its graphic sex talk. The anal sex discussion in season 1 set the tone for many dissections of bedroom habits never before heard on television. Scenes of the women gathered at a restaurant, talking about their sex lives, became known as "chat and chews" on the set. In them, the women spoke about threesomes, vibrators, and oral sex, setting a new agenda for brunches throughout the nation. King often joked, "We are saying stuff the audience is thinking, but we're like a week ahead of them saying it."

King had safeguards to keep the writers from following the temptation toward shocking words for shock's sake. He thought the best antidote was truth. If the group started to run into trouble as they brainstormed the beats of a story line, King would say, "Wait a minute. Let's go back to the day you pitched it. The original story was this." Usually the problem was obvious: They'd strayed way too far from that original inspiration. "Always go back to what actually happened," he said.

It wasn't just *Sex and the City*'s sex talk that shattered standards for decorum on television; it was its specifically gynecological talk. In season 2's "The Cheating Curve," Carrie gets her diaphragm stuck inside her—a story line inspired, King swears, by a woman he knew. She asked a friend to pull it out for her. "Now that," says King, "is friendship."

But when he told the story to Star and the other writers, they balked. "Hey, it's real," he said to them. Still not convinced, the writers asked around for more backup proof. Then when a woman on the crew copped to it happening to her as well, it made the script, with Samantha—of course—swooping in for the save with the addition of the outrageous line: "And I just got my nails done."

Such moments made Samantha—the dirtiest talker of them all—a breakout character, the kind of woman television had never seen before, and the kind of character viewers couldn't help but talk about. Samantha was, as King says, "the leader of the rebellion." Cattrall's portrayal made Samantha an instant classic TV character. King called her "the Lucille Ball of the bedroom." She had a talent for making every sex scene, every orgasm, funny and memorable. Almost everyone who worked on the show reached for one phrase to describe Cattrall: "game for anything."

Dennis Erdman, who had pushed partner Darren Star to pursue Cattrall's casting and later directed some episodes, saw the fruits of his effort when he was on set for the filming of the second-season opener. "Take Me Out to the Ballgame" has Samantha "coaching" her lover into being better in bed. She straddled this guy, yelling, "Fuck me, you big stud, fuck me!" Then she stopped, concerned. "Oh, no, it's 'Fuck me, fuck me, you big stud,' isn't it?" she asked the script supervisor. Satisfied, she went right back to the scene and delivered the line as written.

Cattrall—who eventually received a Golden Globe and five Emmy nominations for her portrayal—embraced her role in eradicating taboos around sex. She felt that presenting these issues with humor helped viewers talk about problems and solve them. She saw their work on *Sex and the City* as part of a tradition that began with Mae West and Madeline Kahn, who combined saucy and funny with aplomb. Channeling the role of Samantha gave Cattrall the courage to strip down for sex scenes—in these moments she was the bold Samantha, after all, not Kim Cattrall. And she saw the scenes as an acting challenge: How do I fall onto the bed differently this time?

In fact, Cattrall would even capitalize on her status as the high priestess of sex ed by writing a book with husband Mark Levinson in 2001 called *Satisfaction: The Art of the Female Orgasm*, which reviewers treated with surprising respect, calling it a "worthwhile read" and a "thoughtful manual."

"Women who have been 'sexually free' or 'promiscuous' have been punished through the ages," Cattrall said. "Whether it's *Looking for Mr. Goodbar* or Mata Hari or Sappho, whatever the scenario has been about a woman being sexual and being up front about her sexuality, each time she was punished, killed, or abused for it—until recently." That is, until Samantha.

• • •

When the second season of *Sex and the City* began to air in the summer of 1999, it marked a true breakthrough moment for the show. The show was nominated for its first Outstanding Comedy Series Emmy that summer, and Sarah Jessica Parker was nominated for Outstanding Lead Actress in a Comedy Series.

The Vibratex Rabbit Pearl vibrator became a sensation after being featured on an episode of *Sex and the City*. The New York City sex toy store the Pleasure Chest reported a flood of requests. *Rolling Stone* named Cattrall its "hot woman of a certain age" in 1999. The magazine called her "the most womanly temptress to strut through TV land in years."

High on its new cultural cachet, HBO threw dozens of *Sex and the City* screening parties throughout the United States as the new season kicked off in July 1999. Fans attended even in scorching heat; they swarmed clubs such as the Tongue & Groove in Buckhead, Georgia. "I feel like they really are saying the things we're all thinking," fan Alana Peters, a twenty-nine-year-old software consultant, told the *New York Times*.

The parties celebrated the show's popularity, despite HBO executives' fears that it wouldn't play with viewers outside New York City. Media reports documented followings in Cleveland, Providence, and Baton Rouge. Ratings bore this out. *Sex and the City* beat competition airing at the same time on broadcast networks in homes that had HBO across the country. Cable viewership had risen 11 percent over the previous year, while network ratings were down by 6 percent.

As the *Times'* Nancy Hass wrote, "Like *Seinfeld* the show seems to belie the conventional television wisdom that Middle America will reject any show too clearly set in Manhattan. Such logic is responsible for the flatness of sitcoms like *Friends* and *Caroline in the City*, set in Manhattan but looking suspiciously like the San Fernando Valley, where they were actually shot, down to the slightly dated slip dresses, ubiquitous Gap cargo pants, and perky mating rituals."

Male critics, in particular, still didn't get it. Many continued to respond with condescension and vitriol, while others did not get the joke. The *Washington Post*'s Tom Shales returned in 1999 with a new take on his previous year's disdain: "The series reportedly has a substantial following among gay males," he wrote, "perhaps because the women talk tirelessly about men." He harped again about Parker's breasts in the opening credits and his professed displeasure with her looks, describing her hair as "hanging down in hideous gnarled strands."

Psychologically, this seems related to his other complaint: the series's penchant for male objectification. "[U]ndraped males are as likely to appear as undraped females," he wrote. "On the season premiere, for example, the ladies find themselves in the New York Yankees' locker room, ogling and giggling." He's shocked—*shocked!*—by Samantha's joke in that scene that a player's "cup runneth over."

Shales didn't mischaracterize the show's approach to men. He just missed its point. Parker herself said that the women are "multidimensional, but the men are objectified the way we often are." The male characters often lack even names: Marathon Man, Mr. Pussy, Groovy Guy. But, as Carrie says, sometimes men are like accessories: "You know it's not your style, but it's right there, so you try it on anyway." Women were capable of using men the same way men used women. It had long been true; *Sex and the City* simply let men in on the bitter truth.

The *Chicago Tribune*'s Steve Johnson, meanwhile, seemed annoyed to find himself enjoying the show: "Back for a second season of women's locker-room talk is *Sex and the City*, the HBO series that is almost saved by its dirty-words-from-pretty-mouths aesthetic and the bubbly, blithe presence of Sarah Jessica Parker. Because both of these things are unusual for a television comedy, you can be misled into thinking *Sex and the City* is pretty good. It is, instead, pretty titillating and engaging, which I think are two ways of saying the same thing, but also pretty hollow and predictable in its portrait of the desperation of the over-30 single woman." One wonders where all of this "desperation" is coming from, given that the entire point of the series is the women's lack of desperation. Miranda prioritizes her career over relationships; Samantha prioritizes sex over relationships; Carrie is anxious about Mr. Big, but indifferent to other suitors; only Charlotte expresses an old-fashioned interest in securing a husband.

The show would continue to fight with dismissive, confused, and sexist critics throughout its run. In fact, the second season self-consciously satirized some of these responses. In one episode, Carrie is the subject of a *New York* magazine story, which she thinks will be a glowing portrait of single life but ends up featuring her on the cover looking haggard with the headline "Single and Fabulous . . . ?" In another, Miranda complains that her friends talk about men too much. "All we talk about anymore is Big, or balls, or small dicks," she says. "How does it happen that four such smart women have nothing to talk about but boyfriends? It's like seventh grade but with bank accounts."

But while critics whined about reverse sexism and scoffed at its frivolousness, *Sex and the City* was making history.

5

A Very High Altitude

· · · · · · · · · · ·

By the third season, *Sex and the City*'s writers and directors knew what viewers wanted, and they knew how to give it to them. Sometimes it was the impossibly luxe lifestyle. Sometimes it was the characters' intimately embarrassing moments. Sometimes it was romance.

In a few magical moments, it was all three.

As director Allen Coulter prepared to film the third-season finale in Central Park, he knew he had one of those on this afternoon in 2000. He saw it as his Howard Hawks moment: a picturesque romantic standoff between equals, a throwback screwball scene that was sexy but not explicit. That is, if Hawks had been forced to shoot on location with paparazzi clicking through every scene, catching his every move, as scores of fans mobbed the periphery.

Large crowds now gathered everywhere *Sex and the City* shot, particularly for this scene, in which Big and Carrie meet at the lakeside

101

Boathouse restaurant after he's gotten married to a younger woman named Natasha and engaged in an affair with Carrie. Miranda has just advised Carrie, "Don't let him kiss you. That seems to be where you get into trouble." Naturally, the first thing he does is try to kiss her next to the lake; when she swerves to avoid him, they both fall in. Coulter wanted to make this look as good as a classic Katharine Hepburn–Cary Grant showdown.

It made sense that *Sex and the City* would evoke Howard Hawks. The director became famous for his strong-willed, bantery heroines in films he made throughout the 1930s and 1940s—Hepburn, Rosalind Russell, and Lauren Bacall in classics such as *Bringing Up Baby*, *His Girl Friday*, and *To Have and Have Not*, among many others. Film critic Molly Haskell wrote about the type that became known as the Hawksian woman: "The charge leveled by feminists that Hawks's women must model themselves after men to get their attention is largely true. . . . But the behavior of his tomboys and bachelor girls is also an explicit challenge to traditional stereotypes of what a woman is and should be. Their aggressiveness arises from a variety of motives and instincts, from ambition, energy, intelligence, sexual insecurity, and from a frustration, perhaps, from being so long excluded from the world of action and camaraderie and non-sexual love that Hawks's cinema celebrates." Her description fit *Sex and the City*'s heroines just as well—except the "non-sexual" part, of course.

This Hawksian moment in Central Park required plenty of technical finesse. Coulter had frogmen in the water to be ready for any emergency. The water had been tested for disease and given a clean (or at least clean enough) bill of health. The crew covered the bottom of the lake with wire mesh so neither Parker nor Noth would step on, say, broken glass from park litterers. Parker wore a pink, floral silk chiffon dress by Richard Tyler, chosen with care by Patricia Field's assistant, Rebecca Weinberg—it was sexy but still daytime-appropriate, and would look pretty even when wet.

In addition to the crowd, swarms of paparazzi had become the norm at *Sex and the City* location shoots like this, which often led to scuffles and curses between the show's crew and the photographers. The crew had learned they couldn't ban the cameras from a public space because of the constitutional right to freedom of the press. So the photographers would get as close as they could, while the crew would work to keep them as far away as possible. Often crew members would stand holding up black cloth to block the actors from public view for hours at a time as their arms shook from the effort. The cameras would click-click-click away regardless to get what they could while distracting the actors and disrupting the scene's soundscape.

In these situations, Parker tried to remind herself that the crowds and attention were a good sign, an indication of how strongly viewers now connected to the show. She had them to thank for the show's success. But in the case of the Central Park shoot, the onlookers added to the cast and crew's anxiety about the scene, which would be complicated to pull off.

As Parker and Noth prepared to shoot with Coulter, Noth thought of the sensation of clicking up the roller-coaster hill, knowing you're about to drop and scream. This specific scene may have been causing his anxiety, or perhaps it was the altitude to which the show had ascended. Probably a bit of both.

When the moment came and the couple took their plunge, it looked great on camera. However, a piece of wire from the protective mesh sliced Parker's foot open upon impact. Noth choked on a mouthful of water.

The stars laughed about it, although Parker required a tetanus shot. The scene had turned out Hawksian indeed, and it gave the crowds of onlookers something to see, too. Only one trip to the doctor required.

Filming on the third season of *Sex and the City*, the show's biggest spectacle to date, was wrapped.

• • •

By this time, as the third season was shooting, the four main actresses could no longer go out in public without being approached by fans, especially in boutiques, where they had to take their sunglasses off if they wanted to browse. In those more intimate settings—perhaps because of shopping's strong connection to *Sex and the City*—women would stop them to gush over the show, to recite their favorite lines. The actresses knew it was flattering, but it felt intense. Sometimes they just wanted to get a new dress in peace.

Even some of the major male actors, like Chris Noth and David Eigenberg—Mr. Big and Steve—found themselves upgraded to first class on airplanes and stopped on the street for a discussion of their characters' relationships on the show. Noth got to star in the Broadway play *The Best Man* as a Mr. Big–like character, a role he knew he wouldn't have landed, he said, if he "had not gotten some fame."

For the summer 2000 season, HBO threw a glitzy premiere party at the United Artists 64th Street movie theater in Manhattan. Sure, the show was often called *Dirtysomething* and the *Washington Post* continued to take shots at it (a 2000 review described it as "teetering . . . on classy soft porn"). But that year it also won two Golden Globes: one for Parker as lead actress and one for the series. Pop group Destiny's Child made a music video tribute to the show, from the HBO logo and opening credits to Beyoncé, Kelly Rowland, and Michelle Williams brunching and strutting down the street, for their song "Girl."

In the surest form of flattery, Hollywood began its *Sex and the City* imitation in earnest. ABC brought us *Talk to Me*, which followed a radio host played by Kyra Sedgwick as she tried to get over a breakup "like a man" by having meaningless sex. The "like a man" plot line swiped directly from *Sex and the City*'s pilot; the part where she broke into tears while in bed with her conquest did not.

The brighter side of the rush for the "next *Sex in the City*" was a marked increase in female involvement behind the scenes of sitcoms. Terri Minsky, who had been involved in the early days of *Sex and the City*, created *The Geena Davis Show*, where 75 percent of the staff was female. Women executive-produced at least six shows on the air in the next year, with predominantly female staffs: *Madigan Men*, *Girlfriends*,

Tucker, *Three Sisters*, *What About Joan*, and *Gilmore Girls*. More women rose to top network leadership positions than ever before: Susanne Daniels at the WB, Gail Berman at Fox, and Nancy Tellem at CBS.

Sex and the City fever had helped push many of these developments forward. "Absolutely that series affected us," said Stu Bloomberg, entertainment cochairman at ABC. "A lot of women at this company live for that show." Broadcast networks were panicking over cable encroachment; their ratings had dropped so much that they no longer insisted every show have wide appeal. "Niche" shows—which was how they saw female-driven shows—could attract a passionate following even if they didn't draw every gender, age group, and region.

More fans joined the *Sex and the City* "niche" every week, and the media finally began embracing the message that meant so much to King and Star: As *USA Weekend* said at the time, *Sex and the City* told viewers that "being single is no longer a disease." While other shows had focused on foursomes of single women, like *Golden Girls* and *Designing Women* in the 1980s, those highlighted women beyond middle age, women who had at least attempted traditional married life before they ended up single after deaths and divorces. *Sex and the City* told women beyond "ideal" marriage age, but not yet to middle and older age, that there was still no hurry to settle down.

Sex and the City began to gain international audiences as well. It aired in Australia, Ireland, and the United Kingdom, among other countries. The series had gone from something people on the street in New York City didn't even recognize, to a "niche" show, to a national sensation, and finally to a global event with finale parties in Paris, London, and Berlin.

It grew to be a particularly large hit in Japan. "In Japan it was very powerful because young women were finding their voice and being more demanding in relationships," says Veronica Chambers, who wrote about the phenomenon in her book *Kickboxing Geishas: How Modern Japanese Women Are Changing Their Nation*. The show particularly resonated with female Japanese culture in two ways, she says: its fairy-tale princess underpinnings and its emphasis on "freedom of expression through fashion" at a time when the Harajuku fashion movement in Japan emphasized similarly exaggerated and theatrical looks.

Sex and the City had everyone's attention, but what next? The strategy for the show as it matured was to shift the focus from the sex and dresses that made it famous to deeper character issues that would stand the test of time. The third season folded more drama into the comedy than the seasons before it.

Of course, there was still plenty of fun. In two episodes toward the end of the season, the girls go to Los Angeles with Carrie to investigate a Hollywood offer to option her columns, just as Bushnell once had. Matthew McConaughey plays the douchiest possible version of himself in the episodes, with *Buffy the Vampire Slayer*'s Sarah Michelle Gellar as a young movie executive, Carrie Fisher as herself, and Vince Vaughn as Carrie Fisher's house sitter.

Those episodes proved to be a sunny, self-referential free-for-all that traded on the show's cachet to lure big-name guest stars. But before the show could enjoy this confection, they had to get through the hard stuff.

ROOMS (AND LIVES) OF THEIR OWN

Virginia Woolf wrote in her essay "Professions for Women" in 1931: "You have won rooms of your own in the house hitherto exclusively owned by men. You are able, though not without great labour and effort, to pay the rent. . . . But this freedom is only a beginning; the room is your own, but it is still bare." At the time of her creation, Candace Bushnell's print alter ego, Carrie Bradshaw, as portrayed by the media, often ended up at the single girls' table with the British sensation Bridget Jones. Single women hadn't progressed much since Woolf's time, according to the neuroses on display in Fielding's work and the suffocating sense of hopelessness in Bushnell's. Women had rooms of their own, but they used those rooms mainly to moon over men. Bushnell and Fielding, as leaders of the "chick lit" trend, ushered in a proliferation of single, professional heroines, but emphasized old-fashioned ideals of love and marriage once again, dressed up as modern with stilettos and booze and jobs.

However, *Sex and the City* the television show, as it reached velocity in its third season, reminded Parker more of books about bold female characters that are wonderful to read regardless of whether those characters are "likable" or morally perfect: *The Scarlet Letter*, *Olive Kitteridge*, *Jane Eyre*, *Pride and Prejudice*, *The Bell Jar*, *Breakfast at Tiffany's*, *Anna Karenina*. Young women across America who wanted something beyond marriage and kids suddenly had a vision for who they wanted to be: a Carrie, a Charlotte, a Miranda, or a Samantha. In varying ways these four characters began to fill that room once imagined by Woolf.

They started out obsessing about men, of course. But they added their own shadings and nuances to the singleton stereotype as they began to explore both the good and bad parts of being unmarried. Then they took this a step further, examining the costs and rewards of coupledom and marriage. The process started with the introduction of Steve and Miranda's relationship, and continued in the third season with a crisis in which Charlotte learns to be careful what you wish for.

Charlotte rants in the first episode of the third season, lamenting that her Prince Charming has yet to make himself known to her: "I've been dating since I was fifteen. I'm exhausted. Where *is* he?" She would find him, or at least a version of him, but it would not be the happy ending Charlotte hoped for.

She was soon to meet Dr. Trey MacDougal, played by the Ken-doll-handsome Kyle MacLachlan, most famous for his role on *Twin Peaks*. Trey proves to be rich, WASPy, and impotent—that last fact she discovers almost, but not quite, too late, just before their wedding. She marries him anyway in a quaint uptown church, wearing a beaded tulle gown by Vera Wang.

Davis was relieved: Like Charlotte, she enjoyed having a steady beau. She didn't like acting opposite a different guy every episode.

Yet Charlotte and Trey's imperfect relationship shifted the show's focus away from the idea of finding a Mr. Right—whom Trey was turning out not to be for Charlotte—to the more complex idea of finding the right life for yourself. Charlotte had to look beyond the romantic ideal encoded in her upbringing; finding a handsome prince had not solved all of her problems. In fact, he had only created more problems. The single female heroine was evolving beyond both the Hawksian woman and Bridget Jones.

That heroine could evolve on *Sex and the City* because the women who wrote for the show put more of their lives and hearts into it than ever: not just bad dates, but heartbreaks. Jenny Bicks benefited from expert training when she was a sitcom writer—in how to write jokes, in how to write tight—but *Sex and the City* changed her life by allowing her to be herself. Cindy Chupack had the same experience. She wrote about what mattered to her, and found out it mattered to millions of others, too. "It was such a moment in the zeitgeist," as Chupack says, "and also a moment in my life when I needed that support."

Fans were feeling the same way as they watched. "As many times as these women fall down—meet the wrong sociopath, have weird sex, get their hearts broken—they always manage to get back up and try again," Naveen Kumar later wrote on the website *Refinery29*. "It's inspiring. After all these years, I still believe in the show's campy powers to lift me out of a funk."

• • •

Halfway through its third season, *Sex and the City* made the cover of *Time* magazine's August 28, 2000, issue—the magazine's first ever to feature a cable show. The four actresses stare at readers over the cover line "Who Needs a Husband?" "More women are saying no to marriage and embracing the single life," the subhead says. Then, of course, it undermines all that empowerment with a parting shot: "Are they happy?" Inside the issue, amid analyses of the upcoming US presidential contest between George W. Bush and Al Gore, and chronicles of the rise of Silicon Valley and a company called Enron, four articles attempt to answer that question. Single mothers, having given up on partnership and gone to sperm banks, discuss their tribulations. Writer Walter Kirn bemoans what he sees as modern women's pickiness:

> Whatever it is that women want in men, two things are certain: a) it changes annually, and b) women never seem to find it. In the '70s, they looked for sensitivity. Then came a backlash. Strength was the ideal; then strength and sensitivity combined. And a willingness to commit, of course—without being clingy. Clinginess was fatal. A little success and power were welcome too, as long as the man in question wasn't controlling. Now, it seems that what's wanted is a soul mate, a sort of buff Buddha who's terrific in bed, who's on top of his health, his finances, and emotions, and can serve in a pinch as a spiritual adviser. It's a testimony to women's romantic natures that they really believe such men exist out there.

The feature on *Sex and the City* itself strikes the most respectful pose of all the single-ladies coverage: "In its first two seasons *Sex* became a pop-culture icon for its astute bedroom politics, for the saucy *Seinfeld* banter (laced with corny double entendres) of its glam foursome, but above all for recognizing that a woman can live well without being at either end of a man's leash," critic James Poniewozik wrote. He called the show's third season "exceptional." "It proves these women's ability to cut deep that they've been called both 'evil, emasculating harpies' (*USA Today*) and male fantasies." The answer to the cover's taunting question seems to be that real single women still are not as happy as they think they are—but those fictional *Sex and the City* ladies are!

The *Time* package expressed the complications of both the making of and reaction to *Sex and the City*. The events of the third season in particular allowed for discussions about complex women's issues long kept out of television: for instance, whether it's antifeminist for a woman to choose to be a full-time homemaker, as Charlotte does in this season after falling for her dream WASP, Trey. She snaps, "The women's movement is supposed to be about choice. And if I choose to quit my job, that is my choice. . . . I choose my choice!" In another story line, Miranda considers abortion after an unplanned pregnancy with Steve, just because she's not sure she wants a child—not because of financial insecurity. And Carrie's controversial affair with Big had viewers debating whether it was okay for a woman to be more commitmentphobic than a man.

Charlotte's "choice" line, in particular, hit deeper than just a joke. It was so meaty, it could have fueled another *Time* magazine cover story—in fact, the idea of professional women who "opt out" of careers would inspire many trend pieces in the years to come. The line also anticipated what would be termed "choice feminism" by author Linda Hirshman in her 2006 book, *Get to Work: A Manifesto for Women of the World*. Hirshman first applied the concept to women like Charlotte, those who wanted the option to stay home without being judged for it.

But the term would come to describe the wider, increasingly pervasive idea that anything a woman chooses for herself is feminist. Unfortunately, this free-for-all approach to feminism doesn't acknowledge that "choice" is a fraught term: It assumes that what a woman does is not influenced by sexist social norms, when in fact women can be sexist, too. And that doesn't apply just to overtly antifeminist women like 1970s anti–Equal Rights Amendment activist Phyllis Schlafly.

Even a woman who thinks of herself as generally in favor of equality can gravitate, as Charlotte does, toward unrealistic ideals of feminine comportment. The show leaves little doubt that the pressure to marry is intense for all women, and marrying well is Charlotte's raison d'être until Trey. Of course choosing a handsome husband and then choosing to stay home, away from the pressures of her job, feels good to Charlotte in the moment. It's what she's been taught to work toward for her whole life. But that doesn't mean her choice is inherently a feminist act; in fact, it's been guided by patriarchal forces, whether Charlotte knows it or not.

Still, the idea of choice feminism satisfies many—the women who get to do whatever they want and call it a positive political action, as well as the corporations who capitalize on feminism by persuading women to choose their "empowering" strip-aerobics classes, pop albums, lingerie, or deodorant that's "strong enough for a man, but made for a woman."

Sex and the City celebrated every possible aspect of choice feminism, which tends to dovetail nicely with consumerism; society embraces women's liberation most when it's about liberating women from their money. Women could be feminists by buying their own expensive shoes, bikini waxes, and cosmopolitans, even by exercising their right to opt out of work. Yet if this approach allows women a free feminist justification for any and every decision, it also provides a new way to pit women against each other. We can fight over which of us is doing feminism wrong—stay-at-home moms versus working mothers, singles versus marrieds, plastic surgery enthusiasts versus those who judge them—while corporations sell us empowerment. This approach also represents a key portion of what's derisively known as "white feminism," which focuses on the concerns of wealthy white women—like having the choice to stay home or work for a living—to the detriment of more critical issues facing women of color and working-class women. Feminism is not just "a lady doing what she wants."

Sex and the City, for all of its excellent and addictive qualities, served as a weekly commercial for white ladies doing what they want as the ultimate liberation. Its portrayal of women as layered characters, flawed and sometimes unlikable, freed the women of television and the women who watched them to embrace more than the traditionally feminine role meant to delight men at all costs. But the show also equated feminism with wearing expensive clothes and sleeping with lots of men. While this was a step up from single women as cat ladies, it provided only a limited view of liberation in which patriarchy hasn't lost much ground: Femininity, glamour, and heterosexual coupling still rule, because they make women who grew up around them feel good, and men still get to have unfettered sex with sufficiently feminine, attractive, adorned women.

Sex and the City had taken a step in the right direction, but it was hardly a feminist utopia.

AN AFFAIR TO REMEMBER

From the beginning of *Sex and the City*, its most devoted fans obsessed about the characters' personal decisions: Should Miranda give the puppyish Skipper a chance? Should Carrie have kept the money a guy left her by the bedside when he thought she was a high-class hooker? What should Miranda do about her nosy housekeeper, Magda, who insists on replacing her coffee with tea and her vibrator with a statue of the Virgin Mary? These questions enlivened our brunch conversations and sometimes even helped us figure out where we stood on everything from basic dating etiquette to sex work to opting out.

But none of these debates matched the intensity of feeling unleashed by one of the major story lines for the third season: First, the writers would introduce Mr. Big's first serious rival for Carrie's affection, a sensitive carpenter named Aidan, played by John Corbett. The actor was known for his role on the quirky early-'90s dramedy *Northern Exposure* and served as the antithesis of Noth's Mr. Big. He had wavy sandy hair, an easy smile, and an outdoorsy, hippie vibe. Though Parker knew of him and his work, she was surprised by the strength of some women's ardor when she mentioned Corbett would play her new boyfriend.

Corbett *was* Aidan. When the *Sex and the City* producers first offered Corbett the role, he wasn't sure he wanted to do it. He was building a house in West Virginia and he didn't want to stop just to work on a show he'd never seen. He also resisted the idea of getting naked on-screen, and the first draft of Aidan's debut script had him taking a bath with Carrie. He couldn't do it, he said, as long as his mother was still alive.

But he agreed to meet with Parker to discuss the role. "As soon as she opened to door to her house, I fell in love," he said. Luckily, that bath was scrapped, too.

Viewers' affection for Aidan only intensified the audience's feelings about the second half of the season, which features Carrie cheating on everyone's favorite new boyfriend, Aidan, with the now-married Mr. Big.

On the one hand, plenty of viewers remained Team Big. Around this time, King went to dinner with Noth and Parker, riding in the backseat of Noth's 1970 vintage Mercedes while the TV couple rode in front. When they stopped at a red light, a couple in the next car spotted them and said, "Ooh, it's real! I knew it!"

But viewers lashed out against Carrie after the affair, trotting out the age-old sexist trope that affairs are always the woman's fault. (The sentiment, expressed mostly through letters, emails, interviews, and hearsay at the time, solidified later into a "Carrie Bradshaw Was an Impossibly Awful Human" genre of blog posts during the show's afterlife.) "It's funny because it's like, 'Hey, he's the one who's married. She's not married,'" Bicks says. "There was such a double standard going on."

The story line marked a departure for the show in several ways. It veered melodramatic, more *Melrose Place* than comedy, and more deeply felt than *Melrose*—the series's first dabble in what would become its signature mix of comedy and drama. This plot moved the show's heroine from mere party-girl behavior to morally questionable territory. And the soft-focus, heavy-breathing scenes of the sex between Big and Carrie were the show's only sexy sex scenes—played as hot, guilty flashbacks, not a standard romp through sexual indignities and peccadilloes.

The Big-Carrie affair also prompted the first of several devastating fights between Carrie and Miranda, an emotional explosion that would become a signature of the series and mark its deepening portrayal of female friendship. "You don't want it to be too safe and too lovey-dovey," Nixon said. "These women love and support each other unconditionally, but they also have very different points of view and are bound to clash."

• • •

While *Sex and the City* pushed boundaries with the painfully realistic Big-Carrie affair, it also strained the limits of political correctness with a few third-season episodes that, especially when viewed in retrospect, clumsily addressed identities beyond its straight (and occasionally gay), white, cisgender norm.

In "Boy, Girl, Boy, Girl," Carrie dates a younger man named Sean who casually tells her that he's bisexual. She announces this to her friends with a very specific phrasing: "He's a bisexual." Not just one aspect of his identity, but an entirely "other" being. Samantha—so sexually liberated that she would later have a relationship with a woman—cracks, "I could've told you that, sweetie. He took you ice-skating, for God's sake." Despite this stereotype-dependent joke, she at least also calls him "evolved." Miranda disagrees, trotting out a *Seinfeld* joke to object to his "greed": "He's double-dipping."

When Sean takes Carrie to a party where several of his friends display sexual fluidity, she refers to herself as "Alice in Confused Sexual Orientation Land," which is odd, since these characters seem to know *exactly* their place on the Kinsey spectrum. The festivities culminate in a game of spin the bottle and a kiss between guest star Alanis Morissette's character and Carrie. Normally an open-minded sex columnist, Carrie flees the party, overwhelmed by her shock. She really shows her cards when she calls bisexuality "a layover on the way to Gay Town."

Kate Silver blogged at *Persephone Magazine* about her experience watching the episode with a group of girlfriends: "My straight friends were laughing along with the jokes, not aware that the excessive bisexual bashing—not to mention the usage of a part of my identity as a plot device—was making me feel ill. The ignorance and privilege of Carrie and her friends was being reflected perfectly by my own friends."

In "No Ifs, Ands, or Butts," Samantha dates a black record producer named Chivon whose sister, Adeena, disapproves of the interracial relationship. The episode is laden with stereotypes: Chivon works in hip-hop and takes Samantha to a club with a metal detector; Adeena is a chef known for her high-end soul food and, apparently, her overbearing attitude. The women discuss Chivon's ample endowment. Adeena and Samantha's showdown at the club is the rare physical fight between two women on the show, complete with hair pulling and an admonition for Samantha to keep her "little white pussy" away from Chivon. Samantha's rejoinder: "Get your big black ass out of my face."

Stereotypes and epithets aside, Carrie's ultimate conclusion in this episode reveals that the show doesn't grasp the racial divide it's depicting. When Chivon quite reasonably and respectfully breaks up with Samantha by explaining that he has to prioritize his relationship with his sister, Carrie's voice-over swoops in to declare that "Samantha knew the real problem wasn't her little white pussy. It was the fact that Chivon was a black pussy who wouldn't stand up to his sister." In the end, the episode equates these racial differences with its other plot lines, all tied together with a "deal-breaker" theme: Aidan's demand that Carrie stop smoking and Charlotte's requirement that her date improve his kissing technique.

Ultimately, the episode's attempt at inclusion only made things worse. "This type of pandering to racial stereotypes—a controlling black woman who emasculates a black man—does not represent progress from the preceding seasons' virtual omission of other racial groups," Adia Harvey Wingfield wrote at RacismReview.com. "Racist stereotypes are not, in my view, better than nothing at all."

Journalist Veronica Chambers, who'd become a fan and had written about the show for *Newsweek*, remembers watching the episode, particularly Adeena's "sista with attitude" character, as she says, and thinking, *Ugh*. "So many of my black girlfriends were dating interracially," she says. "We just rolled our eyes. Who cares if Samantha dates a black man?"

THE JOB A MILLION GIRLS WOULD KILL FOR

Despite these misfires, by season 3, *Sex and the City* was the most desirable place to work for young female TV writers. Determined to be among them were twentysomethings Julie Rottenberg—a thin, pale redhead with curly hair—and Elisa Zuritsky—who had curly brown hair and apple cheeks that made her look even younger than she was. In fact, they believed the show might be their last shot at their dream careers in Hollywood, even though they'd barely gotten their first.

The two had been friends since age nine, when they met in an acting class in Philadelphia. They were so intertwined, it was easy to lump them together as one entity, but they had plenty of differences: Rottenberg was the pessimist, the worrier, the extrovert. Zuritsky hoped for the best and believed in it, but she was the more reserved in social situations.

They'd maintained their bond since childhood, and had written their first movie script together around 1998, when they were in their twenties. They bought a book about how to write a screenplay and pecked out a romantic comedy on a Mac desktop computer at Zuritsky's family's beach house on the Jersey Shore. The two of them had lugged the computer from home to the vacation spot just to do it, carrying the contraption, as Rottenberg says, "like it was a dead body." The screenplay took its inspiration from Zuritsky's previous job, when she wrote a column called "Celebrity Date" for the *New York Post*. She would do celebrity profiles by going on date-like interviews. The screenplay, called *Puff Piece*, followed a young woman with a similar column.

They wrote it and then returned to their day jobs: Rottenberg edited comic books (back when comics didn't have the cool factor they would later acquire), and Zuritsky edited the entertainment section at *Nickelodeon Magazine*. They didn't know what they were waiting for, but they weren't quite ready to make a big play for their dream careers writing plays or TV or movies.

Eventually, Rottenberg's plays and animation work got the attention of an agent, who set up a meeting for her with a TV executive where she could pitch some show ideas. She cobbled together a cheap trip to Los Angeles by tagging along with Zuritsky, who was staying there in a grimy hotel room to cover the Kids' Choice Awards for *Nickelodeon*.

When Rottenberg went to the meeting, the executive asked if she had any show ideas. Rottenberg surprised herself when she blurted out, "I do, but I would have to come back with my partner." Who might that be? Rottenberg trembled with the thought that this was the biggest lie she'd ever told. But when she said it, the lie came true: Elisa Zuritsky.

Rottenberg and Zuritsky met with the executive together when she came to New York City for the networks' upfront presentations to advertisers in the spring. They had crammed to come up with show ideas: One was about Tekserve, the computer repair shop in Manhattan. One was about a columnist, similar to their movie script. And one was about a woman who sublets an apartment and inherits the previous tenant's problems along with it.

• • •

That pitch session resulted in a small development deal with Studios USA, but their fate really changed when Darren Star read one of their scripts, which he admired for its authentic voice. They were taking meetings during a trip to Los Angeles, talking with networks on a possible pilot deal, when they got a call from their agent. "Darren Star read your stuff and he wants to meet with you," he told them on the phone. Star wanted to meet that Friday.

Rottenberg replied, "Unfortunately we can't do that. We have to leave on Thursday. Our flight is on Thursday."

"Change your fucking flight," their agent said. "Sleep on my kid's floor if you need to, but do not miss this meeting." But in Rottenberg's worldview, you just don't change a flight. You'll get charged.

That said, they were rushing back home for what? To do nothing. To wait for a TV deal to happen or maybe not happen. They changed their flight and stayed at a friend's place, in her basement.

The next morning, they met with Star, Michael Patrick King, Jenny Bicks, and Cindy Chupack. They couldn't believe they were meeting the writers of their favorite show, the names from those opening credits. They saw it more as a fan experience than anything else, unable to comprehend that they might land a job there.

When Star first met them, he thought, *Wow, they're really young.* His second thought was, *Wow, they're really young to be that talented.*

After the meeting, Rottenberg and Zuritsky's agent called them: The *Sex and the City* producers loved them, he said, but didn't have a job available. Rottenberg and Zuritsky figured that was just a polite kiss-off. The end of their *Sex and the City* dreams.

Months went by before they heard from their agent again. Now it was: "The *Sex and the City* producers intend to hire you."

Zuritsky, afraid to trust the news, asked, "Don't people just say that?"

"Not really."

Michael Patrick King wanted to meet with them in New York.

Their hopes up, they headed to Pastis, a bistro in the Meatpacking District, for the meeting. They got there an hour early, so they decided to sit at the bar, sure they'd see him if he came in. They waited fifteen, thirty, and then forty minutes past their meeting time. No King. Finally, Rottenberg ran outside to a pay phone and called King's assistant. "He's there!" the assistant said.

When they went back in, they found him seated patiently at a table. Somehow they hadn't recognized him—his hair was a little different from the last time they'd seen him—and he hadn't seen them. They were amazed—and relieved—that he had waited so long.

They made it through the lunch, but they were trembling and nauseated as soon as they got out. They had almost fucked up the chance of a lifetime.

A week later, Rottenberg and Zuritsky were spending some time back at the Jersey Shore beach house when they heard from their agent that King wanted to read their work again because he was choosing the next season's writers. "He's putting the room together," the agent said. "He just wants to make sure all the voices work together."

They lay on the floor of the house, despondent. They had been through so much rejection in the entertainment business in general, and received so many confusing signals from *Sex and the City*, that this call read as bad news. No one ever wanted to read your work over again. They either liked you or they didn't. King was just not that into them. They were sure of it.

But they were wrong.

About ten days later they got the official offer to become staff writers. They were so stunned by it, they felt like they couldn't tell anyone. It felt like a lie. They would have accepted positions as production assistants, bringing people coffee. Being writers was just too much, too surreal to be true.

Besides, their agent still wanted to negotiate their contract, which made them nervous. They preferred to just take the job. "This is why you need an agent," he told them. Zuritsky felt like he would blow it. She thought, *He'll ask for too much, and they'll say, "Fuck you, little bitches, you don't deserve anything."*

Then they got the real offer, which was even better. And even more inconceivable.

Rottenberg happened to be throwing a huge party at her apartment that night. She didn't know what to do about her news. She didn't tell anyone, but she drank so much tequila, she spent most of the evening crouched over her toilet.

She and her parents didn't even mention her new job to any of the rest of the family gathered for Rosh Hashanah dinner later that week. It seemed too unfathomable to share.

Zuritsky had gone home to Philadelphia for the Jewish holidays, too. Her parents hadn't seen the show, so the family crowded around a tiny television in the kitchen to catch an episode of *Sex and the City*. It was the one in which Samantha has her pubic hair shaved into a lightning bolt. "No, but it's a great show!" Zuritsky protested as she anticipated her parents' thoughts. "Critically acclaimed! This is a big deal for me."

Afterward, they could only mutter platitudes: "That's so wonderful. Congratulations."

Rottenberg and Zuritsky searched for a three-month sublet in Los Angeles for the writing phase that would precede the fourth season in the fall of 2000. They had to muster up their New Yorkiest stories while surrounded by the palm trees and crowded freeways of Los Angeles.

They were joining TV's most fashionable phenomenon at its height. As King said to the writers, "This is a very high altitude."

Then they heard King say something terrifying: "So this thing is going to end after season six. We have about three more seasons in us." *Oh, my God*, Rottenberg thought. *I just got here, and it's all going to end.*

• • •

When production began on the scripts for the fourth season of *Sex and the City* on the East Coast, Rottenberg and Zuritsky took their place in the Silvercup Studios offices. The office given to them sat on the loft level, where the spaces were delineated by translucent walls. They called the space "the dentist's office."

When the two—whom the other writers dubbed "the twins," despite their contrasting looks—started their new job, they remained sure someone would whisk it away. They'd heard stories about television writers who handed in a draft of their first script and got fired. Worse, King did often joke about that in the writers' room: When someone pitched an idea he didn't like, he'd say, "Mmm, that's not going to work. You're fired." Rottenberg and Zuritsky fretted that, at some level, he meant it.

But then, Zuritsky landed her first joke in a script: Carrie walks a runway, then trips, prompting the line "She's fashion roadkill." The room loved it. Rottenberg and Zuritsky finally began to accept that they might just make it in show business after all.

STAR'S DEPARTURE

In 2000, Star was considering his own future. *Beverly Hills, 90210* and *Melrose Place* had made him rich, but *Sex and the City* had earned him respect, as noted by men's magazine *Details* in a 2000 profile. And Star's thoughts had begun to inch forward to other projects past *Sex and the City*.

Star felt like he had done all he could with *Sex and the City*, so after three seasons—two of them running the show, and one handing over the top job to King—Star planned to depart. He didn't mind leaving it to run on its own; by now he felt it was a perfect machine. He had done the same with *90210*, which was just then, during *Sex and the City*'s third season, signing off the air.

He had tried to make a deal to create more series for HBO, but the network couldn't accommodate that the same way that broadcast networks and studios could. NBC studios, for example, might produce a show that the NBC network didn't want, but the Fox network did. HBO wasn't set up to produce shows that might be shopped to other networks as well; their model was to create only HBO-appropriate shows. Still, Star felt grateful, he says, to have such capable hands in which to leave his creation.

After his departure from *Sex and the City*, he created *The $treet* for Fox, set at a New York stock trading company and starring Jennifer Connelly and Tom Everett Scott. (It was billed as "the male *Sex and the City*.") To the WB, he brought a comedy about the production of a teen drama, *Grosse Pointe*, which starred Lindsay Sloane and Bonnie Somerville as parody versions of *90210* stars Tori Spelling and Jennie Garth.

Over the next three seasons, Star would still read *Sex and the City* scripts and look at edits of the episodes sometimes, and King would often keep him posted on what went on. Star even occasionally weighed in on story lines, though he was happy with King's direction.

King now ran the writers' room alone, developing ways to prioritize openness and safety. It had become a mechanism for transmuting the staff's weekly heartbreaks into TV magic that would touch millions weeks later, and he knew he needed to be careful to maintain that alchemy. Every morning, a writer would come in with some tragic date story, and King would call it—"That's a Miranda," for instance—and it would go up on the white dry-erase board to be spun into one-liners and catchphrases and scenes everyone would soon be talking about the Monday after its Sunday airing.

Taking over the show translated into a very New York kind of reward for King: entrée into the glamorous upper echelons of city life. King, like most of the writers, had once experienced the city as a broke young person, barely scraping by. So he appreciated it even more when every door was suddenly open to him, Michael Patrick King, executive producer of *Sex and the City*. He called it the "I Am Chosen New York."

Sex and the City shared a glimpse of that "I Am Chosen New York" with the unadmitted masses, and the picture it painted made everyone who watched want a taste. *Sex and the City* had formed its own economy, and it did not come cheap.

6

Shopping and Fucking

· · · · · · · · · · ·

If the *Sex and the City* women were consuming something, viewers coveted it, stalked it, bought it, made it, or devoured it.

Take the case of the cupcakes.

In one third-season episode, Carrie and Miranda sat on a bench
in front of a picturesque café window that displayed voluptuous cakes
and, prominently, the Magnolia Bakery cookbook. The pink-frosting-
swirl-covered vanilla cupcakes and the redbrick building made a
perfect painting of a camera shot. There, the two women discussed
Carrie's crush on Aidan Shaw, the hunky carpenter she'd just met.
But the scene at the small West Village establishment went by so fast
that it seemed like a smart move by the store owners to display those
cookbooks in the window, or viewers might miss where those cupcakes
could be bought.

It turned out there was not a chance of that happening. Instead, the few seconds of girl talk over dessert ignited a cupcake fad, and a retail war that has raged to the present day.

Magnolia Bakery opened at the corner of Bleecker and West 11th Street in 1996, a joint venture between high school friends Jennifer Appel and Allysa Torey. They took over a space well-known around the neighborhood for its previous tenant, a bird shop full of talking parrots. Their original intent was a neighborhood bakery, making little daily batches of baked goods and using an old-fashioned cash register for the tiny transactions. But then, in 1999, Appel left to open her own solo shop uptown, Buttercup Bake Shop, with hopes of bigger business.

She missed out on Magnolia's breakthrough moment. One year after Appel's departure, Torey won the small-business equivalent of a lottery she hadn't even entered, and didn't necessarily want to win: *Sex and the City*'s producers asked to use her shop in a scene.

Carrie and Miranda's thirty seconds with the perfect *Sex and the City* baked good—petite and pink, but still an indulgence—launched not only a Magnolia trend, but a nationwide cupcake trend. For once, fans could afford something the *Sex and the City* girls indulged in on-screen. (Cupcakes cost $1.25 each when the store first opened.) Lines snaked around the block at Magnolia, full of tourists. (This was still happening at least four years later, according to a *New York Times* report in 2004.) Magnolia had to hire a "bouncer" to maintain order.

• • •

This kind of popularity spike had become de rigueur for products and places name-dropped on *Sex and the City*. By its fourth season, it had popularized products like the high-end Rabbit vibrator, which marked the series's first product explosion after it was featured in a first-season episode, "The Turtle and the Hare," in which a skeptical Charlotte is turned on to mechanical pleasure after she sees the "cute" vibrator at the Pleasure Chest sex toy shop in the West Village. While the Vibra-tex Rabbit Pearl had already been the shop's bestseller—and thus the proprietors had recommended it to the *Sex and the City* writers when asked—soon other vibrator companies copied the design to meet demand. The Rabbit grew to be the top-selling sex toy of all time.

But *Sex and the City*'s selling power hardly stopped there. Cafeteria restaurant, Cipriani, the Pleasure Chest, Jimmy Choo shoes, tutus, Fendi baguette bags, Tao (the club, not the Chinese philosophical principle), and Sushi Samba all became part of the *Sex and the City* economy. Fancy Manhattan restaurants with inflated prices like Pastis and Buddakan thrived after *Sex and the City* exposure, even years after the series's end, attracting tourists from across the world and opening spin-offs in cities like Dallas and Las Vegas to reach more fans. When Carrie got a Brazilian bikini wax, depicted on-screen during one of the LA episodes in all of its painful glory, the brutal hair removal process became a mainstream phenomenon.

The "choice feminism" *Sex and the City* espoused had claimed the right for us to consume to our empowered little hearts' content. As author Laurie Penny later put it, *Sex and the City* taught us that "the ultimate freedom we were permitted as women [was] shoes and shopping and fucking." Young women who came to New York in search of the *Sex and the City* lifestyle, however, would find apartments as luxurious as Carrie's hard to come by and impossible to afford, especially with all that shopping they still had to do.

And *Sex and the City*'s implausibility hardly ended there: All four of the main actresses were thin, white, attractive women—"relatable," and maybe even "not traditionally pretty" by Hollywood standards, but by real-life standards, they had the creamy skin, enviable bone structure, perfect teeth, and slim bodies TV usually demands of its female inhabitants. Cattrall and Parker in particular represented nearly impossible body standards, and their frequent half-clothed romps and skimpy outfits called more attention to their sculpted-to-perfection midsections. This only became more infuriating when Carrie blurted out lines like, "Shopping is my cardio!"

What did this mean to those of us trying to live the *Sex and the City* life? It represented an extreme fantasy in which freelance newspaper columnists can afford uptown apartments (her rent: an unlikely $750 per month) and a closet full of Manolo Blahniks (standard price in 2000: about $500); in which professional women have enough free time and funds to consume cupcakes, cosmopolitans, designer clothes, cosmetic procedures, yoga classes, and bikini waxes; in which life is a series of fabulous parties, fashion shows, and dates with wealthy men. In other words, we couldn't help but wonder: Why can't I eat this cupcake, drink this cosmo, *and* be a size zero like Sarah Jessica Parker? And where did all my money go?

FASHION SHOW

The fashion helped define the characters, from the tulle skirt in the opening sequence to Carrie's crop tops, Samantha's siren dresses, Charlotte's classy chic, and Miranda's power-bitch suits. The time spent on the stars' looks was not to be questioned. "There was a lot of hair and makeup time and wardrobe changes," director Michael Spiller says, "and no one was saying, 'Make these things happen faster.'"

Parker became a fashion-world idol, her own style inseparable from her character's distinctive mix of vintage and designer clothes. "I think the chic aesthetic that we see in New York is what separates women in this city from another city," said Parker, who had a say in the overall look of the series as a producer.

Of the many complaints lodged against the series over its run, one of the most enduring is that Carrie Bradshaw, freelance newspaper columnist, could not afford the designer wardrobe she wears on-screen. Costume designer Patricia Field reasoned that Carrie could hit up sample sales, borrow designer clothes, or get discounts. And this seemed plausible since much of the wardrobe, at least in earlier seasons, came from Field's thrift shop scrounging. Besides, Carrie does reveal in season 4 that she has only $957 in savings, no assets, and credit card debt (she mentions hitting her limit); she's also shocked when she does the math and realizes she's spent about $40,000 on shoes in her adulthood.

In short, the show strongly implies that there are hidden depths to her financial liabilities. Like many New Yorkers, she's living on borrowed credit and faith. Her rationale seems to be that she deserves to look good—she earned it emotionally, if not financially: "It's really hard to walk in a single woman's shoes," she opines at one point. "That's why we need really special ones now and then, to make the walk a little more fun."

But by the third season or so, many designers were doing everything they could to make their creations accessible to *Sex and the City*'s costume department—unlike other shows, this one did not have to purchase much of its clothing. The show often used designer samples, like a runway show would. *Sex and the City*'s cachet, along with Parker and Field's relationships with designers, got them clothes no other show could have. This stretched *Sex and the City*'s budgets much, much further than Carrie's ever could.

Of course, some designers, like Christian Louboutin of the famous red-soled shoes, did make the show pay for their goods. The Frenchman never saw the show and later said, "Nothing is great publicity when it doesn't pay." That said, Field did persuade Louboutin to make custom mules just for Carrie. Still a pretty big deal, even if the show had to pay (base price: around $3,500).

Writer Amy B. Harris became obsessed with getting onto the exclusive waiting list for a Hermès Birkin bag, a list one could end up sitting on for years. She pitched it as a plot line. But her inquiries into the list for research purposes bumped her to the front of the line; as soon as the company heard she was a writer from *Sex and the City*, she won the privilege of paying $5,000 for a new purse. In the show, Samantha ends up using client Lucy Liu's name to move herself up on the list.

At this point any of the four main characters, but especially resident clotheshorse Carrie, could spawn the most unlikely of trends. Carrie's barely-there slip dresses proved one of the easiest to adopt on a real-life budget. She also made crop tops, previously the purview of teen Britney Spears acolytes, safe for women over thirty. At Parker's suggestion,

Carrie began wearing a giant fabric flower with nearly every outfit. Viewers were smitten. Field said she was "totally shocked" the flowers became a trend; but like cupcakes, the flowers allowed for a simple, affordable entrée into *Sex and the City* life.

Other *Sex*-inspired trends included a revival of Ray-Ban aviators, nameplate necklaces, glittery tube tops, short shorts, rubber nipples, plaid, Birkin bags, plastic horse-head bags (Field sold them in her store), and thigh-high boots. The show also introduced high-end designer names to mainstream audiences—Roberto Cavalli, Anna Molinari, Dolce & Gabbana, Fendi, Prada, Jimmy Choo, Manolo Blahnik.

In one absurd scene that encapsulates the show's entire vision of New York City fashion, Carrie is mugged at gunpoint in a SoHo alley while wearing a Cavalli animal-print silk dress. The mugger demands her bag, and she corrects, "It's a baguette." He then commands her to hand over her watch, her ring, and her Manolo Blahniks—by name. It's hilariously self-aware, allowing the city to punish Carrie just as the puddle splash does in the opening credits, and acknowledging its ridiculousness through Carrie's voice-over: "Just when the city was getting safe, I was getting mugged." In SoHo, no less.

To handle all of her clothes, Carrie's otherwise unremarkable seven-hundred-square-foot apartment has an eleven-by-four-foot walk-in closet that viewers became more familiar with than the closet of any other TV character in history. *The Mary Tyler Moore Show*'s Mary Richards and Rhoda Morgenstern could have died and gone to heaven in this closet; Rhoda lived in a space not much bigger than this closet. The set decorators took meticulous care to maintain the realism in this space, where we often saw Carrie among such items as a rhinestone Dolce & Gabbana coat, a horse-patterned Chloé dress, and a black Prada dress. Fendi baguettes and Dior saddlebags were among her purses. The crew would shift items around constantly to make the closet look lived-in.

If you asked anyone—especially nonfans—what *Sex and the City* was about, they were as likely to mention shoes as they were to mention sex or the city. Shoes didn't simply adorn the feet of the characters; they were a source of excitement, plot, and conversation. Witness Carrie's rapture when she discovers Manolo Blahnik Mary Janes—which she previously believed to be "an urban shoe myth"—in the *Vogue* fashion closet. Or her lust over the flouncy pink Louboutins she greets with, "Hello, lover." Or her despair over the loss of a pair of open-toed silver Manolos when forced to take them off at a friend's apartment for a party.

Before *Sex and the City*, Manolo Blahniks had long enjoyed a reputation as the highest of the high in shoe art among the fashion elite. As Sarah Niblock wrote in the academic book *Reading Sex and the City*, "Manolo Blahnik is considered the Michelangelo of footwear, for the transformation his grand designs can wield on almost any pair of legs." Now featured weekly on a TV show, this Spanish designer's name frequently fell from the lips of mall shoppers throughout the country—just because Sarah Jessica Parker liked the shoes and Pat Field knew the company's CEO, George Malkemus. Or, as Field liked to say, "I know the boys." Fashion-forward pop star Rihanna would later recall falling in love with Manolos when she watched *Sex and the City* as a teenager; she'd go on to collaborate on several popular collections with the designer.

King saw the show's shoe fetish as symbolic, a metaphor for women's growing financial power: "She maybe can't get Mr. Big, but she can save for the shoes." Shoes also resonated with fairy-tale implications: Why wait for Prince Charming when you can buy your own glass slipper?

When it came to fashion vision, Field and Parker proved to be a perfectly matched pair. Parker got to live out some of her more outrageous fashion fantasies through Field's outfits for the show. "Carrie dresses more quirkily than Sarah Jessica, but that quirkiness is in Sarah Jessica, and she expresses it through Carrie," Field said at the time. Parker countered: "Pat gives me credit for things that may have been her ideas, and I give her credit for things that I think in the end were maybe my ideas. We just work well together."

Once the show hit its stride, Carrie's everyday outfits could cost about $2,000 total. When she wore a Christian Dior newspaper-print dress with a Chahan Minassian necklace and Bea Valdes bag in the seventeenth episode of season 3, the entire ensemble totaled more than $23,000. She wore this ensemble, by the way, to track Big's estranged wife, Natasha, down at lunch to apologize for the affair with Big. This could be defined as fashion overkill.

At these outrageous price points in particular, *Sex and the City* began to function as much like a fashion magazine as it did a television show. It helped to spread haute-couture ideas to young women far from the fashionista-heavy cities of New York and Los Angeles at a time before fashion blogs did so. My sister, Julie, used to sneak around our mom to watch *Sex and the City* at seventeen not because she wanted to see the R-rated content, but because she wanted a vision of fashion beyond *Vogue*. "In the Midwest, we didn't get any of these trends in stores for a long time, so I started making clothes," she says. "I wanted something with the signature big fake flower on it, so I went to Target and bought a clearance pair of black strappy stilettos and hot-glued black fake roses on them that I dipped in glitter." She grew up, no surprise, to be a costumer for the NBC drama *Chicago Med*.

• • •

The show's glamorous depiction of the city had outshone even that of creator Darren Star's initial vision. The series might as well have been a production of the New York tourism board, it made the city look so inviting. An on-location shoot could boost a business overnight, but the process was growing even harder for the *Sex and the City* crew. Director Michael Engler remembers a shoot in Bryant Park when he appreciated how big the show had gotten. As he says, "There wasn't a person who hadn't heard of it."

He also remembers the frustration of the simple lunch scene that featured the four women in that park, just behind the city's landmark central library—a common filming spot for the show. Fans had been a moderate annoyance when the show shot on location in the earlier seasons. By season 4, they had become a mob. Hundreds of fans gathered along the park's edges as they tried to get a glimpse, along with dozens of paparazzi. It was nearly impossible to shoot without including some of the crowd. The *Sex and the City* women now got a street-side reception to rival the Beatles, which was a particular challenge since nearly half of the show was shot on location. And while those scenes attracted many curious onlookers, "real" New Yorkers grew annoyed by the increasing inconveniences caused by more security, protective crew, fans, and paparazzi.

The chaos paid off in some ways for the city. *Sex and the City* had given new life to filming in New York. The city was famous for its film cameos, from *The Apartment* to *Annie Hall* to *When Harry Met Sally*. But television production had remained centered in Los Angeles. Even shows set in New York like *Friends* and *Seinfeld* were shot on West Coast lots. *Sex and the City*'s New York shoots, along with *The Sopranos* nearby in Queens and New Jersey, revived the local TV industry, which would experience a boom with later shows like *30 Rock*, *The Good Wife*, *Gossip Girl*, and *Girls*.

Sex and the City made New York City look so good that other productions were willing to endure what became known as "Fraturdays"— shoots that stretched overnight from a full day Friday into Saturday morning due to the extra challenges associated with filming in the city instead of on set. Locations meant longer hours, and multiple locations meant lots of longer hours. A typical week began at a 7 a.m. Monday call time, which would turn into a twelve-hour day. Workdays could stretch up to eighteen hours, workweeks to a hundred hours. With shooting going through the week until Saturday morning, the weekends were reserved for what director Michael Spiller called "set lag." You'd stay up through Saturday to see your significant other, kids, or friends, and then, as he says, "stumble through Sunday and do it all over again on Monday."

And once you'd filmed in a restaurant, you never wanted to go there again. No offense to their food; it was just that you had gone into their kitchen with folding tables and chairs, and had been stuck there for at least a daylong shoot.

The weather was often cold, too. Although the show was set in what the producers called "perpetual spring," filming usually started in late February or the beginning of March, when temperatures were still in the forties. The women shivered in their skimpy outfits during take after take.

Of course, it wasn't all bad for the cast and crew. Location shoots required scouting, so they would expense extravagant evenings and lunches at posh restaurants and nightclubs. The thought process, Spiller says, was: "We're going to see the sunrise here in two weeks, so let's live while we can."

With the boost *Sex and the City* gave the local economy, it became as associated with the city as the Chrysler Building and the Brooklyn Bridge. It was more than Parker could have dreamed of when she first took the role that was so unlike her. She liked to say that what she and Carrie have in common is that they look alike, "and we both have enormous affection for our city and we're sentimental about it." Now she was the city's number one ambassador.

Sex and the City also made writer Jenny Bicks proud to be a native New Yorker. Like a typical New Yorker, she was game for making fun of the city and its inhabitants; she was the go-to source for details about Trey MacDougal's Upper East Side life. She named his mother Bunny MacDougal (to be played on the show by Frances Sternhagen) and suggested Bunny's penchant for pearls and Chanel. She delighted in sharing her knowledge of the city with her fellow writers and saw the show as a love letter to her city.

NEIGHBORHOOD NEMESES

Writing a neighborhood into the show could, by season 3 and after, push it over the brink. That meant great things for real estate values, and bad things for New Yorkers who enjoyed being able to get a table without a reservation.

In the third season, for instance, Samantha moves to the Meatpacking District, just south of the gay neighborhood of Chelsea and north of the perpetually cool West Village. Even though Meatpacking had been sashaying toward becoming party central since before *Sex and the City* premiered, the show would be blamed for "ruining" the historically industrial area.

And if everyone in those Meatpacking clubs was drinking a cosmo, that came as no surprise. No show had more clearly made a drink happen than *Sex and the City* with its cosmopolitans. The mix of citrus vodka, Cointreau, cranberry juice, and lime juice—or some version of it—first became popular in the gay strongholds of Miami and Provincetown, then took hold in Manhattan in 1987 at the trendy Tribeca haunt the Odeon. The cool kids like Bushnell and her ilk would have known it from there, and it made its first appearance on *Sex and the City* near the end of the show's second season in 1999. Fans embraced it: Like cupcakes, drinks offered a simple, affordable way to get a dose of *Sex and the City* glamour.

This helped boost drinking culture, which had long been an integral part of New York City life, but spread to other places as well. Going out with the girls was now equated with sipping pink cocktails, not drinking herbal tea or sharing lattes at a coffeehouse like the characters did on *Friends*. Gay writer Ginger Hale wrote on *Autostraddle* about how her alcoholism began during the show's heyday: "Even the women on *Sex and the City* were living the fabulous single life, going out somewhere amazing every night and guzzling Cosmos by the barrel," she said. "If the straights were doing it, well then, we were not to be outdone because we were not normative; we were rebels! The reality was that I had become another queer substance abuse statistic and there was nothing fabulous about my life. Or at least everything that was fabulous about my life was being drowned in alcohol."

Sex and the City life came with a price, one way or another.

SEX AND THE CITY *and* US

THE BUS TOUR

Nothing encapsulates the marketing of the *Sex and the City* lifestyle better than the *Sex and the City* bus tour.

In June 1999, Georgette Blau was walking uphill on a Manhattan street just after she moved to the city from Connecticut, and she thought about the 1970s sitcom *The Jeffersons*, in which a couple, George and Louise, were, according to their theme song, "movin' on up to the East Side, to a deluxe apartment in the sky." She thought tourists might enjoy visiting the site of the Jeffersons' upward mobility, as well as a variety of other famous filming locations. So she started a company to conduct bus tours of spots in New York City that had been featured in television shows and movies.

Soon she sold out buses of thirty people or more who wanted to see famous TV sites throughout the city. As *Sex and the City* rose in popularity, Blau considered a tour dedicated just to the show. She decided to launch one with a target date of September 13, 2001. Blau was in her office putting the final touches on her *Sex and the City* tour scripts when the terrorist attacks of September 11, 2001, struck downtown. New York City was in mourning. Blau had spent the four prior months planning the tour, but she knew that now she'd wait longer, as long as it took for life to feel normal again.

The tour finally launched in the middle of season 4, in early 2002, just after the company's similar tour of sites from *The Sopranos* in New Jersey. Blau had narrowed ninety-five *Sex and the City* locations down to a dozen, working on a five-foot-square map. The tour started with the Pleasure Chest, the sex toy shop in the West Village, as an ice-breaker. It moved through the major elements of the show: a little eating (cupcakes), a little sex (vibrators), a little drinking (cosmos at a bar), and a little shopping (Bleecker Street).

After more than three seasons, the audience for *Sex and the City* had grown from 3.8 million viewers for its debut to 6.5 million for its fourth-season premiere. The series's cultural cachet was ripe for commercial development, and the tour became a symbol of its salability.

But the bus tour's early days were not without their share of speed bumps.

• • •

The *Sex and the City* bus tour stoked tensions between Magnolia's estranged founders, and between Magnolia and its neighborhood. The bakery's two original owners, Appel and Torey, had split up over differences in business approach—Appel wanted to expand, Torey wanted to keep things local—just a year before *Sex and the City* came calling. Blau's tour featured Magnolia as a stop, but Torey didn't want to change the store's twelve-cupcakes-per-order limit. At first, the tour would send a few employees in to order a dozen cupcakes each in an effort to feed all of the day's tourgoers. Torey, who liked the shop best when it was a small neighborhood operation, asked the tour to place advance orders or stop coming in altogether. The tour ended up ordering from Appel's Buttercup instead.

This resulted in the awkward spectacle of tourgoers standing across the street from Magnolia, the vanilla scent of baked goods undoubtedly wafting over, while they chowed down on Buttercup cupcakes. Some of the tour guides, according to a *New York* magazine report, even explained the discrepancy to tourgoers by implying that Appel and Torey had been onetime lovers who broke up their business after breaking up their relationship. Blau told the publication that wasn't in the official script, but Torey found out about it when an employee's wife videotaped her own tour experience. "They completely badmouth us, they get the cupcakes from somewhere else, and then they take all their cupcake boxes from Buttercup and stuff them in our garbage pails," Torey told *New York*. "So we have to go out and dump the garbage because they're overflowing with Buttercup boxes."

Frustrated by the crowds, Torey put up signs in the shop emphasizing the dozen-cupcake maximum. She cut back her own time in the shop to just a few days a month and retreated upstate to write cookbooks the rest of the time. She had grown up in a Catskills hotel and worked as a jazz singer before she opened Magnolia, so she was used to a slower-paced life. Torey told *New York*, "A lot of people are very business-oriented. They just want to open more places and make more money, and that's how they think. That's just not me."

Appel, meanwhile, began to pursue her own franchise options.

• • •

Businessman Steve Abrams had a house upstate in Sullivan County, New York, where he was part of a dinner-party circuit that included Torey. Torey's cooking, her baking especially, impressed Abrams. But he didn't know that she *was* Magnolia Bakery. They didn't talk business.

Then he found out: She was the force behind the cupcake craze, behind that whole *Sex and the City* thing. He had watched the show, understood its appeal.

Abrams asked her if she would someday consider licensing the Magnolia brand to him for a few stores. He felt the business could grow by marketing to *Sex and the City* fans throughout the United States and the world. A Magnolia cupcake wasn't just a cupcake: It was a symbol of an enviable lifestyle, a stand-in for designer clothes and dinners at exclusive restaurants.

It didn't take long for her to come up with her answer. She asked if he wanted to buy the whole thing: the store on Bleecker and the Magnolia name.

He took the deal, and she was gone, back upstate. Out of the business. She bought a farm and adopted a baby.

Abrams turned her six-hundred-square-foot, $500,000-per-year bakery into a multimillion-dollar business. The cupcake craze would play out worldwide for the next decade-plus because of one scene on *Sex and the City*.

While cupcakes had long been part of American culture, overseas

Sex and the City audiences learned about them from the show. Russians and Koreans had not spent their childhoods eating cupcakes at school birthday parties. But more than a decade after the *Sex and the City* appearance, the Korean outpost of Magnolia Bakery would still attribute 70 percent of its sales to cupcakes.

The *Sex and the City* economy chugs on throughout the world and remains vibrant in Manhattan: The bus tours still fill up daily, Magnolia is still known for its appearance on the show, other cupcake businesses proliferate, and on any given day you're still likely to catch four young women taking a selfie in front of Carrie's brownstone stoop in the West Village or near the Manolo Blahnik store in Midtown—kept locked and guarded even during business hours.

As *Sex and the City* reached the heights of its commercial power, the writers decided such superficial victories weren't enough: They wanted to tell more difficult, more real stories. And they would reach into the darkest, funniest, and most humiliating parts of their own lives to do so.

7

Van Talk, Real Talk

· · · · · · · · · · ·

The more real *Sex and the City* got with its story lines, the more viewers responded. That reality, it turns out, always started in the van.

The women who wrote for *Sex and the City* lived in Manhattan, mostly downtown, and they needed to get to Silvercup Studios in Queens, to the city's northeast, for work every day. A ten-seat white van—the generic kind often favored by movie kidnappers—picked them up and drove them to the outer borough as they talked about whatever had happened to them the night before. They called it "van talk." They would go over their dating and relationship stories, detail by gory detail. By the time they made it to Queens, they knew which parts of their bad dates they wanted to extract for scripts that day.

A young guy in his twenties, an Italian American from Brooklyn named Bones (given name: Michael Buono), served as their driver. He quietly and patiently drove while the writers chattered about everything that had happened to them the night before or, on Monday mornings, over the weekend.

The women lived their lives like lab rats, if lab rats were also the scientists running the experiments. Everything was up for analysis, processing, and distillation into a script.

Each of the writers had her role to play. Cindy Chupack started every relationship as a Charlotte. But she knew she could sometimes become a Miranda with the impediments she placed in her own way. Or become a Carrie by overanalyzing things. Or become a Samantha, when she thought, *Fuck it, I don't need a relationship.* But she spent most of her time as a crazy optimist. She always wanted it to work out. She was the one in the van or the writers' room who said, "Well, maybe this one *can* end happily ever after. Maybe he *is* into you." Like Charlotte, Chupack was the last one to let go of the dream.

Jenny Bicks identified with Miranda. She felt it acutely when Miranda considered an abortion after getting pregnant with Steve's child. She felt it even more when Miranda's mother died in the episode "My Motherboard, My Self." Bicks could imagine, like Miranda, buying an apartment by herself and worrying about being alone for the rest of her life. It was the old worry: *Who's going to find me when I die?* The anxiety remains relevant whether it's Sally Albright, Bridget Jones, or Miranda Hobbes doing the worrying.

Julie Rottenberg, on the other hand, had a boyfriend at the time of the show, with whom her writing partner, Elisa Zuritsky, set her up when she was twenty-five. Rottenberg still felt ambivalent about marriage, however. "I was so fucked up about it," she says now. Those feelings, too, made their way into scripts.

As the writers' van talk grew more serious, so did the show they were making. *Sex and the City* dramatized hard truths along with displaying the latest Jimmy Choos or Dior: People with good intentions cheated. Mothers died; cancer was a bitch. Men were disappointing. Singledom was hard, but so was marriage. Children were even harder. Sexuality was complicated. "People watch the show and think, *Yeah, that's me. That's my situation,*" creator Darren Star said. "I think the show has empowered a lot of people."

The 2001–02 season marked a turning point for *Sex and the City*, with the writing reflecting the harsher realities of the writers' lives while the cast and crew lived with the harsher realities of working on a closely watched show.

THE FEUD

First came reports of "major tension" between Kim Cattrall and Sarah Jessica Parker. In February 2001, *New York* magazine's "Intelligencer" gossip column quoted an "insider" who said Cattrall's scene-stealing as Samantha had upset Parker, claiming the two didn't want to be in the same room together at a recent party. Both of their publicists denied the rift, though their responses focused mostly on the women's professional relationship, not their personal feelings for each other. Parker's spokesperson said, "Sarah's a businesswoman. She's a producer of the show—she wouldn't eat her young. Kim is part of a successful formula—who would screw with that?"

Media around the world couldn't resist the idea of a *Sex and the City* feud, and the story quickly spread: The *Times of India* reported it later that year, but mentioned that Cattrall was "surprised" at the rumors of "jealousy and payment wrangles" because the cast spent most of their spare time on the set singing show tunes together.

The rumors mystified many in the cast. As David Eigenberg says, "All that bullshit about the girls not getting along was such a load of crap. . . . I wasn't around them all the time, obviously, but the girls all sat together and genuinely liked each other, laughed with each other."

True, Cattrall and Parker didn't grab drinks together after their nine- to eighteen-hour workdays. But if they couldn't be in the same room, they wouldn't have continued to appear in so many scenes together, Parker says. TV shows with warring costars knew how to separate them. One sign was a sudden shift to lots of phone-conversation scenes instead of in-person ones. Cattrall told the *Guardian* there was one explanation for the persistent speculation about their relationship: *"The Sopranos* never had any questions asked about whether or not they like each other, because they're not all women." Parker echoes that sentiment: "Nobody ever said to Jimmy Gandolfini, 'Why aren't you hanging out with Nancy Marchand on the weekends?'"

Parker describes her relationship with Cattrall, and her other costars, as a connection different from any other, one without a proper label. They were not sisters, nor best friends. Parker understood it sounded bad, especially when speaking of a relationship between women, to admit, "We're not best friends." They were colleagues of a type few people get to experience. They relied upon each other for years and lived through a unique trajectory only those four people could understand. That didn't require that they always greet each other in the morning with hugs and spend their downtime together. Were they sometimes annoyed by each other? As Parker says, "Abso-freakin'-lutely." But, Parker adds, "that is a testament to the depth of that relationship, because you don't get annoyed by somebody when you're being polite"—that is, when you don't share an intimate connection.

The specter of the feud harried all four *Sex and the City* stars. Interviewers inevitably asked about it. Sometimes they even grilled Parker on specifics: Did she get Cattrall a Christmas present? If not, why not? It upset Davis, who was protective of her costars. Nixon, having known Parker since they were both ten years old, served as a reliable sounding board for Parker and tried to avoid answering media questions about it herself.

The rumors rattled Parker. She resented the implication that she was difficult or mean. The idea was, as she says, "anathema" to everything she had cultivated in her professional life. She tried so hard to treat everyone on set kindly, no matter how tired she was. "In my entire life, I would never, ever throw a temper tantrum," she says. "I've never had the courage. I would be ashamed." Her publicist talked her down with each new feud report: "You have to let it go."

SEX GETS REAL

The show's tone turned heavy on-screen as well in the fourth season, which started to air in June 2001: Carrie turns thirty-five and reunites with Aidan, whom she'd crushed by having an affair with Mr. Big. Miranda struggles with the prospect of motherhood and fights off feelings for her child's father, Steve. Samantha meets the first man we've ever suspected could be her match: hotel magnate Richard Wright.

Charlotte is divorcing Trey, her seemingly perfect man, though she has an even more immediate problem. One of the show's writers, whose name we needn't know, pitched the idea of giving Charlotte a "depressed vagina," vulvodynia, as a result of her marital struggle. The writer had once received this diagnosis herself.

When the episode aired, the story line evoked strong reactions. Some viewers wrote in to praise *Sex and the City* for bringing the problem out in the open. Others wrote in to complain that it didn't belong on a comedy show, as it was no laughing matter. Several media accounts took the show to task for underplaying vulvodynia, which Charlotte's doctor describes as merely uncomfortable. The *Chicago Tribune* published this account: "The pain can get so bad, you can't sleep, you can't walk, you can't sit, you can't do anything," said Lauren Kunis, a New Yorker who was diagnosed with it in 1999. "When you're dealing with that pain 24/7, you just want to be dead."

By the fourth season, the writers had become comfortable enough with each other, and the show, to share almost anything. When they'd first started, they'd come from shows that had nothing to do with their own lives: sitcoms about families, teen dramas. They had approached *Sex and the City* gingerly at first. Sure, they could use their own experiences as single women in their thirties, but would anyone else care?

With the show now at peak popularity, not just in America but around the world, the answer was a definitive yes. Millions of women related to what the writers had given them so far; now the writers were ready to get even more real. Consider the litany of humiliations, trials, and tragedies that Miranda alone experiences in season 4: a boyfriend who takes loud shits with the bathroom door open, a boyfriend who requests rim jobs, a neck spasm that requires Aidan to rescue her while she's naked in the bathtub, her mother's death, Steve's cancer, and her own accidental pregnancy while the infertile Charlotte pines for a baby. To think even half of this came from real life is sobering.

After each morning's van therapy, the writers arrived at the studio around 10 a.m. and headed to King's office for what King called "host chat." Earlier in the show's run, the writers ambled in for a hazier start time, with no official plan to come together to brainstorm. Eventually he invented "host chat," every morning from 10 to 10:30 a.m., a general discussion of people's dates, thoughts, and feelings, a sort of part two of what happened in the van, with the addition of King and anyone else who didn't ride in with Bones. At 10:30 a.m., serious discussion of story lines, outlines, and scripts would begin, with the writers all squeezed onto the plush love seats in King's cozy office.

Host chat, a reference to the chatter you might see at the beginning of a talk show, and "hosty" for short, became such a success that the writers brought it into their own lives for years to come, code for talking something out and analyzing it: "Let's have a hosty break." "After this weekend, I have so much host chat."

THE TWINS' DEBUT

Writers Julie Rottenberg and Elisa Zuritsky's first full script assignment for *Sex and the City* came midway through the fourth season—they had joined at the beginning of the season, contributing jokes and brainstorming until it came time for their first independent effort. And it turned out to be a doozy.

When they first started the job, they had pitched thematically linked stories about tech support—Carrie's computer crashes—and bra support—Miranda has a spiritual connection with her aggressive bra saleswoman. Rottenberg drew on an experience of her own with a devastating Mac crash while she dated a tech guy who was overeager to help. Tekserve, a computer repair shop in Chelsea, had served as a spot of both comfort and terror for her and many New Yorkers. And Zuritsky was inspired by an experience with a very hands-on bra saleswoman at Saks Fifth Avenue in Philadelphia. When King looked up at the whiteboard full of ideas for the season, he linked Rottenberg and Zuritsky's concepts with a major plot point: Miranda's mother dying. "Support," King said. "I can think of no better way to bring these things together."

They had their assignment: the episode that would become "My Motherboard, My Self," in which Carrie resists Aidan's attempts to help her with a crashed laptop and Miranda breaks down over her mother's death when faced with an extra-helpful, motherly bra saleswoman. The episode ends with Carrie, Charlotte, and Samantha traveling to Philadelphia to support Miranda at the funeral.

Soon "the twins" had to turn in their first draft.

King enjoyed walking TV newbies Rottenberg and Zuritsky through the entire process, from script to finished cut. The job had turned out to be as great as the women had expected: Everyone they worked with was smart and funny. They spent their days sharing crazy dating and sex stories. They'd often retreat to the bathroom just to catch their breath and reorient themselves: Was this really happening? And now their boss wanted to help them learn, instead of berating them for everything they didn't know.

King helped them craft their first script every step of the way. Still, Rottenberg and Zuritsky felt sick with nerves when they turned their first draft in. The show had started production for the season, which meant little time for do-overs. King sat down with them and went page by page to give notes: more of this, less of that.

They revised and turned another draft in. This time he and Chupack sat down with them and offered more notes: move this, add this, subtract that. They had heard horror stories from other TV writers about showrunners who rewrote their scripts without consultation.

That wouldn't happen here. Sure, some of the best jokes in this and others of their scripts might be written by King, Chupack, or another writer. But at least they felt like the work with their names on it had come mostly from them.

Lucky for Rottenberg and Zuritsky, the deft stage director Michael Engler came to *Sex and the City* in 2001 from the theater. He had watched the show for the first three seasons, interested particularly because he knew Parker and Nixon from the New York theater circuit. He also loved King and Star's work. He thought the show was experimenting in an interesting way as it found a new approach to TV: The tonal range swung wider than most shows, from romantic to dark to comic to slapstick to aspirational to soulful. It made him want to direct television.

"My Motherboard, My Self" became the second of his two episodes. He loved the way the funeral brought all of the characters' story lines together for an emotional wallop at the end. Even Samantha's typically sexpot story line—she panics because she's stopped having orgasms—hints at a knot of darkness below her surface. In fact, the loss of sexuality is both its own kind of death and a prelude to death itself.

The episode—improbably the work of three relative newcomers to the show—made an instant impression with viewers. In the annals of the show's tearjerkers—Aidan and Carrie's breakups chief among them—this one hit the hardest and reached the deepest. Breakups were sad, but a natural part of single life, and sometimes maybe, just possibly, reversible. "My Motherboard, My Self" was the rare *Sex and the City* episode that acknowledged the women's families while it still prioritized their friendship circle. It spoke to its audience's primal fears: losing a parent and ending up alone in the end.

It was the kind of episode you remember watching for the first time, the kind of episode that makes you see an entire series differently from then on, like supporting a friend through the worst and finding new depths to your relationship thereafter.

BRUNCH BATTLES

Often the writers argued over a relationship or sex issue: whether women *did* want to be "rescued" by men, whether married women and single women could remain friends, whether it was possible for a heretofore straight woman like Samantha to have a genuine love affair with another woman. (*Yes* was the consensus, and that woman would be played in season 4 by Sonia Braga.) Those would also become the heated debates the characters would have at brunch, and thus Carrie's couldn't-help-but-wonder questions. The room served the same purpose for the writers that the coffee shop did for Carrie and her friends.

The most intense fight was too big to boil down to a brunch conversation: whether Carrie belonged with Big or Aidan or someone else or no one. Those who had been around since the show's early days—Bicks, Chupack, King—carried a torch for Big. Those who had arrived later didn't love the untouchable commitmentphobe as much, but they weren't sweet on Aidan's season 4 return, either. Fans, however, had written in begging for Aidan to come back.

Rottenberg and Zuritsky argued against Carrie's reconciliation with the dreamy furniture-maker: He left. It didn't work. Let's move on. They liked the character and the actor; they just didn't buy that Carrie would get back together with him, or vice versa. They were proud of the accurate portrayal of the couple's first breakup at Charlotte and Trey's wedding, soon after Carrie confesses to cheating with Big. They felt sure Aidan and Carrie did not belong together, and got depressed at the thought of them reunited. They did not believe viewers *really* wanted the two back together; those fans writing in just *thought* they wanted that. And the writers *and* fans were so wrapped up in these characters that it was easy to forget that this was a work of fiction.

King encouraged Rottenberg and Zuritsky: "Keep fighting for what you believe in." As they took his advice and argued with the other writers, King would often poke his head into their office at the end of the day and say, "You guys are doing great! Keep fighting!" He said any story would get better with arguments. He knew fans would scrutinize every plot turn, so fighting about it beforehand would strengthen it to stand up to the ultimate test with viewers.

Of course, Rottenberg and Zuritsky lost that Aidan fight.

• • •

King's commitment to realism came down to the tiniest details. The writers' room often had to work out the mechanics of a sex scene before a script was crafted, as when Bicks ended up with a water bottle between her legs, squirting King in the face to determine the correct staging of a female-ejaculation moment.

The more outrageous the story line, the more of it had to come from reality. Anything that would prompt a "really?" response had to have happened to someone in the writers' room or to someone they knew—one degree of separation. Like Carrie, Bicks was once awakened in the early morning in New York City by roosters crowing; it turned out a local shelter had rescued them from a subway cockfight ring. Like Miranda, King did feel judged by the phone answerer at his favorite Chinese restaurant laughing at his serial takeout orders for one. Chupack did once receive a breakup message from a boyfriend's doorman.

King did have a fight with a group of what the show, in its circa-2000 parlance, calls "transsexual hookers." They were making noise late at night on his street, just as Samantha experiences in a third-season episode. King says he lifted the lines directly from life, right down to the filthiest of the lines the prostitutes lob at each other: "He was all up in my stuff once. I told him, 'You better get that thing out of my ass or I'm gonna shit on it!'" It would go down in *Sex and the City* history as another of its blundered attempts at addressing nonwhite, genderqueer characters, but at least it ends with Samantha and her noisy neighbors mending fences and finding common ground.

These ideas from real life would go up on a white dry-erase board as they emerged in the room. King calls it the "therapeutic alchemy of turning humiliation into gold." King passed New York's Lesbian, Gay, Bisexual & Transgender Community Center and saw an announcement about the "gay prom"—that went up on the board. Chupack had a boyfriend who had been in a mental institution. Up on the board. Bicks went to a party where her shoes were stolen. Up on the board. Only one story made it up onto the board, stayed until the end of the series, and never made the leap into an episode: a joke about a guy who seemed to orgasm but left no evidence of it, so he may have been faking—"Casper the Friendly Cum," they called him.

More serious issues required deeper, more difficult discussions. After Miranda found out she was pregnant, the writers knew she should at least consider an abortion—that discussion was hard, airing out everyone's feelings on a topic often fraught with ambivalence even among liberal women who consider themselves pro-choice. During these debates, they suddenly felt the difference between being pro-choice in theory and considering why a white, wealthy, privileged, independent woman might want an abortion. Complicating matters further, the writers knew they wanted Miranda to have the baby for story line purposes.

While plenty of therapy happened in the van, and even more in the official writers' room at Silvercup, writers' meetings could happen at any time and in many places. If the production was on location in the East Village, meetings would convene in a restaurant at lunch- or dinnertime. Seven writers would cram around a table with King, each with her notebook full of pitch ideas and script problems. As they talked, they would often hear New Yorkers at the next table chatting about the most recent *Sex and the City* episode to air. Someone would catch a "Carrie and Samantha . . ." and then shush the other writers, eager to hear what viewers said next.

When it came to assigning scripts to writers once the story lines were solidified in the writers' room, King had another rule: Give it to whichever writer or writers had the most intense emotional reaction to the subject at hand. It was the instinct of an evil godfather that would push many of the women to confront their stickiest hang-ups through the scripts they wrote.

. . .

As the writers' past dating lives unspooled on the show, some of them were coupling up in real life. Rottenberg now lived with the man she would eventually marry, which made her a good resource for the couple-driven story lines. But most of the writers remained single, their present dating lives continuing to furl out in front of them, a stream of material to collect and use, collect and use. As they searched for mates, their experiments in dating as lab rats were confounded by a glaring factor: They were not normal daters. Like Candace Bushnell, they had become professional daters of sorts. Their profession was bound to come up on their dates and to thus scramble their suitors' feelings. It was an era in which everyone had strong feelings about *Sex and the City*.

Writer Elisa Zuritsky went out with one guy with whom she clicked early and had several fantastic dates, filled with laughter. He hadn't seen *Sex and the City*. She lent him her DVDs. The next date, not so much laughter.

"I have to say, I'm a little intimidated," he said.

"That's ridiculous," she said. "Nothing is real. It's a TV show. It's fictional." Of course, that wasn't precisely true. But it didn't matter; the affair fizzled thereafter.

Zuritsky came to believe that the kind of men she liked best were also the kind of men who were most scared of being made fun of on a future *Sex and the City* episode. And the kind of men she liked least were the kind who *loved* the idea of dating a *Sex and the City* writer and ending up on an episode.

She tried to lie. But she couldn't keep that up. As she says, "It was like, whatever threat a successful woman was before, also give her an internationally acclaimed television show about sex that's honest . . ." She had just turned thirty, and she wanted to find someone. But her job, which was otherwise ideal, served as "an insecticide" for good men.

She had never worried about her dating life before *Sex and the City*. Now she felt marooned "on a total desert island of desperation."

She couldn't help but wonder: What if everything she'd imagined for her life, a husband and kids, was just a fantasy that had been programmed into her? What if every assumption she'd made about her life trajectory was wrong, and *Sex and the City* was here to deliver the message?

• • •

Permanent endings emerged as a major theme in the fourth season. Aidan and Carrie unravel as they try to cohabitate—her closet stuffed full of clothes, with no room for his. In an epic fight set in that iconic closet, Aidan pulls out a shredded Roberto Cavalli top and asks when she has worn or will wear, for instance, *that*. "Don't do that," she warns. "Don't mock the clothes." Especially not the Cavalli.

Still, she agrees to get rid of the shirt, but flies off the handle when Aidan's dog, Pete, chews up her turquoise Manolo sandal circa 1996; she declares that the dog owes her $380.

During the course of the fight, she discovers that Aidan comes with his own space-hogging accoutrements, namely lots of toiletries, including a variety of Speed Stick scents and Rogaine. "It's preventative," he protests. The moment offers a sophisticated social commentary on Aidan, who has been presented as a male archetype: Big calls him "Paul Bunyan" in a moment of jealousy, partly because Aidan represents a rough-hewn masculinity that's the exact opposite of Big's Master of the Universe machismo. But in the closet scene, Aidan is revealed to harbor his own vanity. He's a hypocrite for judging Carrie's.

Along with its important character development, the scene was also the only one in the entire series that was completely reshot.

During the first time through, King realized something crucial: "Pat Field is a true genius, with a wildly creative sensibility, but every now and then, that sensibility would be a little too wild for a scene." She sent Parker to the set ready to shoot the important closet fight scene wearing a circus top hat and a shirt with a frilly collar. Corbett wore a T-shirt emblazoned with the word "CHASTITY." As soon as King saw them, he knew no matter what their lines were, all viewers would notice was: *Top hat, frilly collar, CHASTITY. Wait, what is she mad about? Top hat, frilly collar, CHASTITY.*

Every now and then, Field would delight King with a little fashion surprise, dressing an actor in an outfit he did not expect, had never even seen but would totally love. This was not one of those times.

Hair, makeup, and wardrobe prep had taken two hours by the time the actors arrived on set. The cost of sending them back to change into different outfits would be significant. "I don't think this is right, but we're here," King said. "Let's film it and see it."

They filmed it. They saw it. *Top hat, frilly collar, CHASTITY.*

So King asked to do it all over again.

Parker went back to wardrobe to start the process from the beginning. So did Corbett.

This time, when Parker finally returned, she wore a turquoise tube top and a scarf tied around her arm. Corbett wore a plain T-shirt, and the dialogue took center stage. The scene became one of King's favorites in the series.

• • •

As Aidan and Carrie's second attempt at a relationship hurtled forward, more cringe-worthy scenes accrued. Aidan and Big mud-wrestle at Aidan's country house, as directed by Michael Spiller: "If I had any antipathy—and I didn't—toward Chris Noth, this was a chance to work it out," the director says. " 'Clean him up, we're going again!' "

Carrie and Aidan get engaged, but Carrie finds herself unenthused about getting married. She calls herself a "deadbeat bride," trying to convince herself and others that it's the idea of a wedding, not the marriage or the man, that's the problem. To force herself into wedding planning, she goes to a bridal store with Miranda to try on the worst dresses they can find, just for a laugh. But when Carrie emerges from the fitting room in a frothy nightmare, she collapses as she hyperventi-lates and breaks into hives.

In Carrie and Aidan's final, heart-wrenching season 4 scene as a couple, the setting, script, director, and actors combined in unexpected ways to make a special kind of magic.

Late one night, the sun far past set, King heard that director Alan Taylor had chosen the Columbus Circle fountain as the shoot location for Carrie and Aidan's second breakup. He bristled at the thought and hurried to the location. King arrived on the set and, after taking it in, felt it wouldn't work: He was convinced the fountain's running water would make a racket in the background of an emotional scene.

King went to the fountain, where Taylor was already setting up shots, to have him change the setting, but Taylor implored him: "Look at the location!" King took a few minutes alone, in front of the fountain, his arms crossed across his chest, wondering, *Am I right? Is he right?* Finally, he said, "Okay. Let's do it."

The shoot resulted in one of the show's most memorable scenes and a perfect encapsulation of the series: a gorgeous piece of film whose dialogue tears your heart out. Aidan and Carrie break up for good in front of that fountain after Aidan, exuberant from a night on the town at a fancy party, pushes Carrie to run off to Vegas and get married right away. She resists, and he finally sees: She doesn't want to marry him. At all.

In the final result, the dialogue comes through just fine, only a soft hiss from the fountain underneath. The kicker came from a line that was in an early version of the script, in which Aidan says, "I can't be-lieve I'm back here again." The writers had cut it out of the final version of the script. But after filming was done on Parker's side of the scene, at 5 a.m. with the sun rising, Corbett remembered the cut line. "I feel like I need to say it," he told King and Parker.

The cameras captured Corbett doing the line just in time, before daybreak. But then the sun peeked up over the horizon before Parker could get a reaction shot on film. Viewers would see no reaction to Aidan's impactful line. The scene was unlikely to work without that.

The magic happened in the editing room. As King looked over the night's footage, he found a moment from deep in the wee hours when Parker had flubbed a line. Exhausted, she looked down, disappointed in herself, the sadder version of that gut-punched look at the end of the pilot episode. That would become Carrie's reaction to Aidan's line. The moment evoked tears and stuck in viewers' memories.

"As progressive as our society claims to be, there are still certain life targets we're all supposed to hit: marriage, babies, and a home to call your own," Carrie says in voice-over as she ponders her confused reaction to Aidan's push for happily-ever-after. "But what if, instead of breaking out into a smile, you break out into a rash? Is it something wrong with the system, or is it you? And do we really want these things, or are we just programmed?" This line of thought echoed what was going through many young women's heads as they watched— Rottenberg's, Zuritsky's, and mine among them.

These seemed like meaningful questions, and they were. That is, until the city, the country, and the world collapsed in downtown Manhattan and made everyone rethink everything.

8

9/11 Hits Home

. . . .

In September 2001, *Saturday Night Live* returned to the air after 9/11 with a tribute to FDNY and NYPD officers, who were gathered onstage with an introduction by Mayor Rudy Giuliani, followed by Paul Simon singing one of his great homages to the city, "The Boxer." *The Daily Show*'s Jon Stewart opened his first show back with an emotional monologue, punctuated several times by his own tears.

These shows trafficked in current events, and they had addressed the worst event in recent American memory poignantly and perfectly. As the *Sex and the City* writers and producers watched, they wondered how they could ever come close. They wondered if they could just move past it without comment. They wondered how they could go on at all.

But if the city was the fifth lady of *Sex and the City*, then the show could not continue without an acknowledgment of what had just happened to her. When two of the four large planes hijacked by Osama

155

bin Laden's al-Qaeda terrorists hit the World Trade Center's 110-floor Twin Towers that sunny morning, they killed more than 2,700 people; more than 6,000 were injured. At least 200 people trapped in the burning towers fell or jumped to their deaths. The casualties included more than 400 emergency workers who arrived on the scene to rescue people. The iconic skyline had a festering hole in it, now known as Ground Zero, while a miasma of toxic dust and debris engulfed the southern tip of Manhattan. Heartbreaking "MISSING" posters papered walls throughout the downtown area in search of lost loved ones.

Even as the initial chaos calmed, normalcy seemed far away. Smoke still rose from downtown weeks later as makeshift memorial piles of American flags, flowers, and photos of the lost grew around it. Vendors set up folding tables to sell Twin Tower memorial figurines, snow globes, framed photos, hats, and T-shirts.

It wasn't until life began to stabilize that the *Sex and the City* writers and producers started to ponder what this might mean for their show. Bridges and tunnels opened again. *Sex and the City* showrunner Michael Patrick King, his writers, and Sarah Jessica Parker—a producer and the city's self-appointed protector on set—knew they needed to find their own way forward. No one was awaiting the show's specific commentary on the attacks, and King and Parker didn't want to co-opt the attacks or exploit them. But they had to acknowledge the attacks in a show *about* this city.

And time did not stand on their side: They had already shot and edited the six-episode second part of the fourth season, which included Aidan and Carrie's dissolution, Charlotte and Trey's separation, and the birth of Miranda's baby. They had finished the whole thing in a pre-9/11 mindset, wrapping on September 1. It was set to run the following January. They were going to have to work with what they already had, and do what they could to make it feel appropriate to this astonishing shift in national mood. They had to switch their usual rose-colored lens on the city closer to the black of the moment.

The first and easiest fix: erasing the towers from the horizon during a romantic scene in the first episode, in which Samantha and new love interest Richard dance by a rooftop pool. A harder problem arose from a second-episode shot of a souvenir snow globe of the Twin Towers— of all the New York City landmarks, somehow *this* was the one they'd chosen—with Carrie's poignant voice-over: "That's the thing about relationships: Sometimes they look prettier from the outside. And what's inside can be different than what it seems." That would stay, King reasoned, not only for its accidental emotional resonance, but because it felt even more realistic post-9/11, as if Carrie had meant it as a tribute.

Similarly, the finale, entitled "I Heart NY," carried an unintended emotional wallop in the new environment. The title alone had caused debate among the writers when King crafted the script before 9/11. Amy B. Harris remembers several of her fellow writers questioning whether it was too "cheesy." King answered definitively: "I heart New York, she hearts New York. I don't care if it's cheesy."

In the episode, Big tells Carrie he's leaving town to move to Napa. They have a "final" date that celebrates classic New York, ending with an undisputably cheesy carriage ride through Central Park. The key scene became one of King's favorites in the entire series: Carrie and Big, Parker and Noth, doing the twist in an empty apartment to "Moon River," a nod to *Sex and the City*'s spiritual predecessor *Breakfast at Tiffany's*. The aesthetic evoked pure, old-school New York. The melancholy of Big's impending departure undercut everything, while the two characters' innate coolness remained. As King rewatched it, he thought, *Yeah, that's perfect. The way they played it, the way she looks. The way they danced.*

Carrie leaves the date to be by Miranda's side as she gives birth. By the time Carrie returns to Big's apartment the next morning, he's gone. On the street, autumn leaves begin to fall as "Moon River" plays again. She concludes with a voice-over perfect for the times, even though it was written before the attacks: "Seasons change. So do cities. People come into your life and people go. But it's comforting to know the ones you love are always in your heart. And, if you're very lucky, a plane ride away."

Parker recorded that voice-over at a recording session a week after the attacks. Harris accompanied her to the downtown studio, where the smell of the burning World Trade Center wreckage still hung in the air. The women couldn't believe how prescient King's script had been.

In the final, second edit of the season, completed between 9/11 and *Sex and the City*'s January air date, the approach became clear, and surprisingly simple. All "real" shots of the towers were cut, including in the opening credits, where they'd appeared behind Sarah Jessica Parker's name—the only change to the credit sequence in the show's entire run. Everything else remained, and the result was a season that, with what happened to be a darker and more thoughtful turn for the show, turned into a tasteful, subtle tribute to the city in those tender months after a devastating loss.

• • •

The fall 2001 Emmy ceremony added to the melancholy of the time. The awards show was postponed from its September 16 date to October 7, only to be rescheduled again when the war in Afghanistan began. It was finally held on November 4, hosted by Ellen DeGeneres, whose delicate performance on the night got her a standing ovation at the end of the show.

Like *Sex and the City* and every other Hollywood product at the time, the awards show had to balance being entertaining with respecting the seriousness of the time. DeGeneres joked about the lack of jokes to be told in a post-9/11 atmosphere, resorting to a parody of tired comedic tropes: "Cats and dogs are different, aren't they? How about those men, am I right, ladies?" She delivered jokes only those present could truly appreciate: "They can't take away our creativity, our striving for excellence, our joy. Only network executives can do that." And she underlined the cultural differences that had contributed to America's conflict with the terrorists, referring to her role as host: "What would bug the Taliban more than seeing a gay woman in a suit surrounded by Jews?"

During the ceremony, *Sex and the City* became the first cable series ever to win a top award when it took the Outstanding Comedy Series trophy. DeGeneres joked, "When those four women get together and talk about men, I tell ya . . . I have no idea what they're talking about."

. . .

The national mood grew more complicated by the time writing began for the fifth season of *Sex and the City*. Fear of terrorism was on the rise, war had begun, and Americans were afraid of anthrax in the mail. What was a show that prided itself on its glittery version of this city to do now? As media pundits wrung their hands about whether it was still okay to laugh, escape, or have any level of fun as a result of entertainment, the *Sex and the City* cast and crew weren't sure: Were they suddenly irrelevant, or more relevant than ever?

The writers gathered in October 2001, just one month after the attacks, to start writing the fifth season, which would air the following summer. Like most Americans at the time, they still could think of little else besides 9/11. They pitched terrible Age of Terror puns: "We're going to smoke men out." They made "manthrax" jokes. They talked a lot about the city's boom in life-affirming sex.

They took a middle path once it was time to write the scripts. The "manthrax" joke made it into an episode, along with a reference to the women's plan to "throw some much-needed money downtown" to honor President George W. Bush's plea to citizens to support the country by shopping. Here was some political material tailor-made for *Sex and the City*.

The first episode back, "Anchors Away," centers on a Fleet Week party, an idea pitched by new writer Liz Tuccillo. Like many New York women, she enjoyed the crowds of young military men who descend on the city for the annual event. The episode serves up the kind of tribute only *Sex and the City* could, with the women making out with sailors in the name of national pride. As a final grace note, Carrie meets a cute officer from Louisiana, but rebuffs him when he complains about New York: "I can't have nobody talkin' shit about my boyfriend," she says.

Once again, *Sex and the City* delivered the right tone for the right time. About this scene, the *New York Times*' Julie Salamon noted, "Both she and the city seem more fragile, yet still willing to believe in possibility. At this moment, that sense of optimism is almost as seductive as sex."

Salamon's review declared the show more relevant than ever: "It's a different show than it was, not as lighthearted, but it's still involving and inventive. Chastity hasn't replaced promiscuity. There's still plenty of sex and plenty of talk about sex."

• • •

"Anchors Away" marked Tuccillo's first episode on the job. A playwright with pale skin and dark, shoulder-length hair, she had wanted to write for the show since she'd started watching earlier that year.

A New Yorker from childhood, Tuccillo at first had wanted to be an actress, and had started auditioning for plays in the city at just ten. As a teenager, she attended the prestigious High School of Performing Arts, known for its depiction in the movie and TV show *Fame*. She went on to get a degree in experimental theater from New York University and start a theater company with some friends.

That didn't pay the bills, though. As she continued to audition postcollege, she worked an overnight shift doing word processing for a law firm, answered phones at *Spy* magazine, and temped. She got small parts: a Scott Baio movie called *I Love N.Y.*, an after-school special. But her career stalled there; she couldn't seem to get the kind of agent she needed to book significant jobs. She thought if she could write her own material, that would help her show off her skills. At age twenty-nine, she began writing monologues and scenes; immediately, she experienced support and encouragement from other actors, something she'd never gotten as an actress. She wrote a play called *Fair Fight* about competitiveness behind the scenes of an awards ceremony, which was produced by the Naked Angels theater company. Her next work, *Joe Fearless*, told the story of a basketball superfan attending the NBA finals. It was staged in June 2000 at New York City's Atlantic Space.

The next year, she started watching *Sex and the City*. She knew someone who knew King and asked for an introduction. He wasn't looking for more writers, but he agreed to meet her for lunch in the West Village as a favor. The lunch date fell in the days right after September 11, and both were feeling, as Tuccillo later said, "raw." A boyfriend had just broken up with her after the terror attacks had made him realize he wanted to reunite with his ex-wife. She was spending her evenings hosting gatherings at her home where police and firefighters could have a few beers after their long days of working at the World Trade Center site.

King and Tuccillo talked about "loss and love and just being a New Yorker," Tuccillo said. They connected, and she impressed King with how "entrenched" she was in the city, how keyed into the show's themes she was.

"You're formidable, Liz," he said.

He orchestrated a follow-up meeting for her with executive producer John Melfi and Cindy Chupack. Soon Tuccillo had a job offer. She started in Los Angeles the day after the show had won its Emmy. Emmy Awards were proudly displayed on the writing room table when she arrived. She had no idea what was in store for her, no idea how a writers' room worked, and no idea what she was going to say when the meetings began.

But soon enough, she got it: All she had to do was talk about dating and men and life in New York. The rest would take care of itself.

Her presence paid off right away with "Anchors Away."

• • •

The journey toward dark complexity that the show had begun in the fourth season would continue from there. As it headed into what would end up being its final two seasons, *Sex and the City* folded brutal, real-life scenarios into its fairy-tale New York. The fifth season's story lines reflected the anxiety of the time. Carrie says at the beginning of the season that she's "fresh out of great loves." The only sign of hope is the heart-shaped locket she wears. In fact, the only thing going well is Carrie's career: She has regular freelance assignments from *Vogue* and a book deal.

None of the core women are in settled relationships. Samantha had begun what at first seemed like a promising affair with powerful hotelier Richard Wright, played by handsome character actor James Remar, whose long list of TV credits ran from *The X-Files* to *7th Heaven*. Richard, a multimillionaire who can have any woman he wants and shows little interest in love, makes a worthy adversary for Samantha. When they first meet, she pitches her PR firm to represent his hotel chain; he makes her cry when he initially rejects her for the job because she once slept with his architect.

He eventually hires her, and the two become sexually involved. They then pursue a monogamous relationship, starting with their romantic rooftop dance scene set to Sade's "By Your Side," in which Cattrall conveys her fright at feeling attached to a man. But by the beginning of season 5, he has proven himself unworthy of her trust, making her greatest fear come true by cheating on her.

Carrie, meanwhile, meets Jack Berger, a sensitive, scruffy novelist played by Ron Livingston, known best as leading drone Peter in the cult comedy *Office Space*. But any rays of hope he might cast on Carrie's love life are, like Richard's, snuffed out: He has a girlfriend.

Charlotte faces her own romantic challenges. In the first post-9/11 episodes, she helped her husband, Trey, overcome impotence, only to find he didn't want a baby as much as she did. (He even tried to placate her with the "joke" gift of a cardboard baby. It did not go over well.) They separated after being photographed in their apartment for *House & Garden* magazine. The fifth season brings her Harry Goldenblatt, her sweaty, crude, bald divorce lawyer played by Evan Handler. He's clearly attracted to her, and she's surprised when she gives in to his advances and has great sex. But in a very un-Charlotte-like move, she insists the relationship be limited to the bedroom.

SEX GROWS UP

The characters' serious life challenges reflected more than just the dark mood of post-9/11 life: Real life was also progressing for those behind the show. Life milestones—marriage, children, and death—wreaked joy and havoc, and also brought with them a clear message: If such changes were happening for the cast and crew who poured their lives into the show, the show was probably due for some maturation as well. It was time for *Sex and the City* to grow up.

First, the writers lost a friend and collaborator with the death of comedian Judy Toll on May 2, 2002. Toll, who had pioneered the subject of women and sex on-screen with her script for the 1988 film *Casual Sex?*, was a friend of King's from his UnCabaret comedy days in Los Angeles. She had contributed to the annual Los Angeles brainstorming sessions for *Sex and the City*. With King, she cowrote the fifth-season episode "Cover Girl," in which Carrie is horrified to see the nearly naked photo of her that the publisher has chosen for the cover of her book. Toll died shortly afterward from complications related to melanoma at forty-four. The script went into production the day after her death.

Happier news came with word of *Sex and the City* author Candace Bushnell's marriage, which marked the end of an era. Now forty-three, she exchanged vows and platinum Tiffany rings with Charles Askegard, a thirty-three-year-old ballet dancer, on July 4, 2002, on a Nantucket beach. Though the wedding was last-minute and barefoot, the *New York Times* nonetheless managed to cover it. He wore a white Prada suit; she wore a white Ralph Lauren cocktail dress, a garland of pink roses in her hair.

The couple had met just eight weeks earlier at a $3,000-per-ticket spring benefit for the New York City Ballet, after Bushnell ended a longtime relationship with a Brit. At the end of that benefit, Bushnell took the six-foot-four dancer downtown to the club Bungalow 8.

"One has to be open-minded when the right man comes along," she told the newspaper. "And I know it's freaky, but this just seems like the natural thing to do. My friends didn't even say to me, 'So *soon?*'"

Darren Star and Jay McInerney mingled among the twenty-five guests at the wedding. McInerney cracked, "Candace Bushnell gets married—it's like Johnny Carson retiring." They toasted with pink champagne.

Meanwhile, Parker announced she was pregnant with her first child, which forced the upcoming fifth season to be cut short. She could hide her baby bump behind tent dresses and oversized purses for only so long. The writers would have eight episodes, instead of the standard eighteen, to face the post-9/11 world.

• • •

As the show grew more serious around this time, *Sex and the City* also started to gain serious recognition as not only a quality television show, thanks to the Emmys, but also a socially significant one.

A 2002 *New York Times* piece by Alan James Frutkin named the series the best gay show on television: "*Sex and the City* is clearly not a show about gay life (although gay viewers joke that while it concerns four primarily heterosexual women, it's really about gay men—who else could have so much sex with so little guilt?). But since its 1998 premiere, it has featured story lines portraying contemporary gay life with a wit and depth that the more overtly gay *Queer as Folk* hasn't achieved."

Michael Musto, a *Village Voice* columnist, added that *Sex and the City*'s gay characters were allowed to demonstrate their gayness: "Most gay characters in prime time aren't allowed to be sexual. They're only gay because they say they're gay."

The show became such a gay cultural touchstone that several gay men told me they're just as likely to be asked by a date, "Which *Sex and the City* lady are you?" as straight women are to be asked by a friend.

Grad student Adam Neal came out as gay late in *Sex and the City*'s fourth season. And the show helped him figure out the shades of his own sexual identity: "The ladies dealt with topics nearly all gay men face," he says. "Bad kissers, uncut versus cut, bi versus gay, and even what positions and orifices are palatable. As I watched the ladies, I would ask myself, 'Am I the kind of gay who'd do *that?* Or even *that?*'"

He still remembers the "tuchus-lingus" episode about Miranda's lover requesting a rim job. When Charlotte said, "Trey likes it," he surprised himself by thinking, *Well, if Charlotte's cool with it . . .* He says, "A whole new world opened up for me, so to speak."

New York City student Moises Mendez—who was just one year old when the show premiered—continues to consult *Sex and the City* as his own oracle of dating in Manhattan as he enters his twenties. "Whether it be bad kissers, commitmentphobes, or just downright assholes, it seems to me that Charlotte, Carrie, Samantha, and Miranda always knew what to do," he says. "And the bad ones never stopped them from dating."

The *Times* also reported that *Sex and the City* was continuing to successfully inform teenage girls about sex and relationships. Many watched it with their parents, who used it as a jumping-off point for discussions. Others watched in secret. The girls said they admired the main characters' glamour, power, and friendship.

Parker was often mobbed by groups of teenage *Sex and the City* fans. Writers added occasional teachable moments for its surprisingly robust audience of younger viewers. An April 2000 *New York Times* story reported that girls as young as thirteen were having oral sex, which inspired the episode "Hot Child in the City." In it, a teen girl hires Samantha to plan her bat mitzvah and turns out to be sexually precocious, which prompts Samantha to caution her against growing up too fast. The episode helped the show win a Sexual Health in Entertainment award for an "exemplary job incorporating accurate and honest portrayals of sexuality."

Cattrall explained that the episode was the only time she ever said to the producers, "I'm not doing that." In the original draft, the thirteen-year-old girl (played by Kat Dennings) and Samantha competed over their knowledge of fellatio. Cattrall refused to do the scene as written. "This isn't about being conservative," she said. "A woman would just never do that unless she's mentally ill." King changed it to a scene that made the episode one of Cattrall's favorites, with Samantha saying, "Ladies, aren't you a little young for that kind of talk? I'm serious. You have your whole lives to talk that way."

The show's more adult sexual moments struck home with young viewers as well. Julie Eisen, who grew up near Philadelphia, started watching the show when she was fourteen, sneaking down to the basement to catch episodes. She learned a major life lesson: Masturbation is normal. The only thing she knew about masturbation before watching was that a girl at her overnight camp was bullied for "fingering herself." Julie didn't understand why the girl would do that, but she did get the idea that doing it was shameful. Afterward, Julie caught the vague platitudes in teen magazines about how it was "perfectly normal," but she still didn't understand the how and why.

Sex and the City, on the other hand, was, as she says, "like, 'Duh, we do this.'" She learned that women had "goody drawers." She definitely caught onto what masturbation was all about during Charlotte's Rabbit obsession. Samantha set aside entire days to masturbate. "It was nothing but another component of their active sexual selves," Julie says.

Teenage Julie became "a vocal advocate of masturbation" to her friends, she says. When her female friends were having sex but had no idea what orgasms felt like, Julie would ask, with the confidence of a sex educator, if they masturbated. When she saw their uncomfortable facial expressions, she insisted they try it. "How else could they tell their partners what felt good?" she says now. "The show modeled sexual agency for me when I was fourteen. And I am forever grateful for it." It's no coincidence that Julie Eisen grew up to be a health-communication specialist.

The show had begun its transition, at least in some circles, from a fluffy, girly joke to an acknowledged generator of social change.

GETTING THROUGH

Still, the fifth season felt, from the inside, like an awkward slog through a necessary transitional phase—from pre-9/11 to post-9/11 life, from semiadulthood to real adulthood, from fairy tale to reality.

Julie Rottenberg and Elisa Zuritsky found themselves writing the most frustrating episode of their careers thus far: "Luck Be an Old Lady," the season's third, in which the girls go to Atlantic City to celebrate Charlotte's thirty-sixth birthday. It had started as a vague idea—they go to Atlantic City, then stuff happens!—and had never taken a clear form. The joke was supposed to be that other shows do Vegas, and *Sex and the City* would do the East Coast equivalent. But Atlantic City matched the mood of the season as a depressing place. As Carrie later put it in the episode, "People go to casinos for the same reason they go on blind dates—hoping to hit the jackpot. But mostly, you just wind up broke or alone in a bar."

Every time the episode came up in the writers' room, Rottenberg thought, *Ah, I don't understand that one. Good thing somebody else will be writing it.* But when it came time to assign the script, King looked right at her and Zuritsky: "Julie and Elisa. You're going to write that one."

They didn't understand why they were stuck with it: Maybe because of their connection to the Jersey Shore, near Atlantic City? Of course, they had started the job so recently, Rottenberg says, "I would have written an episode about the garbage truck if you told me to." Besides, with the abbreviated season, every writer wouldn't necessarily get an episode, so they knew they should be grateful.

They got through it, but it was laborious. They never really felt like they solved the central problem of the episode, but it was memorable for its location and its refreshing sense of frivolity in a fairly dramatic season. Fans particularly loved the girls' dressing-down of a male casino customer who calls out to Miranda, "Hey, Red, move your fat ass!" Miranda: "My ass is fat because I just had a baby, you asshole!" Samantha, to the guy: "What's your excuse?" Carrie: "Yeah, ya havin' triplets?"

And Carrie does make one of her most poignant observations about friendship: "Friendships don't magically last forty years. You have to invest in them. It's like your savings: You don't expect to wake up one day when you're old and find a big bucket of money waiting there."

The seventh episode of the season proved taxing for director Michael

Engler. In "The Big Journey," Samantha accompanies Carrie on a terrible cross-country train trip to San Francisco for a book-tour stop; they discover that even luxury accommodations on a train are cramped and that the only men on board are a tame bachelor party full of loyal husbands. (Key Samantha zinger: "I'm starting to understand why there was a murder on the Orient Express.") Engler struggled to pull off the technicalities of shooting on a train. The crew crammed into the train cars for days. They even had to shoot a scene in the cramped train bathroom. In true *Sex and the City* fashion, they shot on a real train, though at least it wasn't moving—it was stopped in the station in front of a green screen, with the passing scenery to be added later in editing.

The eighth and final episode came as a relief. "I Love a Charade," written by Chupack and King, does not concern itself primarily with its four main heroines. The focus is on the girls heading to the Hamptons for the wedding of gay piano-bar entertainer Bobby Fine to society lady Bitsy Von Muffling. While there, Charlotte tells the girls about her relationship with Harry, whom she's now decided to date openly. And Carrie runs into Jack Berger, who reveals he's broken up with his girlfriend. She's convinced he gives her that rare sparky feeling, what she calls "zsa zsa zsu." But few watching were as excited as she was: "A boring downer" is how *Vanity Fair* later described Berger.

At the wedding the women are touched by the obvious affection between the bride and groom, prompting us to speculate what on earth the show is trying to tell us. Is it that we should settle for love without sex? Is it that none of us has a clue what to do about love, marriage, commitment, and the rest of our short lives? Is it that life is meaningless anyway in the wake of a massive tragedy like 9/11, so human companionship is the best we can hope for in our empty husk of being?

While the filming of that episode lasted, like so many, until dawn, at least the cast, crew, and producers got to be together in the Hamptons—and the season was over. They found comfort in the togetherness at such a time. And they found more comfort in taking a break before they had to figure out how to make one last season of this damn show.

9

Happy Endings

. . . .

Sex and the City writer Jenny Bicks had breast cancer.

That could mean only one thing: One of the *Sex and the City* women was also getting breast cancer.

Michael Patrick King, Bicks's boss but also one of her best friends, walked into the office one day and told her, "We're writing about your cancer." She'd had cancer for about a year, and everyone at the show knew. But this took revelation to a whole new level.

"What?" she said.

But she knew resistance was pointless in the face of King's determination. And he was right. It was a good idea. So in the next breath she added, "Ugh, all right."

Bicks was reluctant, but she respected King's instinct to make the most of a good story. It was a chance to switch the conversation about breast cancer from pink-ribbon platitudes to stories more grounded in reality: the hot flashes, the good and bad wigs, the postmastectomy breast implants, the sexual side effects. We all knew about the brave bald women going through chemo, but we rarely talked about the moment when your hair falls out midcoitus with your much-younger boyfriend.

Samantha went through the disease much differently from Bicks. Samantha whipped her wig off in front of hundreds of people as she gave an inspirational speech. Bicks had only wished she could do such a thing.

Actress Kim Cattrall was just as game for cancer as she had been for the comic sex scenes she'd elevated to an art.

Once again, *Sex and the City* had allowed Bicks to write her life into comedy, and to make Samantha the brave, ballsy cancer fighter that Bicks hoped she could be. By writing about it with her friends—her fellow *Sex and the City* writers—Bicks shared her burden with those closest to her in a way few people experience. They could all talk about it without getting mired in the pain. They could support her without constantly asking, "What can I do to help?" Instead of putting on a brave face at work and pretending nothing was wrong, she could let her coworkers protect and take care of her.

The story line made for some of the show's most poignant moments of friendship among the four main characters, while still allowing it to maintain its acerbic bite. Take, for instance, how Samantha reveals her diagnosis, which happens to coincide with Miranda's wedding to Steve: First, she methodically tells Carrie in a cab on the way to the ceremony, saying she's afraid she'll blurt out, "I have cancer," during the festivities. She then does, in fact, blurt it out to Charlotte during the reception. Finally, Miranda insists the other three tell her why they're so glum. Samantha apologizes for ruining Miranda's "special day," and Charlotte tells Miranda to go back to her people—her family and Steve's. "*You* are my people," Miranda tearfully insists.

If there was a good way to have cancer, this was it. Bicks even began to hear from others diagnosed with cancer that seeing Samantha deal with it had made a difference to them. She got to go to the Emmys in a

• • • • • • • • • • •

The dawn at the end of a long night of shooting the fifth-season finale in the Hamptons: Kim Cattrall hugs writer Elisa Zuritsky, with Amy B. Harris. *Courtesy of Julie Rottenberg*

• • • • • • • • • • •

Rehearsing a scene from the fifth-season finale wedding reception: Groom and bride Nathan Lane and Julie Halston, Cattrall and Cynthia Nixon with a doll in place of Miranda's baby, and Kristin Davis and Evan Handler. *Courtesy of Julie Rottenberg*

Writer Cindy Chupack, executive producer Michael Patrick King, actor Sarah Jessica Parker, and co–executive producer John Melfi during a lunch break on the fifth-season finale shoot. *Courtesy of Julie Rottenberg*

Nixon and her actor baby, Joseph Pupo. *Courtesy of Julie Rottenberg*

Three women with cupcakes during On Location Tours' *Sex and the City* bus tour of Manhattan sites from the show. *Courtesy of On Location Tours*

Chupack, script consultant Greg Behrendt, and writer Liz Tuccillo in front of the white board, planning out season 6, where highlights include "Aidan Crash," "Good Date, Bad Sex (3 times)," and "TiVo: Jules & Mimi." *Courtesy of Julie Rottenberg*

"Great Sexpectations"
Sex and the City
Episode 602
Outline
Cindy Chupack
January 22, 2003

1) INT. CORNER BISTRO – NIGHT (N1)

CARRIE and BERGER are having a burger, fries and a beer and making each other laugh. In these first three scenes we see them sparking, connecting and talking, talking, talking. *The only thing as delicious as those first few bites of a truly great burger are those first few dates with someone truly great... like Berger. Everything is fresh, everything is a first, everything is foreplay.*

2) INT. BED, BATH AND BEYOND – DAY (D2)

We find Carrie and Berger amid a rack of shower curtains. *Even a trip to Bed, Bath and Beyond can become an ecstatic errand.* Carrie surveys a shower curtain with fish on it: "I don't see you as fish guy." Berger: "The problem with the fish is then you're into a whole fish theme. Fish soap dish, fish soap..." Carrie: "Do you have a theme now?" Berger: "Yes, mildew." She laughs. They come to one with a map of the world on it, and Berger tells her that's what he has at home, but on his, China is covered in mold. Carrie: "And here they thought communism was a problem." He says he doesn't get why the names of the countries are on the outside. "They should be on the inside so the showeree can learn where Dubai is while lathering up. Who do I talk to about that?" Carrie: "This is very intimate, you know, shopping for a shower curtain." Berger: "Wait until I get you into bedding." She smiles. He pulls a curtain around them and kisses her. It's very flirty and fun and sexually charged.

3) INT. ODEON – NIGHT (N3)

The kiss continues as Berger and Carrie close down a restaurant. They make out in their booth as a COUPLE OF WAITERS put chairs up on tables around them. They stop kissing and start immediately talking again (picking up the conversation right where they left off) and then they start kissing again. Finally Berger says: "We should get out of here before they turn the lights off." The lights go off. They are left with only candlelight. He puts down a big tip, pulls Carrie up, and they walk out laughing about whether it's still a public display of affection if there's no public left. *The wait staff couldn't wait any longer and neither could I. I wanted Berger in my bed, bath and beyond... immediately.*

4) INT. CARRIE'S BEDROOM – LATER THAT NIGHT (N3)

Carrie and Berger are in her bed, undressed, about to have sex. He's kissing her neck as he gets on top of her, and she's trying to enjoy it, but unfortunately the whole thing feels more awkward than hot to her. She's not in a comfortable position, he's not making much eye

. . . .

Chupack's outline for the sixth-season episode "Great Sexpectations." The note at the top for a dialogue idea: "The penis isn't always the hardest thing in a relationship." *Courtesy of Cindy Chupack*

Parker waiting to shoot on location in Manhattan. *Courtesy of HBO®*

Chris Noth and Parker in a scene from the Paris-set finale. *Courtesy of HBO®*

Behrendt and Tuccillo at the premiere for *He's Just Not That into You*, the movie adaptation of the book they cowrote, which was inspired by a *Sex and the City* line. *Getty Images*

Harris discusses her *Sex and the City* prequel TV series about a teenage Carrie Bradshaw, *The Carrie Diaries*, at the New York Television Festival in 2012. She's with *Carrie Diaries* star AnnaSophia Robb and *Sex and the City* author Candace Bushnell. *Getty Images*

Sex and the City creator Darren Star and costume designer Patricia Field at the second-season premiere of their more recent collaboration, the TV series *Younger*, in 2016. *Getty Images*

Instagram star Carrie Dragshaw (Dan Clay) in a classic Carrie look. *Courtesy of Dan Clay*

• • • • • • • • • • •
Sarah Jessica Parker, Kristin Davis, Kim Cattrall, and Cynthia Nixon at the premiere for the 2010 film *Sex and the City 2*. *Getty Images*

wig. She didn't triumphantly toss it at the crowd, but it still represented one of the least-sucky ways she could think of to go through cancer.

Better still: Like Samantha, she survived.

• • •

The writers' transmuted personal story lines turned into great television every week, but King and Sarah Jessica Parker, in her capacity as a producer, had a feeling they should end the show soon. *Sex and the City* had reached the top of its game and they wanted to go out while it was still at its peak. Every year got harder—the location shoots crammed with fans and photographers, the rumors about cast strife, the real-life challenges of maintaining relationships and families with such a brutal filming schedule—but mostly they wanted to end it while the creative quality was high.

King and Parker decided *Sex and the City*'s sixth season would be its last, airing in two parts, during the summer of 2003 and the winter of early 2004. They planned to leave the party while it was still a party. The previous two years had gone by in a blur of paparazzi flashbulbs, magazine coverage, and rabid fans. King obsessed over media lists of which shows were falling out of favor, those "Why is this still on?" lists. He worried he would see *Sex and the City* on one, under the heading "Over." He also felt a natural end coming. He first proposed stopping to Parker after the fifth season wrapped: "If it goes any further," he said, "it will become a different show." It would be a show about marriage, motherhood, and middle age.

Besides, this moment was the time to go out on top in terms of popularity, or nearly so. The sixth-season premiere marked the first time ratings went down compared with the previous season premiere. King's instinct had been dead-on. His show would never appear on an "Over" list. In the final season, thanks to the announcement that it was ending, *Sex and the City* achieved the kind of ubiquity few pop cultural phenomena do. Now they had to give fans a worthy final season and a finale for the ages.

With the end in sight, media scrutiny grew even more intense, as exemplified by the uproar that greeted star Cynthia Nixon when she experienced major changes in her personal life.

When Nixon left her male partner of fifteen years during the show's final season and began dating a woman, Christine Marinoni, press attention would not let up. Paparazzi huddled outside her home waiting for a shot of the star with Marinoni, whom she'd met while working as an activist with the nonprofit Alliance for Quality Education in 2001. Both of them campaigned to reduce public-school class sizes in New York City. They became closer friends as Nixon split in 2003 from her partner and the father of her two children, Danny Mozes.

When Nixon and Marinoni became an item and press attention flared, Nixon hired a publicist for the first time. She asked the publicist: What was the plan here? She didn't want to lie or hide, though that's what he suggested. So she signed on with another publicist, one who helped Nixon publicly confirm the relationship and come out as bisexual, saying she had "nothing to hide" and was "very happy."

The tabloids, and even the mainstream press, could not resist this story: A star from TV's most-discussed show, which was somehow simultaneously the straightest and gayest show in history, had an offscreen subplot worthy of the series itself.

• • •

The writers took the show's impending conclusion as an invitation to stage an all-out assault on the heroines' lives and relationships. Samantha dealt with her breast cancer *and* the terror of falling into a trusting, supportive, monogamous relationship with a hunky actor/waiter named Smith Jerrod; Charlotte faced infertility during the most unexpectedly satisfying relationship of her life; Miranda struggled with single motherhood; Carrie fell into a no-win relationship with novelist Jack Berger, and then into an authoritarian relationship with an older artist played by Mikhail Baryshnikov. The stakes had never been higher for *Sex and the City*'s heroines. The writers, too, faced their riskiest maneuver yet. They had to stick the landing.

As the series wound down, Carrie faced a problem that resonated heavily with the show's theme of how women's professional ambition affects their romantic lives: Berger, the fellow author for whom she'd fallen, couldn't handle her success, which outpaced his. This gave him a vulnerability, a multidimensionality, that her other great loves never quite had. King calls Berger "the most thoroughly written man that we've ever created."

Alas, he was not long for this world. As King likes to say, "We brought in Berger to kill him. He was a marked man." While they didn't literally kill the character, they did kill the romance. It was the *Sex and the City* equivalent of a *Sopranos* hit job.

Berger had another purpose, too, though no one had realized the magnitude of it at the beginning.

This destiny was discovered over a lunch break during the *Sex and the City* writers' seasonal brainstorm in Los Angeles. As straight male script consultant Greg Behrendt remembers it, he was snacking on a cookie in the hallway when writer Jenny Bicks asked him to come to her office to talk over a dating problem. She'd asked a guy she was seeing to come upstairs to her place after a date. He'd declined. "Do you think that's bad?" she asked.

Behrendt wanted to simply stare at her, mouth agape. What do you say to that? Do you say, "Oh, he probably had a lot on his mind"? Instead, he stated what he saw as the obvious truth: "He just doesn't like you. Sexual attraction is a big part of the deal. I don't care if you have to fly the fucking space shuttle the next day, you come up if you're into it."

He'd learned this himself while courting the woman he would marry. He understood what he'd do to win a woman he loved. A man makes the extra effort if he's falling for someone.

Fellow writer Liz Tuccillo joined the conversation and was thrown by Behrendt's brutal honesty when he reiterated: "He's just not that into you."

When they returned to the writers' room after lunch, Tuccillo brought the conversation up to the group. She couldn't get over those words: "He's just not that into you." For the rest of the day, even if they had managed to move on to another topic, the questions would come back to variations on "he's just not that into you" from the writers' dating lives: "So if he says he doesn't like me, then he doesn't like me?" "If he doesn't call, then he doesn't like me?" Behrendt saw in this discussion a larger truth about the ways men and women had been taught to view their romantic relationships. The women who didn't see this—who didn't see that he just wasn't that into them—wanted hope more than they wanted truth.

Julie Rottenberg and Elisa Zuritsky wrote the episode in which this discussion appeared, called "Pick-a-Little, Talk-a-Little." Berger gives Behrendt's advice to Miranda when she wonders what to do about an ambivalent guy: "He's just not that into you," he offers.

Miranda feels liberated. Why not just move on from someone who isn't trying?

As the script progressed, Tuccillo visited Rottenberg and Zuritsky in what they called their "dentist's office" at Silvercup Studios. She said, "Guys, I think this 'He's just not that into you' thing could be a book. This is huge. This is *Oprah*. This is the *Today* show. Would you like to write it with me?"

Rottenberg's reaction was something like, "Mmmph." Zuritsky offered a dismissive "Good luck!"

They looked at each other quizzically after Tuccillo left. How on earth could that be an entire book? A *Sex and the City* episode, sure. An episode they hadn't even named "He's Just Not That into You."

Public reaction to the episode, however, indicated that Tuccillo was onto something. The day after it aired, "He's just not that into you" became an instant catchphrase. Berger had made his mark.

But soon afterward, his number was up as a marked man. He was transformed from Miranda's savior to a national enemy with one cowardly gesture when he broke up with Carrie via a Post-it note: "I'm sorry. I can't. Don't hate me." (Samantha comments, "The motherfucker's concise.")

Tuccillo later explained that, with this infamous breakup, Berger was the perfect embodiment of the typical man who thinks he's being the good guy and ends up much worse for it: "By trying so hard not to be the bad guy, by not breaking up when they should, by not being brave, they end up being like the worst guy in the world. I think the 'Don't hate me' is a very common thing with men—never wanting to seem like the bad guy."

The incident causes a crisis of faith unlike anything Carrie has experienced, even with Big. While the writers had brought Berger in to take him out, he also came with an important purpose: to give Carrie what appeared to be a real shot at a relationship. She had bounced between two classically masculine extremes: businessman Mr. Big and earthy furniture-maker Aidan Shaw, both of whom towered over her physically and emotionally. In Berger, Carrie seems to have found her equal. They both write for a living. They banter like a couple straight out of a Howard Hawks film. This makes his kiss-off all the more powerful.

The writers wanted Berger to leave Carrie in the most craven way possible, to contrast with how much work she'd done to keep the relationship going. The Post-it idea had presented itself from the beginning, though the writers hadn't realized it at the time. During Carrie and Berger's first phone call, he lies in bed and fidgets with a pad of Post-its. As King watched it back for break-up ideas, he thought, *That's the gun. He's going to shoot her in seven episodes.* Chekhov's doctrine delivers again.

• • •

With Berger out of the picture, Carrie's final *Sex and the City* suitor would be a great artist so far along in his career that she could never eclipse him: Aleksandr Petrovsky, played by Russian ballet legend Mikhail Baryshnikov.

Baryshnikov came with a reputation and presence beyond anything *Sex and the City* had experienced. Sure, Candice Bergen and Valerie

Harper, among other American TV greats, had guest-starred. But Baryshnikov, like Petrovsky, brought the weight of the rest of the world with him. Known as one of the greatest dancers in ballet history, he was born in what is now Latvia, then in the Soviet Union. He defected in 1974 while on tour in Canada, seeking asylum in Toronto. Soon afterward, he became a principal dancer with the American Ballet Theatre and the New York City Ballet.

Americans first got to know him as the lead in a televised version of American Ballet Theatre's production of Tchaikovsky's *The Nutcracker*, shown on PBS. He performed in two TV specials, dancing to Broadway music in one and Hollywood movie music in another. He was nominated for an Oscar for his first film role, one written for him—that of a womanizing ballet dancer in 1977's *The Turning Point*. He reached ubiquitous fame when he costarred with tap dancer Gregory Hines in 1985's *White Nights*. He'd also appeared onstage in avant-garde productions, including works by Beckett and Chekhov.

It made sense that some of the *Sex and the City* actors were intimidated when he strode into that converted bread factory, Silvercup Studios, to woo Carrie Bradshaw. David Eigenberg, for one, couldn't stop calling him "Mr. Baryshnikov," a level of deference he had not felt moved to offer another fellow actor. Though barely five foot eight, Eigenberg had about an inch on Baryshnikov, and yet he cowered before the Russian.

"David, please call me Misha," Baryshnikov said. Eigenberg was in awe.

Parker effortlessly called him Misha, but she was surprised by the outpouring of strong feeling he evoked in people: "The diversity of people who respond positively to Baryshnikov—from a camera operator to a grip, from a housewife to a journalist, from a plumber to a wardrobe person—is astounding," she says.

The casting came as a surprise to critics. "When exec producer Michael Patrick King told TV Guide Online he snagged a 'big name' for the plum part, we were thinking Tom Cruise, George Clooney, Sean

Penn . . . you know, *movie* stars," wrote columnist Michael Ausiello. In his interview with Parker about the casting, she explained it this way: "When I understood the general description of the part, it was very hard to find anybody that could bring that sort of myth and legend. And while there are enormous movie stars who are extraordinary and obviously thrilling to watch on screen, people don't necessarily just fit the bill because of their name recognition. He is extraordinary, and this character is not like anyone we've ever had on the show before. And this person has to bring with him culture and style and complication and depth and a brand-new point of view about the city. And it is thrilling to think that there is this whole other city that Carrie doesn't know."

Carrie meets Petrovsky at a gallery in New York, and suddenly she's in a relationship we never imagined for her. Petrovsky comes off as bigger than Big and the absolute opposite of Aidan and Berger—commanding, worldly, confident, and terrifying in his hugeness.

SINGLE IN THE CITY

In between Berger and Petrovsky, Carrie still had some time left to make a few more major statements about single womanhood of a certain age. The memorable episode "A Woman's Right to Shoes" features Carrie attending a baby shower where the hostess, Kyra, makes everyone remove his or her shoes at the door. Carrie reluctantly parts with her Manolos, only to find they've disappeared by the time she's ready to leave.

When Carrie requests reimbursement for her lost footwear, Kyra can't believe the price: $485. Looking down from the moral height of motherhood, she lectures Carrie about self-indulgence and frivolity. Carrie grows even angrier as she remembers all the wedding and baby gifts she's given friends over the years, getting nothing in return because she hasn't chosen to marry or mother. She registers at Manolo Blahnik for just one item—the $485 shoes—and informs Kyra that this would make the perfect gift for her wedding to herself.

The symbolism is so heavy it can't even be called symbolism. And women *loved* it. Like so many *Sex and the City* accoutrements before, women rushed out to get this one: But this time, they didn't clamor for the shoes. They registered for whatever they wanted for their birthdays, or for no occasion at all—no occasion to do with men or procreation. Trend pieces have continued throughout the years since its airing to slobber over this idea.

As late as 2017, reports still attributed "sologamy" to this one *Sex and the City* episode. "The commitment can be anything from a quiet private moment in a room by yourself with a candle and a mirror to a full-blown wedding bonanza complete with dress, cake, reception and vows," the UK-based *Sun* newspaper reported. It even mentioned a Japanese travel agency that will organize a self-wedding for about $3,200.

Baltimore high school science teacher Elizabeth Schap calls "A Woman's Right to Shoes" "my episodic soulmate, my life's script. The story spoke to everything I was feeling about being single in a world where no one was." She felt like her family and friends couldn't understand her single life because it hadn't hit any traditional milestones. Since she first saw the episode in her midtwenties, she has made everyone close to her watch it: her mother, her sister, her married friends.

• • •

Writer Cindy Chupack was assigned the script for an episode called "Catch-38," in which Carrie gets closer to Aleksandr, as signified by him giving her the keys and the alarm code to his apartment. But Baryshnikov's character also reveals he's had a vasectomy. If Carrie, who's now thirty-eight, ends up with him for any serious length of time, she must give up children for good.

Chupack, who was thirty-eight at the time, recalls that as she worked on the script, she felt like her fellow writers were interrogating her. She remembers being asked point-blank: "If you had wanted a baby, wouldn't you have had one already?"

She was the Carrie in this scenario, and even before Chupack was ready to decide for herself how strongly she felt about having children, the show forced her to examine her feelings just as it did the viewing audience. Michael Patrick King had once again played matchmaker for a writer and the issues presented in a script assignment.

The plot line reminded Chupack of a past-life reading she once got as a gift. It had been over the phone, which made her question it: How could someone tell what her past lives were over the phone? If she believed in fortune-telling's accuracy at all, in-person seemed like the right way to do it. In any case, the psychic told Chupack that she hadn't had a good relationship since ancient Greece. Chupack jokes that she knew was she in a slump, but ancient Greece? Wow. "You've always had children," the psychic told Chupack. "But in this life, you're supposed to learn how to love and be loved."

She didn't gain total clarity about her own situation as she wrote the episode, but she was proud of a metaphor she slipped in. Just after finding out about the vasectomy, Carrie eats a black-and-white cookie while at a playground with Charlotte. Black-and-whites are a favorite of Chupack's and a classic New York City treat. Chupack's idea: This wasn't a black-and-white issue. She wrote:

> **CHARLOTTE:** But we're thirty-eight, these are the years.
> **CARRIE:** Yes, I know, I've heard! I'm running out of time. I
> don't even have time to eat this cookie.
> **CHARLOTTE:** How is it?
> **CARRIE:** It's so good I forgot to have children.

DR. ROBERT LEEDS

Miranda made progress in her own love life as well, and also answered one of the most repeated—and most warranted—criticisms of the show. She dated her dreamy neighbor Dr. Robert Leeds, played by the black actor Blair Underwood, known for his work in films like *Deep Impact* and on TV's *L.A. Law*.

The show had drawn fire for its whiteness from the beginning, and had made matters worse with Samantha's relationship with black hip-hop producer Chivon. Samantha later dated a Hispanic woman, only to decide she wasn't as lesbian as she'd hoped to be. Since then, *Sex and the City* had rolled with the seismic cultural mood shift of 9/11 seamlessly, but still hadn't addressed its own whiteness. The actresses, forced to answer much of the media criticism, had lobbied for diversity for some time. Nixon spoke candidly in interviews, calling the lack of diversity "irresponsible." She told the Associated Press, "I think it's about time."

The show introduced Dr. Leeds, the New York Knicks' team physician, as Miranda's perfect match: as successful as she, charming, and handsome as hell. Alas, he was not to be her destiny, but a mere prelude to it. His perfection forces her to see that she's meant to be with the less-perfect love of her life, Steve. This becomes apparent when Robert says "I Love You" on a giant, custom-made cookie. She finds she can't say it back because she's still in love with Steve (though, no fool, she does eat the cookie). When Miranda professes her love to Steve at their son Brady's first birthday party, it marks the unceremonious end to her courtship with Robert.

The addition of Robert nodded to, even if it didn't do enough for, the significant black fandom of the show. Many women of color responded to the same qualities in the series that white women did: its freeing depiction of female sexuality, its prioritizing of female friendship, its emphasis on fashion, and its glamorous take on city life. Beyoncé was a fan: "Only time we don't speak is during *Sex and the City*," her future husband, Jay Z, raps during their duet "'03 Bonnie and Clyde." "She got Carrie fever."

"Women of color have laughed along with SATC, we have loved it, we have gotten invested in the characters," Samhita Mukhopadhyay wrote on *Feministing*. "We could relate to endless stories of dating while being savvy, independent, and smart. We even managed to ignore the fact that they have *never* had a prominent person of color on the show. (Let's be real, some of us like shoes and handbags, too.)"

Women of color have spoken and written about how they could enjoy the best of *Sex and the City* even while laughing at and critiquing its whiteness, just as they did with *Friends*, *Seinfeld*, or any number of mainstream shows that were, as usual, predominantly white. "Showing that people of color also have full romantic lives would have made such a difference in making the show not thinly 'politically correct' but a show with a much deeper accuracy to everything it pretended to be about: love, sex, friendship, and New York City," Hunter Harris wrote on *Refinery29*. Still, she added, "These characters provided some central (and corny) metaphors for my life. Cut through the classist and incredibly narrow understanding of New York and it had a real value: It taught me how to have girl talk and what exactly a booty call text was. I also learned that it was okay to desire a full sex life."

Susana Morris, a black English professor at Auburn University, told author Rebecca Traister in her book *All the Single Ladies* that moving to Atlanta in 2002 and seeing all of the "fierce, single black women" reminded her, in a way, of *Sex and the City*. She had enjoyed watching it with her Dominican, lesbian roommate despite the cast's lack of resemblance to either of them. "There is this thing," she said of the parts she did relate to. "It's having friends, going on the town, living it up, finding a network of women."

Many of those women of color watching *Sex and the City* found its formula a little more familiar than most of the white women who watched. They had also watched *Living Single*, a show about unmarried women that was ahead of its time. Starring Queen Latifah and Kim Fields, it premiered on Fox in 1993, a year before *Friends*, and featured six black, single friends—four women and two men. It anticipated the formulas used by both *Friends* and *Sex and the City* with its focus on single life in Brooklyn. It highlighted the women, who were "bodacious and bold," as creator Yvette Lee Bowser described them to *People* magazine. "They weren't playing dumb to get a man."

It hit big in its target demographic, young African Americans. But Fox never marketed it outside that group, so its cultural impact was negligible among the white Americans who dominated mainstream media coverage: To wit, it was the No. 1 show among African American audiences in the 1996–97 season; the same year, it ranked 104th in the overall Nielsen rankings. It won two NAACP Image Awards, but didn't crack the mainstream, white-dominated Emmys (aside from two nominations for its lighting direction).

The parallels to *Sex and the City* are striking: Like Carrie, Latifah's character, Khadijah, works in media, as an editor and publisher. Fields's character, Regine, works in fashion and pines for a man to take care of her. One of their girlfriends, Max, is an attorney, just like Miranda.

Black women who watched both *Living Single* and *Sex and the City* could see themselves in both: "I always say that I'm Khadijah from *Living Single*, but I'm also Miranda from *Sex and the City*," said Issa Rae. She went on to, in 2016, create and star in HBO's *Insecure*, which is proudly influenced by both shows.

Living Single would never get the credit that *Sex and the City* would, and Dr. Robert Leeds wouldn't get enough time to make much of an impact on *Sex and the City*.

THE CONVERSION

Charlotte's final evolution of the series began at Pastis, the Meatpacking District brasserie that was a favorite place for the writers to brainstorm. There, among the French-countryside wooden tables and flea market mirrors, the clinking of glasses and plates and silverware, they came up with the last step in the WASP princess's transformation via love: She would become the perfect Jew.

Her new lover, divorce lawyer Harry Goldenblatt, shocks her when he says he could never marry her because she's not Jewish. She does the only logical thing: She converts. But this wouldn't be just any TV conversion, with a quick ceremonial scene never to be spoken of again. If Charlotte York was going to become Jewish, she would give it her all, and we would do it with her every step of the way, from her relentless pursuit of a rabbi who literally closes the door in her face three times as she seeks conversion to her solo preparation of a traditional Shabbat dinner.

Among the New York City–based crew, suddenly everyone had an opinion. Even the Jews among them hadn't realized the crew was so heavily Jewish until shooting began on Charlotte's conversion sequence. Grips spoke up: "I was raised Orthodox, and . . ." Though the show had hired an official consultant, many more volunteered as unofficial consultants: "Hey, she wouldn't want her head covered that way!" "She would say 'HaShem' instead."

Davis had done her homework, too, listening over and over to a tape of Hebrew prayers to get them just right.

Everyone's diligence paid off, with a story line fans would mention to Davis as their favorite for years to come—more than her first wedding, more than Trey's impotence, more than her infertility.

THE FINAL EPISODES

Writing the finale presented challenges far beyond those of a regular script. King knew he could disappoint at least a few million people who hoped for the opposite of whatever ending he chose.

The writers debated: With whom should Carrie end up? Mr. Big? Petrovsky? Someone else? No one? King says he always planned for Big and Carrie to end up together. He simply wanted to make sure they didn't get together in a traditional way: no spectacular marriage proposal, all of the plot driven by Carrie's choices. It would all hinge on Carrie's decision to follow Petrovsky to Paris, hoping to find her happily-ever-after in that dreamy European city.

The other women would get their own forms of happily-ever-after. In the finale, Miranda invites Steve's mother, Mary (played by the incomparable Anne Meara), to live with them in Brooklyn as she shows signs of dementia. When Miranda's form of a fairy godmother, her housekeeper Magda, sees her giving the disoriented Mary a bath, her reaction is pure pride: "That's love," Magda says, kissing Miranda on the forehead. Charlotte and Harry receive word that they've been approved to adopt a Chinese baby. And Samantha gives her triumphant cancer luncheon speech with support from her sensitive love, Smith Jerrod (played by model and *90210* guest star Jason Lewis). Even more significantly, she sends Smith off to shoot a movie by insisting that he have sex with other women, given her lowered libido during cancer treatment. But she finds herself hoping he won't—and is thrilled when he returns home to say that he prefers to be monogamous with her. Samantha has finally made peace with love.

King added to the already astronomical finale workload with an extraordinary decision to shoot several endings as decoys for the paparazzi and tabloids. They might be able to spot a location shoot and guess from afar what was happening in it, or even get a rogue crew member to spill about a scene, but they wouldn't be able to tell which shoot was real. He peppered the shoots with misdirects: Maybe she'd end up with Big. Maybe she'd end up with Petrovsky. Maybe she would decide to stay in Paris. The actors and writers knew which was real, but the crew— which could include newcomers, freelancers, or just people who want to share secrets with their spouses after all their hard work—would not.

In one alternate scene, Carrie fakes out her friends by telling them she's already married Petrovsky. Then she reveals that he's coming back to the States from Paris so they can have a ceremony with her three best friends as her maids of honor. In another alternate ending, Samantha says Big "went all the way to Paris to choke." Carrie replies, "It's the Big ending we've all been waiting for."

The decoy endings made for some absurd moments. After one long day of shooting in the coffee shop, among Cafeteria's familiar white-paneled walls and white plastic chairs, they still had those alternate scenes to shoot. Writer Julie Rottenberg realized just how obvious they were being. In a real scene, they'd run in between takes to give actors notes. She scurried in with a bogus note for Nixon, who shot her an incredulous look. Perhaps Rottenberg was better off not doing any acting of her own.

King channeled the writing room debate into his scripts for the final two episodes. Carrie and Miranda have a devastating fight when Carrie decides to quit her job and move to Paris. "What are you gonna do over there without your job?" Miranda asks. "Eat croissants?"

"I cannot stay in New York and be single for *you!*" Carrie tells her. It's the quintessential friendship problem in adulthood: We are taught to prioritize romantic relationships over our female friendships. We'd see it as crazy and possibly stupid to stay in a certain place for a platonic friend, even one we've known and loved for years, even when the alternative is a chilly, older Russian artist we haven't known for long.

When Carrie stalks off, Miranda utters another rich line, especially for *Sex and the City*: "You're living in a fantasy!"

Another fraught finale scene happens on Carrie's street—Perry Street in the West Village, that cozy, tree-lined, and brownstone-filled few blocks that had become a second home base for the production over the years. For one last time, it would pretend to be a street on the Upper East Side. Perry was blocked off, as always, and the lights were rigged at the top of the trees. It looked like "this magical terrarium," King says.

In the finale, Big comes by Carrie's place in a typically half-hearted attempt, either at winning her back or at closure. "I came here to tell you something," he says. "You and I—"

"You and I nothing!" she screams. "You cannot do this to me again. You cannot jerk me around." After he claims that it's "different this time," she cuts him off: "Forget you know my number—in fact, forget you know my name. And you can drive down this street all you want—because I don't live here anymore!"

Most of the many nights they'd spent on the street had come in the spring or summer; this time they were shooting in the winter. The final season shot in the bitter cold, often with snow still on the ground. That night, the actors' breaths made little white puffs in the air as they shot on that street for the last time ever.

The "I don't live here anymore" struck Parker in the heart. She *didn't* live here anymore. She was leaving Carrie behind. When the scene wrapped, her only solace came from a surprise visitor: Her husband, Matthew Broderick, had been standing there watching with three friends.

Around them, crew members and producers were crying. Everyone decided to end the night around the corner at the White Horse Tavern, a bar known for its history as a literary hangout in the 1950s and '60s, frequented by Dylan Thomas, James Baldwin, Jack Kerouac, and others. It seemed like the perfect New York place to end the emotional night, except for one thing: The White Horse was closing early, at 1 a.m., to prepare for a city inspection the next day.

The cast and crew of *Sex and the City* began emptying their pockets of all their cash, handing it to the bartender. "Will you stay open for this much?" someone asked, referring to the wads of money. The White Horse stayed open.

• • •

The finale was expected to be widely watched, not just for its melodrama but also for the fashion spectacle of Carrie in Paris.

Patricia Field did not disappoint. She found an enormous, layered sea green Versace ball gown that was particularly memorable among the many memorable costume changes. This extraordinary dress, a Versace that didn't look very Versace, held court among the many outfits Field had pulled as options for the Paris finale. The whole staff, even Field and Parker, knew it was over the top. But Parker said, "Just let me put it on." They photographed it as an option to take to King.

Field and Parker would often have to come up with Supreme Court–level arguments to convince King to approve their more outrageous fashion choices, but this time they knew they had none. Field thought: Okay, maybe when the American fashion plate goes to Paris, she brings "all of her finery." Parker remained more grounded: "We don't have any argument for this. It's just the dream."

Field saw it as perfect for one of the saddest scenes in the series: the main character living what she thought was her dream with the man she thought was her dream—and being devastatingly disappointed. Carrie could wear it in the scene when she's stood up by Petrovsky—all the better, because it would look phenomenal flounced out all around her as she waited for him. Baryshnikov described it as looking like a mille-feuille, the French pastry whose name means "a thousand layers" (and is known in America as a Napoleon). "The more heightened that gown was," Field later said, "the more heightened that sadness was."

As Parker now summarizes their plea to King: "It's just everything she thinks she's running from and everything she thinks she's running toward. It's ridiculous and it's too much. It's not even the person she is; it's who she becomes in Aleksandr's presence."

Finally, Field called King down to her office, a room so stuffed with designer clothing it looked like a department store. In the middle stood the sea green Versace. "This just came from Paris," she said in her smoker's rasp. "It wants to be in the show."

"Pat, it's amazing."

"It's couture."

"Pat, how would she ever get it there? Realistically, she would never be able to pack that."

Field ignored this point. "For the scene where she's stood up. I'm just saying, one-of-a-kind couture."

"She couldn't pack it." He smiled sadly and left.

Then he thought better and returned. "Okay, do it," he told Field. The Versace dress decision was one of King's great takeaways from his entire *Sex and the City* experience: Sometimes what mattered most was the spectacle.

When it came time to shoot that scene at a New York hotel—many of the Paris interiors were shot stateside—Field drove from her new job at the sitcom *Hope & Faith* after a Friday night shoot to catch the *Sex and the City* dress in action. Parker's stand-in was wearing the dress while the scene was set; to Field's horror, the dress was crumpled like an unmade bed.

She interrupted to object, then led the crew in smoothing the dress out to cover the entire sofa. Parker should perch in the middle, among the dress's layers. Then she should get up and go to the window, the gown following her. "That is the way this dress has to be shot," Field remembered saying.

Parker needed to have four crew members help her carry its layers as she wore it. The scene appeared just as Field demanded. No one who watched that finale forgot that dress and the way it looked spread out on that sofa, Carrie waiting among its layers for true love to find her.

• • •

Baryshnikov, Parker, Noth, and the crew headed off to film in Paris in January 2004, a cold and rainy time in the City of Lights.

They shot at the Hôtel Plaza Athénée, where Petrovsky and Carrie stay together. The cast and crew also made the hotel their home for the shoot, so much so that Parker's son, James Wilkie, then fifteen months old, started walking steadily there for the first time. He had taken his first step back home in New York, to the relief of father Matthew Broderick, who didn't want to miss that moment. But James Wilkie became a toddler in Paris, delighting the crew, who felt like his extended family.

At other location shoots around the city, Carrie lunched with Petrovsky's ex at the trendy restaurant Kong. She called Miranda from a pay phone at Place Saint-Sulpice. She shopped (and tripped) at Dior on Avenue Montaigne. She looked on as a *Sex and the City*–like foursome brunched at the nearby L'Avenue. She stepped in dog poop while wearing Louboutins on Rue Servandoni. She strolled Place Dauphine with Petrovsky in one of their final moments as a happy couple.

Carrie had, in fact, gotten everything she'd searched for throughout the series: a famous boyfriend, a romantic city. But now she had become the outsider in a city even more glamorous than New York. She could barely communicate with anyone, she didn't understand the customs, and she lost her trademark "Carrie" necklace, an unsubtle symbol of her identity.

The writers chose the ending that had been there from the beginning: Mr. Big was The One after all. And King went big with Big's grand gesture.

Big asks for Carrie's friends' permission to go sweep her off her feet in Paris. He indicates that he knows his place in Carrie's life—and articulates the series's thesis—when he tells her friends, "You're the loves of her life. A guy's just lucky to come in fourth."

Miranda delivers their judgment: "Go get our girl." Nixon delivers it in such a way that it could make even the most anti-Big among us cry.

Big finds Carrie in Paris and vows to have a word with the Russian when he hears that Petrovsky (accidentally) slapped Carrie. "I don't need you to rescue me," she says, in another of the finale's clear-message moments.

Big at last declares his love at the Pont des Arts: "It took me a really long time to get here. But I'm here. Carrie, you're The One."

Her response: "I miss New York. Take me home."

But the script doesn't leave it at that. The last scene has Carrie alone among the crowds on the street in New York City, heading off toward whatever is next.

It was here that King planted a surprise for the writers, revealing Mr. Big's real name when it comes up on Carrie's pink, bedazzled flip phone: John. The writers learned it for the first time when they read his script. Normally, a detail like that would have been hashed out in the writers' room. But as he wrote, it just hit him: "He *has* to have a name. Now, that he's finally seen Carrie as The One, he's real."

John was the least specific name he could come up with. Just John. Just "man."

King took pride in those final two scripts. "Those Paris episodes," he says, "landed."

Yet the show's creator, Darren Star, had a different reaction. He felt the ending "betrayed what [the show] was about." The series, he said, was supposed to be about women *not* being defined by men. They could fall in love with men, but the message should not be about finding fulfillment with one. Alone on the streets of New York would have been fine. Reunited with her friends, sure. Why did Mr. Big have to be such a big part of it? "At the end," Star says, "it became a conventional romantic comedy."

Star's old friend Candace Bushnell agreed with him, though she understood King's decision. "In real life, Carrie and Big wouldn't have ended up together," Bushnell later said. "But at that point the TV show had become so big. Viewers got so invested in the story line of Carrie and Big that it became a bit like Mr. Darcy and Elizabeth Bennet."

Viewers split along the same lines: Many swooned over the romantic ending. Many others complained that it had betrayed what they loved most about the show. Either way, everyone had a strong opinion about the ending, just as they did about the show.

• • •

By the time the show signed off HBO in 2004, *Sex and the City* attracted 10.6 million viewers for its finale. The final episode was the series's most-watched ever. *Sex and the City* had helped build the cable network into a purveyor of respected television. The show had also gained at least some prestige, not only in the form of Emmys and admiring reviews, but also in academia: UK film studies professors Kim Akass and Janet McCabe edited *Reading Sex and the City*, a 2004 anthology of critical essays that examine the show's place in the literary canon (alongside the likes of Theodore Dreiser's *Sister Carrie*), its relationship to Woody Allen films, and its strong connection to gay culture.

Over the series's six seasons, it was nominated for more than fifty Emmys and won seven, including the Outstanding Comedy Series award in 2001, when it needed such recognition most. King won for Outstanding Directing for a Comedy Series in 2002, and Parker and Nixon won for their acting in 2004.

More recognition, and a clear legacy, would come with time. But not before King and Parker gambled it all on two polarizing movies.

10

Ever Thine, Ever Mine, Ever Ours

· · · · · · · · · · ·

Fans would continue to come to *Sex and the City* for solace and inspiration for years to come, and the first sign that *Sex and the City*'s legacy would not fade quickly came courtesy of Jack Berger, of all characters.

Seven months after the show's finale, a book called *He's Just Not That into You*, written by show staffers Greg Behrendt and Liz Tuccillo, arrived in stores. Readers instantly went crazy. The book became a *New York Times* bestseller, hit No. 1 on Amazon, and saw its print run balloon from thirty thousand to four hundred thousand within six weeks of its release. Oprah Winfrey welcomed Behrendt and Tuccillo to her stage. The *New York Times* admired the book's "evil genius"—"it's never you; it's always him"—and praised the "brilliant" title. "Like most chick lit, this book starts from the position that men are emotional criminals and women innocent bystanders," Rick Marin wrote.

"This has become a given, because women own the terms of debate. We live in a world that revolves around *Sex and the City*, *Bridget Jones* and Oprah." This perhaps understated the continuing power of the patriarchy, but you get the point.

It wasn't supposed to be this way. At least not according to anyone who wasn't Tuccillo, who had seen the idea's explosive potential from the second she heard Behrendt say, "He's just not that into you." Even after *Sex and the City*'s six seasons of worldwide success, young women's market power continued to be wildly underestimated—and once again made the careers of those smart enough to recognize it.

After Julie Rottenberg and Elisa Zuritsky, the writers of the episode featuring the famous line, had shrugged off Tuccillo's book idea, Behrendt had agreed to coauthor. After all, he'd uttered the line first. He had no grand expectations, but it seemed like a fun project. He said he'd be most comfortable doing the project if Tuccillo asked him dating-advice questions from the standpoint of a straight woman who sought the guidance of a straight man. That way, he didn't imply any expertise. His answers would represent no more than his opinion.

A typical Behrendt answer went like this: " 'Busy' is another word for 'asshole.' 'Asshole' is another word for the guy you're dating." Or: "Men are never too busy to get what they want." Or: "Let's start with this statistic: You are delicious. Be brave, my sweet. I know you can get lonely. I know you can crave companionship and sex and love so badly that it physically hurts. But I truly believe that the only way you can find out that there's something better out there is to first believe there's something better out there."

After the episode had aired, Behrendt and Tuccillo had written about a third of the book, signed with an agent, and shopped it around. Rejections poured in, including one that said, "This isn't even a magazine article." Only one publisher, Simon Spotlight Entertainment, a division of Simon & Schuster, offered them a deal for what Behrendt remembers as $35,000.

There was a specific reason Simon Spotlight was the one that got it. The imprint had just started under the guidance of a young editor recently promoted to publisher, Jen Bergstrom. She had worked in the children's division at Simon & Schuster. She acquired the rights to kids' shows such as *Bob the Builder* and *Blue's Clues*, then edited books based on them. In her early thirties and child-free, she couldn't stand the thought of editing another board book—those thick, sturdy books made for babies to chew on and occasionally look at.

She'd gotten an offer for a job elsewhere. So she went to her boss, Jack Romanos, the president and CEO of Simon & Schuster, and told him she didn't want to leave, but she'd have to if he couldn't give her a different job within the company. He asked why she was considering the other offer. "Well, they're going to allow me to start an imprint for media tie-ins of all ages," she said. "I would love to do it here." He asked how she'd brand such an imprint. She explained that even though Simon & Schuster published about a thousand books per year, "As a thirty-something-year-old, I don't want to read any of them. I am sending them to my parents and my aunts and my uncles, but I'm not reading them. You're not publishing for an eighteen- to thirty-four-year-old demo."

He agreed to give it a try. Simon Spotlight was born.

The first book she tried to acquire was a tie-in to *Queer Eye for the Straight Guy*, a surprise-hit cable show about a team of gay men who make over straight men. She lost that bidding war.

When Bergstrom then got the proposal for *He's Just Not That into You*, she missed her subway stop because she was so absorbed in it. She had seen every episode of *Sex and the City* multiple times, but the "he's just not that into you" episode was one of her favorites. She remembered watching it for the first time, epiphanies bursting in her head: *Oh, my God. That's happened to me.* Reading now, she had a vision of the cover she wanted—a big picture of an answering machine with a "0" that indicated how many messages it had. Every night she herself would come home from work and, as she unlocked the door, think, *Please let it be blinking with messages, please let it be blinking with messages.*

After she missed her subway stop to keep reading the proposal, she jumped off at the next stop and called the editor who had received it. To Bergstrom, this was a "profoundly important book: It's telling you, 'Don't internalize someone else's negativity, someone else's opinion of yourself.'" She could think of no better way to launch an imprint that targeted eighteen- to thirty-four-year-olds. "We have to buy this book," Bergstrom told her editor on the phone.

Bergstrom still had no titles with which to launch the imprint. The agent selling *He's Just Not That into You*, a young woman named Andrea Barzvi, had all but given up on the sale. She'd put it back into her desk drawer after several rejections. When she had heard about Simon Spotlight, she sent it over, thinking this new imprint might be the idea's last shot. It was the right shot. When Bergstrom met with Behrendt and Tuccillo, she fell in love.

After she signed Behrendt and Tuccillo, Bergstrom sold the idea hard to her sales team, saying, "You cannot underestimate the power of women in pain." The salespeople wondered: How could she charge twenty-two dollars for this skinny, 176-page book? "We will pay any amount of money to have someone talk us out of the pain, or off of the cliff that is the dating world," Bergstrom said. "Especially in New York."

She rallied the young women in the publishing group to get behind the book. She told the publicity department not to send it to the people in charge at morning shows, newspapers, and magazines. "I want you to send the book to the interns," she said. At *The Oprah Winfrey Show*, she wanted the publicists to find twentysomething staffers who watched *Sex and the City*, who were dating—not Oprah herself; the host had famously been with boyfriend Stedman Graham for nearly twenty years by now. Bergstrom knew the marketing had to get around the snobbery of people who hadn't watched *Sex and the City*, who weren't in the trenches of dating, to reach those who had, and who got it.

When Bergstrom was on vacation in August 2004, while getting a mani-pedi in the Hamptons, she got the call telling her *He's Just Not*

That into You would appear on *Oprah*. She had to admit: She felt important. She was vacationing in the Hamptons, getting a call from her publicity director on her cell phone, telling her they got *Oprah*.

Bergstrom called Romanos to tell him. After a few seconds of silence, he said, "Okay, you've got a bestseller here."

After Behrendt and Tuccillo's *Oprah* appearance, Simon Spotlight couldn't keep the book in stock. Teenage girls, adult women, everyone wanted it. HBO, Sarah Jessica Parker, and Ron Livingston did their part to help talk the book up, but the phenomenon was already happening. Women fought over the book in stores. Behrendt was visiting a bookstore himself, where he overheard a woman asking for it and being told they were sold out. He went out to his car and got a copy for her.

The media coverage of the book shortage intensified the buzz. Larry King called. Every major publication called. Maureen Dowd used a play on the title phrase to characterize her feelings about the two US presidential candidates, John Kerry and George W. Bush: "I'm just not that into them," she wrote, launching the phrase further into the zeitgeist. Behrendt and Tuccillo did two sold-out stand-up shows at New York City's Irving Plaza. They played Montreal's prestigious international comedy festival. Behrendt got a talk show of his own.

More than 1.7 million copies have sold in the United States alone since. It has been translated in twenty-eight countries, including Russia, Uruguay, and Mexico. The book was adapted into a hit ensemble romantic comedy in 2009 and opened at No. 1 at the box office. In other words: One line from a *Sex and the City* episode became a bestselling self-help book, which helped launch a book imprint and then became a hit fictional film starring Drew Barrymore, Jennifer Aniston, and Ben Affleck. Unsurprisingly, the film came from a female-run production company: Barrymore's Flower Films.

Bergstrom, who was "very single" when the book was published, remained so afterward, with an annoying caveat. Whenever she complained to friends about her latest dating travails, now they would say, "Excuse me, Jen, you are the publisher of *He's Just Not That into You* and you *still* do not see where this is going?" Her life had become one big *Sex and the City* episode.

Bergstrom—at thirty-three among the youngest publishers at a top-five house ever—made her imprint a known quantity thanks to *He's Just Not That into You*'s success. "This is a book that had not been taken seriously, in my opinion, by other publishers because they thought it was just silly dating advice that didn't have a big audience," Bergstrom says. "And that's because the people who were making the decisions, with all due respect, were maybe a little over the hill."

From its beginning, *Sex and the City* was dismissed for being too female by the patriarchal powers that be. Once again, with *He's Just Not That into You*, its massive market value had been validated by the right woman at the right time. And once again, that instinct had made a young woman into a corporate star.

• • •

He's Just Not That into You represents just a slice of *Sex and the City*'s continuing cultural resonance. Moments and elements of the show might play as out-of-date now, but that's partly because of how much it helped advance depictions and perceptions of women and sexuality. The *Guardian* named Carrie Bradshaw an "icon of the decade," with an accompanying piece by feminist author Naomi Wolf saying that Carrie "did as much to shift the culture around certain women's issues as real-life female groundbreakers."

Brunch and shoe shopping have become shorthand for "girls' time." Thanks in part to *Sex and the City*, the term "hooking up"—having sex without emotional attachments, like Samantha—went national due to countless trend pieces. By now, everyone knows you can't order a cosmopolitan, lest you out yourself as a *Sex and the City* imitator.

What shocked or thrilled viewers about *Sex and the City* when it premiered has woven itself into everyday life in much of Middle America. Gay culture, for instance, went mainstream—a significant development that would lead to widespread acceptance of gay marriage, and ultimately its legalization in 2015. After New York State made gay marriage legal, journalist Jesse Oxfeld wrote a piece for the *Observer* encapsulating all of these changes. The headline: "Yesterday, an Oppressed Minority, Today, an Old Maid." *Sex and the City* underwent an analogous transformation: yesterday, feminist pioneers, today, basic bitches.

Being single also went mainstream. *Sex and the City* anticipated a seismic shift in American demography: By 2009, unmarried women outnumbered married ones, possibly for the first time in American history. As Carrie once said, "Being single used to mean that nobody wanted you. Now it means you're pretty sexy and you're taking your time deciding how you want your life to be and who you want to spend it with."

As the series continued to run in syndication on cable channels such as TBS and E! in the United States as well as around the world, it gained a new generation of fans searching for guidance in sex, love, and friendship as they entered adulthood. The show also began streaming on Amazon Prime, where it picked up still more young fans.

Watching it from start to finish became a rite of passage for many young women and young gay men in particular. Writer Ryan Roschke was getting over his first breakup at age twenty-two when he started watching nightly: "After I suffered through all my college lectures for the day, I'd watch one or five or ten episodes," he wrote on *PopSugar*. He found inspiration in the characters' resilience: "Time after time, [Carrie] finds herself on the verge of collapse, of utter loss, and she always picks herself up, slips into some Manolo Blahniks, throws on a f*cking fabulous outfit, and moves on. . . . My heart hurt a little less with every passing day. I did what Carrie did: I kept living, and I kept breathing."

THE FEUD RETURNS

Even after it ended, *Sex and the City* couldn't shake reports of the rumored feud between Cattrall and Parker—a keen level of interest that further indicated the show's continuing resonance, for better or worse.

Days after the finale, a *New York Post* story once again mentioned the supposed rift between Cattrall and Parker. *Newsweek* reported that the two didn't greet each other on the set. *Us Weekly* noted that Parker mentioned Davis and Nixon but not Cattrall when Larry King asked if she was friends with her costars. At that year's Golden Globes, the magazine further emphasized, Davis, Nixon, and Parker attended the after-parties without Cattrall.

Rumors flared again when HBO confirmed on May 24, 2004, that it had abandoned plans for a movie follow-up to the series; several reports linked the decision to the rumored cast discord. Cattrall had, in fact, backed out of the movie plans to play Hayden Panettiere's mom in the Disney film *Ice Princess*. "Kim and the girls were promised a script by a certain date," her publicist told *Us Weekly*. "The script never came, so Kim took a movie." *Variety* reported that Cattrall had asked for script approval on the *Sex and the City* movie and the same salary as Parker, but Cattrall's rep countered that all four stars had script approval and salary parity—Cattrall was neither a diva nor an anomaly. Parker did get more money than the others, but as a producer.

A long two years later, reports of the feud were still simmering. In 2006, the *Times of India* ran an account that Davis was "pleading" with Cattrall and Parker to end their bickering so a movie follow-up could be made. However, the newspaper's only actual quote from Davis on the matter was: "If [a movie] happened, I would be the happiest person ever on the planet." As for Cattrall, the paper said she "refused to sign up for the project, infuriating Parker."

Cattrall later acknowledged that she did, indeed, push for a higher salary on the film. "I ain't got no rich husband," said Cattrall, who divorced jazz musician Mark Levinson the year the show ended. "I ain't got no sugar daddy. . . . I felt that with the series I was losing a job, we were all losing our jobs." She further explained to the Canadian magazine *Maclean's* in 2008 that she had needed a break immediately after the finale, especially because of her divorce.

Cattrall at that time was still hurting from the end of the show, which she had hoped would continue longer. She wished she had been more included in the decision to end the series that was made by Parker and the other producers, she later said. She also felt a bit underappreciated at the time of the show, which she has said contributed to both her decision not to have children and the demise of her relationship: "You know your counterpart's making a million dollars an episode. And I knew that we were never going to get that, but I felt that we had worked a lot of nineteen-hour days; I lost a marriage to the series, and a lot of friends. You just have no life."

• • •

Sex and the City's influence on the shows that have followed it is clear. The 2007–08 TV season brought a spate of blatant attempts at *Sex and the City: The Next Generation* to broadcast networks, with *Lipstick Jungle* and *Cashmere Mafia*—both *Sex*-like shows featuring powerful businesswoman-types—and *Big Shots*—a male take on *Sex*. Network executives were unapologetic about the comparison: "I had a clear, emotional reaction to *Sex and the City*," NBC executive vice president Teri Weinberg told *Mediaweek*. "You always ask yourself, 'How do you do that again? How do you create another version? How do you explore relationships from that unique point of view?'"

Lipstick Jungle, incidentally, was adapted from a Candace Bushnell novel, while Darren Star created *Cashmere Mafia*. Star waved off all comparisons. "It's interesting that there can be countless *CSI* and *Law & Order* clones, but when you're doing a series about the lives of women, it's seen as derivative of *Sex and the City*," he told *Mediaweek*. "There's a lot of room to do shows from a female point of view."

But so few had done so before *Sex and the City* that the comparisons were still inevitable, and despite Star's reticence, they were a compliment to his original creation. None of those shows lasted more than a season or two, but they proved that media companies wanted more *Sex and the City*.

Soon movie plans were a go.

In reality, the cast "feud" and salary disputes hadn't been the only roadblocks to a film version of *Sex and the City*. Movie executives hesitated to invest too much in the idea. Few shows had made the transition from TV to film—particularly in a direct iteration, not a remake or a parody like *The Brady Bunch* or *The Dukes of Hazzard*. Even more important, film studios continued to resist female-driven movies. They believed men wouldn't go to see them, and an all-female audience wouldn't be enough to make a profit.

King was convinced he had at least one story left to tell: Carrie getting married. He felt it was an event too big for just a TV movie. He knew it would work as a big-budget film, but he had to convince studio executives that it was worth the investment. When he and Parker pitched it to the studio, he estimated it would make $50 million in its first weekend. The studio estimated much lower—$30 million for the entire theatrical run—but agreed it was worth a shot.

They finally got the green light in July 2007 to bring their glitz to the big screen. This time, Cattrall signed on along with the rest of the core four.

From the first day of filming on location in New York that September, the production was mobbed with screaming fans and paparazzi. Security guards and New York City police officers did their best to maintain order. Every time one of the four actresses said a line, shrieks followed. Cattrall said to Nixon, "Don't you feel like a Beatle? Just let me be John. I want to be John." They all seemed happy to be back, Cattrall later said, despite the chaos.

Patricia Field returned to oversee the costumes, with the fashion more glamorous than even the final seasons of the show. Designers flew in racks full of wedding dresses from across the world to be contenders for Carrie's nuptials. As the winner, Field chose a distinctive Vivienne Westwood with a strapless bodice, exaggerated points swooping up like meringues from each breast, and further draped dollops of meringue dripping down to form the layered, full gown.

Field again talked King into a ludicrous statement item for Carrie:

a teal life-sized-bird fascinator that secured her veil to her head for her intended wedding to Big.

"What do you mean you're putting a bird on her head?" King asked.

"Once again, I don't have a legitimate argument," Parker recalls saying. "But I'm telling you, this bird is extraordinary."

"I've got to see the bird."

They showed him the bird, secured to Parker's head, while she was in full costume in a Park Avenue building's vestibule on location. Parker twirled for King. "She worked that bird like no one's ever worked a bird," King says. He agreed to the bird.

But it was such a bold choice, King felt he had to put the bird into his script. After the first disastrous wedding attempt, with Big bolting before they could exchange vows, Carrie cries, underlining her dedication to Big: "I put a bird on my head!"

Miranda replies: "Is that what that was? I thought it was feathers." The confused thought echoed that of many viewers who eventually saw it in the movie.

The Big-Carrie union eventually becomes official in an understated courthouse outing later in the film. With a wedding and its final outcome to protect, King took similar precautions with the movie to what he did with the series finale, shooting alternate scenes and endings to keep the major plot points secret. He and the actresses often batted away questions about publicly filmed scenes by saying they were "dream sequences." At one point when word leaked to the press that there was a wedding in the movie, Kim Cattrall exited her trailer in Midtown wearing a full wedding gown as she walked to the set—even though, to be clear, her character couldn't have been further from walking down the aisle.

Sex and the City, the movie, premiered in theaters in 2008 with a plot stuffed full of fan service (lots of fashion montages), gross-out humor (there is a trip to Mexico and the requisite digestive issues), friendship, and heartbreak. Charlotte is married to Harry and raising their adopted daughter, Lily; Miranda and Steve are together in Brooklyn with son

Brady; Samantha has moved to Los Angeles to be with her movie-star boyfriend, Smith. And, of course, Carrie and Big are now contemplating marriage. Carrie's move out of her apartment prompts an indulgent fashion montage for the ages, with her modeling several familiar outfits from the series for her friends, including the iconic tutu from the opening credits.

Some of the audience members were thrilled, and others disappointed all over again, with King's insistence on a happy ending for the troubled couple. I, for one, let go of my ideas about what this franchise was supposed to do and enjoyed the nostalgia and fun. I had given up on Carrie's independence with the show's finale. But Mandy Len Catron later wrote in her book *How to Fall in Love with Anyone*, "It is difficult to locate your own sense of value in a world that is still preoccupied by Cinderella stories, where entire shelves of airport newsstands are full of bridal magazines, and even *Sex and the City* ends with a wedding." She makes a fair point, of course.

SEX REIGNS AT THE BOX OFFICE

Individual fans' reactions to the plot aside, with the movie's opening, King found his box office projections proven right and then some. He had a good feeling as soon as he saw lines full of excited women outside Los Angeles movie theaters on opening day, many dressed up beyond your standard multiplex garb. When the show had been airing, he hadn't been able to see his success standing in front of him like this. For the first time, he could sit back and watch his achievement materialize.

When I went with friends in Los Angeles on opening night, women clustered in pods of three to five friends. We had to sit in the front row of a packed theater, scrunching down in our seats and tilting our heads back to see the screen towering over us because everyone else had gotten there so early. The entire place cheered as soon as the updated version of the jazzy theme song began.

The movie made $26 million on its opening night in the United

States and Canada, and $56 million in its first weekend, nearly twice what the studio had estimated for its entire run. It was the biggest opening ever for an R-rated film and a film with a female lead (adjusted for inflation). Analysts were surprised when it beat *Indiana Jones and the Kingdom of the Crystal Skull*.

Reviews were middling to good. The *San Francisco Chronicle*'s Mick LaSalle called it "the best American movie about women so far this year. Indeed, at the rate Hollywood has been going, it may stand as the best women's movie until *Sex and the City 2*, if that ever comes along."

It was dubbed a "surprise" hit—because film executives continued to underestimate the power of female audiences—taking in $415.2 million globally over its run. It changed business practices in the film industry, opening minds to the idea of blockbuster comedies and R-rated films that star women. Thanks to *Sex and the City*, Hollywood discovered it could make money by pleasing professional, adult women. *Bridesmaids*, *Trainwreck*, and the all-female *Ghostbusters* remake followed in years to come.

And now Hollywood, being Hollywood, wanted to repeat this successful trick. Soon plans were under way for a second *Sex and the City* movie.

King pondered how to tackle it, and knew that even in the short, two-year gap between films, the world was changing rapidly. The first movie came out in May 2008, and then the stock market crashed that September. The economy tanked. With a franchise that depends upon extravagance, what's a sequel to do? If people, including the four heroines, couldn't afford as much anymore, King thought, where would they go for a little indulgence? He was also trying to tie the movie into the theme of women's liberation and make it feel current.

He opened the script with the wedding of the TV show's two recurring gay characters, Stanford Blatch and Anthony Marantino, played by Willie Garson and Mario Cantone. For the main story line, King sent the women on an all-expenses-paid vacation, courtesy of Samantha's PR business, to Abu Dhabi. King planned the movie as a commentary on the Middle East's abominable treatment of women. His vision: These liberated American women would laugh in the face of such patriarchy. Samantha would throw condoms at religious men and yell, "I have sex!" It would provide a broad, farcical take on America's volatile, era-defining culture clash with the region. And the vacation plot would cleverly allow the focus to remain on the four women's relationships with each other, unburdened by husbands.

Filming started in 2009 in Manhattan, followed by Monaco and Morocco standing in for the United Arab Emirates. The Emirates declined to allow the movie to shoot there, which further underlined the cultural differences King's script highlighted.

Alas, King's feel for the zeitgeist this time was off.

King is the first to admit it. He says now that he may have "miscalculated what people would be in the mood for." But he stands behind the "beauty and the audacious comedy and culture-clashing danger" of the second film. "Plus," he adds, "the ladies were on camels . . . so lighten up, everybody."

Reviewers savaged the film. LaSalle, who gave the first film a favorable review, wrote: "Twenty minutes in, the movie is already operating at a deficit, and it never recovers. It can't recover, because it never finds something that it wants to say, or a story that it needs to tell." Even *Us Weekly*, normally a cheerleader for the industry, called it "as cheesy as a bad designer knockoff." The publication *Sight & Sound* noted, on the one hand, the "squealing audience stampede" that accompanied their reviewer at a preview. The film, however, was a "trashy, wealth-fetishizing travelogue": "Underneath the laughable jeopardy of the plot (the foursome's biggest terror is that they will be forced to fly home in economy class), the movie teems with large (and largely unexamined) female fears around aging. . . . None of the actresses—weighed down by Patricia Field's fancy-dress fashion-porn costuming and shot from a variety of unflattering angles—gives much of a performance, Kim Cattrall's lascivious Samantha ('He's the Lawrence of my labia') faring worst of all."

Variety's Brian Lowry noted its "not-very-convincing rumination on the treatment of Muslim women—even in what's supposed to be a relatively progressive Arab country—that seems more condescending than stirring." *USA Today*'s Claudia Puig wrote: "With his Cosmopolitan-style approach to all things feminine, director Michael Patrick King is out of his league attempting to comment on the inequitable treatment of Muslim women. He ends up mocking religious beliefs and making Carrie and her friends appear insensitive."

Parker later said that she recognized why fans and critics alike hated the film: "I understand, I actually get it," she said. "I can see where we fell short on that movie, and I'm perfectly happy to say that publicly."

Yet the 2010 release still made nearly $300 million worldwide. Fans were so dedicated that critics didn't seem to affect the box office. That said, it's hard to calculate the cost of making a bad movie: A better film could have made even more money, and it could have secured *Sex and the City*'s legacy. It also could have made *Sex and the City 3* a surer thing.

But if nothing else, *Sex and the City 2* marked a true victory for older women in movies: The characters were all over forty, with one over fifty. None of them played a grandmother, or even a crazy aunt. New Line, the company that distributed the *Sex and the City* films, called them "the Super Bowl for women"—a powerful, if sexist, statement on their economic lure.

• • •

Through early 2018, press reports continued to obsess nearly weekly over whether there would be a *Sex and the City 3* and, yes, that feud.

In late 2016, a new spate of Internet reports speculated about the prospect of another movie. *Radar Online* claimed Parker was holding up the operation because she didn't like the script, which would depict her as "more mature." These reports infuriated Parker. She had never in her life objected to any script King had written. Parker says she was the first to sign on for a third film when he finished a script in mid-2017.

But in fall of 2017, Cattrall publicly said she was hanging up

Samantha's stilettos for good—she had no intention of playing the character again in a third movie or anything else. "That was part of turning sixty," she told Piers Morgan in a TV interview. "How many years do I have left and what do I want to do with it? What haven't I done? I feel that the show is the best when it's the series, and the bonus was the two movies." She insisted her decision had nothing to do with pushing for more money or contract perks.

Parker also expressed her resulting frustration in the press, making it hard to deny some semblance of at least a professional conflict, if not a *feud*, between her and her former costar: "We had this beautiful, funny, heartbreaking, joyful, very relatable script and story," she said. "It's not just disappointing that we don't get to tell the story and have that experience, but more so for that audience that has been so vocal in wanting another movie."

The feud would continue to flare up in the press from time to time in the future, but it seemed likely that any future *Sex and the City* films would not include Kim Cattrall in her career-defining role.

· · ·

With or without plans for a movie, the principals' careers naturally carried on after *Sex and the City*'s end. Executive producer Michael Patrick King returned to HBO in 2005 with *The Comeback*, a mockumentary comedy he created with *Friends* actress Lisa Kudrow. She starred as Valerie Cherish, a sitcom star who tries to revive her career with a reality show. It ended after one season because of an initially middling response from critics and viewers. But its cringe-inducing humor made it a cult hit whose popularity grew over time, and it returned for a second hilarious and heartbreaking season nine years later.

In 2011, King cocreated another female-driven show, this time with comedian Whitney Cummings. *2 Broke Girls* follows two waitresses as they start a cupcake business, one of them played by Kat Dennings— once the rich bat mitzvah girl in the *Sex and the City* episode "Hot Child in the City."

Davis channeled her fame into charity work. She spends a large portion of her time supporting the David Sheldrick Wildlife Trust, which fights illegal poaching of elephants, as well as Oxfam, which combats global poverty, and the United Nations Refugee Agency. She also explored theater, making her Broadway debut in the 2012 revival of political drama *The Best Man* and her West End debut as the wronged wife in a stage adaptation of *Fatal Attraction.*

Cattrall chose to work mostly in productions based in the country where she was born, England, and the country where she was raised, Canada. She spent time onstage in a production of *Antony and Cleopatra* at the Liverpool Playhouse and in *Sweet Bird of Youth* at London's Old Vic. From 2014 to 2016, she starred in the HBO Canada series *Sensitive Skin*, playing a woman struggling with aging after being known for her beauty in her younger years.

Cynthia Nixon starred in movies such as Mark Levin's *Little Manhattan* and continued to live in New York with her two children and girlfriend Christine Marinoni. (The two also had a son together in 2011.) Nixon returned to Broadway in 2006 in the drama *Rabbit Hole* as a woman recovering from the death of her four-year-old son. Her husband was played by John Slattery, who had appeared on *Sex and the City* as Carrie's politician paramour with a pee fetish. Critic David Rooney wrote of Nixon's stage performance: "Creating a field of anxiety around her, Nixon's controlled, naturalistic work is faultless here." She won a Tony for the role, and another in 2017 for her work in the drama *The Little Foxes.*

Nixon also became a prominent marriage-equality activist. She announced her engagement to Marinoni at a 2009 rally: "We could go to Canada, and we could go to Connecticut, and we could even go to Iowa, but we don't want to," she told the crowd. That October she spoke at the giant National Equality March in Washington, DC. Marriage equality became law in New York in 2011, and Nixon married Marinoni on May 27, 2012.

One happy result from the scuttled *Sex and the City 3* plans: It freed Nixon to pursue her political ambitions. In March 2018, she announced she would challenge incumbent New York State Governor Andrew Cuomo for the Democratic nomination leading into that fall's elections. She ran on a progressive platform focused on eradicating income inequality and fixing the ailing New York City subway system, a city-centric approach that Miranda would be proud of. Her candidacy felt like the perfect culmination of *Sex and the City*'s legacy: One of its stars—who played a smart, successful, feminist lawyer—joining a record number of other women running for office in 2018.

SEX GETS ITS DUE

As the mediocre movies faded from view and the original series returned to the center of *Sex and the City*'s critical legacy, its reputation began to recover.

The CW network aired a tastefully sweet prequel series, *The Carrie Diaries*, in 2013. The show was based on Candace Bushnell's novel of the same name, which imagines Carrie growing up in the 1980s in Connecticut's New York City suburbs. *Sex and the City* writer Amy B. Harris, who had been working on the network's series *Gossip Girl*, handled the TV adaptation. She felt the pressure of maintaining the show's legacy: "It made me want to vomit every day," she says. She got through it by reminding herself that King had chosen her, specifically, to create the show.

The show's two seasons follow young Carrie as she falls in love for the first time, considers sex, interns at *Interview* magazine, and helps her gay friend as he comes out of the closet. Harris had to negotiate some tricky story territory: Namely, she decided to follow the book's lead and have Carrie growing up with a single dad after her mother died. In *Sex and the City* the television show, Carrie rarely mentions her family, but when she does, she indicates that her father left the family when she was five.

The resulting series got a mixed reception from critics. "Ironically, since Carrie is still a virgin, there's still something quite innocent about the series," Tim Goodman wrote in the *Hollywood Reporter.* "It's kind of quaint and far less cynical than *Gossip Girl.*" But *New York*'s Matt Zoller Seitz reamed it as an angst-fest whose power was depleted by broadcast-network blandness, joyless and boring in comparison to its adult predecessor. He concludes: "The problem is that *The Carrie Diaries* is an inept spinoff that dishonors its source."

His bashing of *Carrie*, however, hinted at the redemption under way for *Sex and the City* itself.

No less than the *New Yorker*'s Pulitzer Prize–winning TV critic, Emily Nussbaum, rose to the show's defense in 2013 when she read the book *Difficult Men: Behind the Scenes of a Creative Revolution*, Brett Martin's paean to *The Sopranos* and other troubled-white-guy shows that helped launch the so-called Golden Age of Television of the 2000s. Martin had written dismissively of *Sex and the City*: "It might as well have been a tourism campaign for a post–Rudolph Giuliani, de-ethnicized Gotham awash in money. Its characters were types as familiar as those in *The Golden Girls*: the Slut, the Prude, the Career Woman, the Heroine."

While his assessments weren't inaccurate, they emphasize the series's superficial traits and ignore its innovations. Somehow he forgot that *Sex and the City* predated *The Sopranos* and actually launched the network's filmic approach to television, for starters. "The condescension is palpable," Nussbaum writes. She distinguishes *Sex and the City* from the fluff it's often compared with. After Carrie falls for Mr. Big, Nussbaum says, "pleasurable as *Sex and the City* remained, it also felt designed to push back at its audience's wish for identification, triggering as much anxiety as relief. It switched the romantic comedy's primal scene, from 'Me, too!' to 'Am I like *her*?' A man practically woven out of red flags, Big wasn't there to rescue Carrie; instead, his 'great love' was a slow poisoning."

Nussbaum concludes: "So why is the show so often portrayed as a set of empty, static cartoons, an embarrassment to womankind? It's a classic misunderstanding, I think, stemming from an unexamined hierarchy: the assumption that anything stylized (or formulaic, or pleasurable, or funny, or feminine, or explicit about sex rather than about violence, or made collaboratively) must be inferior." She wonders if a different finale would have solidified a different critical fate for the series: "[I]n the final round, *Sex and the City* pulled its punches, and let Big rescue Carrie. It honored the wishes of its heroine, and at least half of the audience, and it gave us a very memorable dress, too. But it also showed a failure of nerve, an inability of the writers to imagine, or to trust themselves to portray, any other kind of ending—happy or not."

The same year Nussbaum's piece ran, Starlee Kine argued on *New York* magazine's *Vulture* site, "What I find so unusual about *SATC* is that it allowed its characters to express that they were dissatisfied and sad. If they felt lonely, they said it, without meta commentary and while still keeping it funny. There's very much a pre-*SATC* world and a post-one, and there is something refreshing and authentic about this show being able to have done this." She even defended the finale as "optimistic and satisfying because it hadn't felt like a foregone conclusion, even though [Big and Carrie had] been getting back together off and on since the pilot."

Besides critical defense of the show's social statements, the Internet is also home to pure, still-budding fandom, as demonstrated by a variety of devotional projects that rethink *Sex and the City* in modern terms. In 2016, stylist Chelsea Fairless and writer-director Lauren Garroni launched an Instagram feed (@everyoutfitonsatc) that tracks every outfit from the series. It had reached 435,000 followers by January 2018. They've embraced Miranda as their spirit *Sex and the City* character— a sentiment common among many younger fans of the show who identify with her intelligence and ambition.

Another Instagram hit known as Carrie Dragshaw personifies the show's queer influence in a bold way never seen before. Dan Clay moved to New York City to seek out the *Sex and the City* lifestyle and found an apartment blocks away from Carrie's apartment exterior on

Perry Street in the West Village. He took on his Internet-famous persona and mass following after he dressed as Carrie Bradshaw for Halloween in 2016. A photo of him in his costume went viral, and he began to pose in a new outfit weekly, gathering 88,000 followers by January 2018. "I watch *Sex and the City* the way that some people read William Faulkner," he told the *New York Post*.

The show continues to demonstrate a direct influence on the next generation of female comedians and writers. It's the obvious forerunner of Lena Dunham's influential, equally loved and loathed HBO show *Girls*. The show began in 2012, telling the story of girls in their twenties who learned about sex by watching *Sex and the City* and are now trying it out to questionable results. Comic Amy Schumer spoofed the *Sex and the City* bus tour in a 2016 sketch in which a cheaper version features only Steve-related sites.

Comedy Central's *Broad City* turns *Sex and the City* inside out, with a focus on the almost obsessive friendship between two Brooklyn women, played by cocreators Abbi Jacobson and Ilana Glazer, and no glamour at all. Its 2016 season premiere paid direct homage to *Sex and the City*, with Ilana's boyfriend, Lincoln, graduating from the same trapeze school Carrie attends in the sixth-season episode "The Catch." Lincoln, a key figure in the show's subversion of gender roles, explains that he was inspired by *Sex and the City*: "The Miranda in me thought I'm out of my comfort zone, but the Carrie in me couldn't resist. So I did it." Abbi responds, "You know what? I'm really a Miranda-Carrie, too, I think with a little bit of Charlotte, even though she really annoys me." The joke is twofold: First, it's Lincoln—a straight black man—who is acting out a *Sex and the City* lifestyle fantasy. Second, the rest of the episode—like most of the show—features decidedly unglamorous New York City exploits. Ilana drops her bike-lock key in a subway grate, which means she must spend the rest of the episode with a heavy bike chain around her waist. She and Abbi endure violence at a sample sale. Abbi gets stuck in a porta-potty. And Ilana (thanks to her bike chain) gets stuck to a van, which drives away with her on its bumper.

The *Sex and the City* heroines, as harrowing as their love lives sometimes seemed, were in little danger of any of these indignities happening to them.

Issa Rae's HBO comedy *Insecure* draws directly from *Sex and the City* for its relationship plot lines and sex dissections among female friends, moving those concepts from white New York of the 2000s to black Los Angeles of the 2010s. The show also takes *Sex and the City*'s approach to character development—and even social statement—via uncomfortable sex scenes. In one, Issa's ex, Lawrence, comes by to pick up a few of his things from their formerly shared apartment, and the two have unexpected, wordless sex on the sofa that lasts mere seconds before he takes off. In another, Lawrence is seduced by a white woman and an Asian woman for a threesome, only to be exposed to their blatantly racist expectations. The results are surprising, riveting, hilarious, and heartbreaking, just as *Sex and the City* was in its heyday.

• • •

The *Sex and the City* actresses are still most strongly associated with their roles on the show, none more so than Sarah Jessica Parker.

In 2016 Parker returned to HBO to star in *Divorce*, a dark comedy about the dissolution of a marriage. Until *Divorce*, she had sworn off television after the roller coaster of *Sex and the City*. She and Matthew Broderick had two more children, twins Marion and Tabitha, in 2009, bringing their total to three. She served as vice-chair of the New York City Ballet and launched a fragrance line and the SJP shoe collection. She opened a boutique in Las Vegas.

When she rejoined the melee on TV with *Divorce*, she found herself on the defensive: "This is not Carrie in the suburbs, Carrie the commuter," she told the *New York Times*. "And I kind of want to get ahead of that, so that there is not this giant heave of disappointment when people find the show is not . . . that same buoyant kind of thing."

Parker says she doesn't mind the burden of such a legacy. Almost daily, young women tag her in Instagram posts that declare their joy over moving to New York City to start their Carrie Bradshaw lives. She worries about them a little. But it touches her heart.

Still, she admits that she tries to steer clear of the *Sex and the City* tour bus that comes through her West Village neighborhood, stopping at the Pleasure Chest sex toy shop and loitering across the street from Magnolia Bakery while passengers eat Buttercup cupcakes. The tour continues to fill up at least once a day—twice on Fridays and Saturdays. Now, many of the tourists come from overseas, including China, the UK, Australia, and Germany. One thing unites them: They found a spark of inspiration in Carrie, Charlotte, Miranda, and Samantha. And they want to experience a little piece of those fictional lives with others who feel the same.

Perhaps that makes sense. Fans discover and rewatch episodes via streaming, DVD, or sanitized-for-broadcast reruns at home on their own. But *Sex and the City*'s true legacy is best enjoyed with friends, or even strangers on a tour bus who also found comfort in four women who dared to be single and sexual on television at a time when few were.

King puts their legacy simply: "You are not alone." Whether you're on the bus tour, watching *Sex and the City* on Amazon Prime while nursing your latest heartbreak, or toasting girls' night unapologetically with pink drinks, Carrie, Charlotte, Miranda, and Samantha are with you. So are the writers and producers of *Sex and the City*. And so are all of us, the fans whose lives changed a little, or a lot, because of this groundbreaking, imperfect, revolutionary show.

Acknowledgments

Everyone I talked to said the same thing: The *Sex and the City* set was a warm, familial place, no matter how intense the media attention got, no matter how glitzy the production looked on-screen. Those at the center of the production—the creators, writers, and actors—welcomed me into that family and generously shared its history with me. I'm overwhelmed with gratitude for Sarah Jessica Parker, Kristin Davis, David Eigenberg, Darren Star, Michael Patrick King, Greg Behrendt, Jenny Bicks, Cindy Chupack, Amy B. Harris, Julie Rottenberg, and Elisa Zuritsky. Not only did they graciously grant me interviews, but they also continued to work with me to nail down the details of their stories. Julie, thank you for the incredibly intimate personal photos, meticulously scanned and captioned. Cindy, thank you for sharing pages from your impressive notebook archives with us.

Those who shared their personal stories of *Sex and the City*'s effect on their lives also helped to illuminate what this show means to people. So did outside expert extraordinaire Veronica Chambers, who had so many informed perspectives on the series that she shows up in several sections: She is a fan, a journalist who covered the show, an expert on Japanese women's reactions to the series, and a cultural critic who edited the beautiful book *The Meaning of Michelle*. If you want to bask in the glow of strong women writing about a strong woman, check out her anthology of tributes to First Lady Michelle Obama.

Thank you to the best reading team around: Andrea Bartz, Erin Carlson, Heather Wood Rudúlph, and A. K. Whitney edited this thing like it was their job. Kristin McGonigle, your beautiful transcriptions saved my life. Moises Mendez became an indispensable assistant. And as always, A. Jesse Jiryu Davis should get as much credit for this as I do, from his all-around support during a particularly hard year, to his meticulous editing skills, to his endurance of a lot of talk about shoes, cupcakes, Big, Aidan, and bad sex puns. I couldn't help but wonder how much couldn't-help-but-wondering he could take.

Agent Laurie Abkemeier made magic yet again. Jon Karp, Karyn Marcus, and the rest of the team at Simon & Schuster have made me happy to have a literary home.

Extra love to my Chicago office, Dave Freiberg and Bill O'Meara, who housed me for a large portion of what turned out to be an insane phase for all of us. The wine, the food, *The Handmaid's Tale* and *First Dates*, the view, the parties, the unwavering support . . . you are my home away from home and my family away from family. And love to my actual family—Mom, Julie, and Scott—who continue to show up and celebrate me even in our most difficult times.

Source Notes

1

The Real Carrie Bradshaw

2 Candy, as her family called her: Bob Morris, "Weddings: Vows; Candace Bushnell, Charles Askegard," *New York Times*, July 7, 2002.

3 magazine had just launched in 1978: *Night* magazine (official website), accessed August 24, 2017, http://www.nightmag.com/night .html.

3 career advice from Barbara Walters: *Ladies' Home Journal*, June 1979.

3 "Calorie Watchers Cookbook": *Good Housekeeping*, January 1980.

3 "Are You Lying to Yourself about Sex?": *Self*, March 1981.

4 "practically skipped up Park Avenue": Candace Bushnell, *Sex and the City* (New York: Grand Central Publishing, 2001), ix.

6 "was doing advanced postgraduate work": Hadley Freeman, "Rereading Sex and the City by Candace Bushnell," *Guardian*, April 19, 2013.

7 "Shopgirls knew that dressing": Moira Weigel, *The Invention of Dating* (New York: Farrar, Straus and Giroux, 2016), 48.

7 "River Wilde": Elizabeth Snead, "The Underside of Big-City 'Sex,'" *USA Today*, December 2, 1999.

7 who drove a Ferrari: Jay McInerney, "Goodbye, Mr. Big," *New York*, May 10, 2004.

8 "drowning": Morris, "Candace Bushnell, Charles Askegard."

9 "The day it became evident": Kate Bolick, *Spinster* (New York: Penguin Random House, 2015), 135.

10 "mildly amusing": Jonathan Yardley, "Naked Ambition," *Washington Post*, August 28, 1996.

10 Jay McInerney and Tama Janowitz: Sandra Tsing Loh, "No One Has Affairs to Remember Anymore," *Los Angeles Times*, July 28, 1996.

10 "opulent debasement that suffuses this collection": "Sex and the City," *Publishers Weekly*, July 29, 1996.

10 "perfectly normal behavior": Alex Kuczynski, "View; Dear Diary: Get Real," *New York Times*, June 14, 1998.

10 "concerns itself almost entirely": Meghan Daum, "Keeping Up with Ms. Jones," *Village Voice*, June 30, 1998.

12 youngest person to run: Bill Carter, "A Soap Opera Ends: Let the Comedies Begin," *New York Times*, August 7, 1996.

12 waiting for her to fail: Lynn Hirschberg, "Jamie Tarses' Fall, as Scheduled," *New York Times Magazine*, July 13, 1997.

14 "California-style": Candace Bushnell, "Darren Does Gotham," *Vogue*, September 1995.

16 "insipid, tiresome": Rita Kempley, "If Looks Could Kill," *Washington Post*, March 15, 1991.

18 a mere $60,000: Emily Gould, "Candace Bushnell Wasn't Paid Much for 'Sex,'" *Gawker*, January 9, 2007.

18 "a unique voice": Anya Sacharow, "'90210' Creator Has Eye for Sex Columnist," *Mediaweek*, March 11, 1996.

19 "could change NoHo": Monte Williams, "Neighborhood Report: Lower Manhattan Update; In-Crowd's Bowery Bar Wins Its Battle," *New York Times*, February 12, 1995.

19 "Everyone and everything": David N. Herszenhorn, "Neighborhood Report: West Village; Shifting Shadows and Multiple Personality of the Meatpacking District," *New York Times*, February 5, 1995.

22 networks had noticed the weakness: Terry Jackson, "There's No Summer Vacation for Network Competition," *Chicago Tribune*, June 10, 1998.

22 less than 50 percent: Ibid.

2

A New Kind of TV Woman

27 "Everything that has happened": Michael Specter, "Bimbo? Sarah Jessica Parker Begs to Differ," *New York Times*, September 20, 1992.

27 "the Kennedy fiasco": Ibid.

27 "lethally charming": Rebecca Wallwork, "Sex and Sarah Jessica Parker," *Daily Telegraph*, May 10, 2008.

29 "I was excited": Amy Sohn, *Sex and the City: Kiss and Tell* (New York: Melcher Media, 2004), 85.

30 "formidably self-possessed": Leslie Bennetts, "New Faces: Cynthia Nixon and Amy Wright, Two Versions of the Sophisticated Adolescent Brat," *New York Times*, December 5, 1980.

30 "I Happen to Like New York": Mervyn Rothstein, "Despite a Dash of HBO Fame, the Lure Is Still the Stage," *New York Times*, November 29, 1999.

30 twenty-five plays: Ibid.

31 breastfed her newborn daughter: Sohn, *Sex and the City: Kiss and Tell*, 86.

36 playing a sexy role at forty-one: Kenneth Whyte, "Kim Cattrall Talks to Kenneth Whyte about Money and Aging, the New Movie, and the One Thing She Wouldn't Do Onscreen," *Maclean's*, April 28, 2008.

36 read a little more than half: Chris Sullivan, "Sex Icon? I've Just Piled on 20 Pounds! Kim Cattrall Says She'll Do ANYTHING to Leave Sex and the City Behind," *Daily Mail*, July 29, 2011.

36 never liked the idea of people who were interested: Whyte, "Kim Cattrall Talks to Kenneth Whyte."

36 didn't like the idea of her playing libertine Samantha Jones: Lisa DePaulo, "Woman on Top," *New York*, October 23, 2000.

37 "I feel like I'm over the hill": Whyte, "Kim Cattrall Talks to Kenneth Whyte."

38 "unfulfilling": Kim Cattrall and Mark Levinson, *Satisfaction: The Art of the Female Orgasm* (New York: Hachette Book Group, 2002), 13.

38 longer to get over: Sohn, *Sex and the City: Kiss and Tell*, 107.

38 "Samantha is street-smart": Ibid., 108.

38 "mayor of Hollywood": Brantley Bardin, "Q&A: Willie Garson," *Out*, June 2000.

39 "I've had a lot of intense": Dennis Hensley, "Chris Noth: Big Deal," *Movieline*, February 1, 2000.

39 smoking "herb": Ibid.

39 "All you have me doing": Ibid.

42 "The overemphasis on danger": Carole Vance, ed., *Pleasure and Danger: Exploring Female Sexuality* (Boston: Routledge and Kegan Paul, 1985), 7.

42 "I don't see how": Mary Cross, *Madonna: A Biography* (Westport, CT: Greenwood Press, 2007), 58.

3

Building *Sex and the City*'s New York

59 "She's actually old-fashioned": Sohn, *Sex and the City: Kiss and Tell*, 22.

60 "*Sex and the City* is about": Ibid., 86.

65 "Pillar Box Red": Patricia Field, "Fashion Icons with Fern Mallis," 92Y, December 14, 2016.

65 one-bedroom apartment: Ibid.

65 a name change: Ibid.

66 "come from our school": Nancy Hass, "'Sex' Sells, in the City and Elsewhere," *New York Times*, July 11, 1999.

66 signature piece of jewelry: Field, "Fashion Icons."

67 "Every woman has a name": Ibid.

67 "they weren't teenagers": Ibid.

71 five dollars in a wholesale showroom: Ibid.

72 debate with King: "Cynthia Nixon (Miranda)," *People Extra: All About Sex and the City*, June 2001.

72 obstruction of a sidewalk: James Barron with Phoebe Hoban, "Public Lives; Out and About," *New York Times*, March 4, 1998.

73 "new millennium Noël Coward": Michael Patrick King, interview by Nancy Harrington, Archive of American Television, May 25, 2011, Burbank, CA.

73 "the opportunity to form this new show": Ibid.

4

The Show Everyone Wants to Live In

78 "find it saucy and smart": "Sex and Sarah Jessica Parker," *Cincinnati Post*, June 5, 1998.

78 "Sarah Jessica Parker has an in-your-face face": Tom Shales, "On HBO, Meaningless 'Sex,'" June 6, 1998.

79 "While this show is probably too depressing": Ellen Gray, Knight-Ridder, "Cable's Summer Fare: Sex, Lies and Videotape," *Chicago Tribune*, September 8, 1998.

80 "so self-consciously arch": Steve Parks, "'Sex and the City' Is Simply Insipid," *Newsday*, May 31, 1998.

80 "Maybe I'm too old": Eric Mink, "'Sex and the City': Even Once Is Too Much," *Daily News*, June 4, 1998.

80 "From the Greeks": Michael Kilian, "Sex, Comedy Come Together Well in 'Sex and the City,'" *Chicago Tribune*, June 25, 1998.

81 No. 10 on the cable Nielsen ratings chart: Brian Lowry, "NBA Finals Lead NBC Past Slumping Opponents," *Los Angeles Times*, June 10, 1998.

82 "The straight types": Hass, "'Sex' Sells."

82 "The reason the show works": Ibid.

87 long-running grudge: Rebecca Traister, *All the Single Ladies* (New York: Simon & Schuster, 2016), 92–93.

87 *New Yorker* TV critic Emily Nussbaum: Ibid., 93.

87 "If *Sex and the City* used shoes": Ibid., 94.

88 Editor Tia Williams had a slightly different experience: Tia Williams, "Commentary: Where Are the Black Women in 'SATC'?" Essence .com, May 31, 2010.

89 "the revolution that reclaimed": *UnCabaret* (official website), accessed August 26, 2017, http://uncabaret.com/.

90 "The creative dialogue": Gary R. Edgerton and Jeffrey P. Jones, eds., *The Essential HBO Reader* (Lexington: University Press of Kentucky, 2008), 199.

94 "David's a real guy": "David Eigenberg (Steve)," *People Extra: All About Sex and the City*, June 2001.

96 Mae West and Madeline Kahn: Sohn, *Sex and the City: Kiss and Tell*, 108.

97 "worthwhile read": Amazon.com review of *Satisfaction*, by Kim Cattrall and Mark Levinson, accessed August 26, 2017, https://www.amazon .com/Satisfaction-Female-Orgasm-Kim-Cattrall/dp/0446690902.

97 "thoughtful manual": "Satisfaction: The Art of the Female Orgasm," *Publishers Weekly*, January 1, 2002.

97 "Women who have been": Sohn, *Sex and the City: Kiss and Tell*, 108.

97 Pleasure Chest reported a flood of requests: David Kushner, "Joystick Nation," *Village Voice*, March 30, 1999.

97 "hot woman of a certain age": "Hot Woman of a Certain Age: Kim Cattrall," *Rolling Stone*, August 19, 1999.

97 HBO threw dozens: Hass, " 'Sex' Sells."

98 Cleveland, Providence, and Baton Rouge: Ibid.

98 beat competition: Ibid.

98 Cable viewership had risen: Gloria Goodale, "Cable Steals the Summer," *Christian Science Monitor*, July 23, 1999.

98 "The series reportedly has a substantial following": Tom Shales, "Cable Gets Fresh, Scores with Viewers," *Washington Post*, June 5, 1999.

98 "multidimensional": Ileane Rudolph, " 'Sex' and the Married Girl," *TV Guide*, June 6, 1998.

99 "Back for a second season": Steve Johnson, "Hollow Ring," *Chicago Tribune*, June 4, 1999.

5

A Very High Altitude

102 "The charge leveled": Molly Haskell, "Masculine Feminine," *Film Comment*, March/April 1974.

102 chosen with care: "Clotheshorse Carrie," *People Extra: All About Sex and the City*, June 2001.

103 Noth thought of: "Chris Noth (Mr. Big)," *People Extra: All About Sex and the City*, June 2001.

103 Parker required a tetanus shot: Sohn, *Sex and the City: Kiss and Tell*, 98.

104 "had not gotten": Sherryl Connelly, "Best Man for the Job," *Daily News*, August 13, 2000.

104 threw a glitzy premiere party: "They're Hot and Heavy for 'Sex,'" *Yahoo! Travel*, May 31, 2000.

104 "teetering": DeNeen L. Brown, "'90210' Creator's New Zipper Code," *Washington Post*, March 17, 2000.

104 75 percent: Hilary De Vries, "Laugh Track," *Chicago Tribune*, February 28, 2001.

104 at least six shows: Ibid.

105 "Absolutely that series affected us": Ibid.

105 "being single is no longer": Stephanie Mansfield, "Sexy Success," *USA Weekend*, May 26–28, 2000.

108 "As many times": Naveen Kumar, "The Problematic *SATC* Scene No One Talks About," *Refinery29*, May 26, 2016.

112 building a house in West Virginia: Sohn, *Sex and the City: Kiss and Tell*, 115.

112 He couldn't do it: Marta Jary, "'She Needed to End Up with Mr. Big,'" *Daily Mail*, August 21, 2017.

113 "As soon as she opened": Ibid.

113 "You don't want it": Sohn, *Sex and the City: Kiss and Tell*, 86.

114 "My straight friends": Kate Silver, "(Straight) Girls' Night: Biphobia in Sex and the City," *Persephone Magazine*, October 18, 2011.

115 "This type of pandering": Adia Harvey Wingfield, "Race and 'Sex and the City,'" *Racism Review*, June 19, 2008.

121 "the male *Sex and the City*": Hilary De Vries, "Television Hit Man," *Los Angeles*, November 2000.

6

Shopping and Fucking

124 Magnolia Bakery opened at the corner of Bleecker and West 11th Street: "About Us," Magnolia Bakery, accessed August 27, 2017, https://www.magnoliabakery.com/about-us/.

124 a joint venture between high school friends: Adam Sternbergh, "Sweet and Vicious," *New York*, September 19, 2005.

124 talking parrots: Melissa Kravitz, "Secrets of Magnolia Bakery," *amNewYork*, May 7, 2016.

124 Lines snaked around the block: Robert Sietsema, "Me and Magnolia: Life Before and After the Cupcake Bomb Went Off," *Eater*, July 14, 2016.

124 "bouncer": Ibid.

124 the proprietors had recommended: Natasha Burton and Carina Hsieh, "A Brief History of the Rabbit," Cosmopolitan.com, February 9, 2015.

125 the top-selling sex toy of all time: Burton and Hsieh, "A Brief History of the Rabbit."

125 "the ultimate freedom we were permitted": Laurie Penny, *Unspeakable Things* (New York: Bloomsbury USA, 2014), 259.

125 "I think the chic aesthetic": Julia Szabo, "Defining the N.Y. Woman," *New York Post*, June 10, 1998.

127 did make the show pay: Whitney Bauck, "Christian Louboutin on Putting Butcher Meat in High Heels, and Other Secrets from His Decades-Long Career," *Fashionista*, May 18, 2017.

127 "Nothing is great publicity": Rosemary Feitelberg, "Christian Louboutin on His Roundabout Route to Shoe Design," *Los Angeles Times*, May 19, 2017.

127 custom mules: Field, "Fashion Icons."

128 seven-hundred-square-foot apartment: "Carrie's Apartment," *People Extra: All About Sex and the City*, June 2001.

128 eleven-by-four-foot walk-in closet: "Carrie's Apartment," *People Extra: All About Sex and the City*.

129 "Manolo Blahnik is considered": Sarah Niblock, "'My Manolos, My Self': Manolo Blahnik, Shoes, and Desire," in *Reading Sex and the City*, eds. Kim Akass and Janet McCabe (London: I. B. Tauris & Co., 2004), 144.

129 "I know the boys": Field, "Fashion Icons."

129 Rihanna would later recall falling in love: Nicole Phelps, "Rihanna Could Collaborate with Anyone, She Chose Manolo Blahnik Because 'His Craftsmanship Is Like No Other,'" Vogue.com, May 1, 2016.

129 "Carrie dresses more quirkily": Sohn, *Sex and the City: Kiss and Tell*, 70.

129 "Pat gives me credit": Sohn, *Sex and the City: Kiss and Tell*, 70.

129 about $2,000 total: Jessica Chou, "Proof That Carrie Bradshaw's Outfits Were Totally Unrealistic," *Refinery29*, October 15, 2015.

129 more than $23,000: Ibid.

133 the Odeon: Marion Bernstein, "Famous Cocktails Invented in NYC Bars," *Time Out New York*, January 20, 2017.

133 helped boost drinking culture: Katy Brand, "Sex and the City Blamed for Death of 'Good Wife'? Bottoms Up," *Telegraph*, April 3, 2013.

133 "Even the women": Ginger Hale, "Sober in the City: Redefining My Queerness on Fire Island," *Autostraddle*, May 8, 2014.

135 stoked tensions: Sternbergh, "Sweet and Vicious."

135 explained the discrepancy: Ibid.

135 "They completely badmouth us": Ibid.

136 "A lot of people are very business-oriented": Ibid.

7

Van Talk, Real Talk

140 "People watch the show": Sohn, *Sex and the City: Kiss and Tell*, 36.

141 "major tension": Beth Landman and Ian Spiegelman, "*Sex and the City*—Who's *Really* Big?" *New York*, February 12, 2001.

141 "Sarah's a businesswoman": Ibid.

141 "surprised" at the rumors: "Cattrall Slams Sex and the City Rift," *Times of India*, July 31, 2001.

142 "*The Sopranos* never": Zoe Williams, "Just Fancy . . ." *Guardian*, January 4, 2002.

143 Several media accounts: Susan Ferraro, "No Laughing Matter," *Daily News*, June 7, 2001.

143 "The pain can get so bad": Wendy Navratil, "HBO Aside, Vulvodynia Can Be Painfully True Story," *Chicago Tribune*, June 13, 2001.

160 "Both she and the city": Julie Salamon, "The Relevance of 'Sex' in a City That's Changed," *New York Times*, July 21, 2002.

160 had wanted to be an actress: Heather Wood Rudúlph, "Get That Life: How I Became a Writer on 'Sex and the City' and an Author of 'He's Just Not That into You,'" Cosmopolitan.com, March 2, 2015.

161 as Tuccillo later said, "raw": Ibid.

161 how "entrenched" she was: Ibid.

161 "You're formidable": Ibid.

163 went into production: Michael Schneider, "Comic-Scribe Toll Succumbs at Age 44," *Variety*, May 7, 2002.

163 platinum Tiffany rings: Morris, "Candace Bushnell, Charles Askegard."

163 "One has to be": Ibid.

164 "Candace Bushnell gets married": Ibid.

164 "*Sex and the City* is clearly not a show": James Alan Frutkin, "The Return of the Show That Gets Gay Life Right," *New York Times*, January 6, 2002.

164 "Most gay characters": Ibid.

165 inform teenage girls: Sarah Hepola, "Her Favorite Class: 'Sex' Education," *New York Times*, June 22, 2003.

165 girls as young as thirteen: Anne Jarrell, "The Face of Teenage Sex Grows Younger," *New York Times*, April 2, 2000.

165 "exemplary job incorporating": Robin E. Jensen and Jakob D. Jensen, "Entertainment Media and Sexual Health: A Content Analysis of Sexual Talk, Behavior, and Risks in a Popular Television Series," *Sex Roles* 56, nos. 5–6 (March 2007).

165 "I'm not doing that": Whyte, "Kim Cattrall Talks to Kenneth Whyte."

165 "This isn't about being conservative": Ibid.

9

Happy Endings

172 press attention would not let up: Matthew Breen, "Cynthia Nixon Is More Than Just *Sex*," *Advocate*, May 10, 2010.

172   "nothing to hide": Sarah Warn, "Cynthia Nixon in Relationship with a Woman," *AfterEllen*, September 24, 2004.

175   "By trying so hard": Sally Holmes, "The Story Behind the 'Sex and the City' Post-it Breakup," Elle.com, December 13, 2014.

175   defected in 1974: Martin Knelman, "Baryshnikov's Defection Is One for the Books," *Toronto Star*, October 5, 2010.

176   "When exec producer Michael Patrick King": Michael Ausiello, "Sarah Jessica Defends Baryshnikov Casting," *TV Guide Online*, August 4, 2003.

178   "sologamy": Helen Thomas, "What Is Sologamy? The New Wedding Trend of Marrying Yourself—All You Need to Know," *Sun*, February 20, 2017.

180   calling the lack of diversity "irresponsible": Lauren Johnston, "'Sex and the City' Diversifies," Associated Press, August 18, 2003.

180   "Women of color have laughed": Samhita Mukhopadhyay, "Sex and the City's Women of Color Problem," *Feministing*, June 3, 2010.

181   "Showing that people of color": Hunter Harris, "For Women of Color Who Love *Sex and the City*," *Refinery29*, July 19, 2016.

181   "fierce, single black women": Traister, *All the Single Ladies*, 71.

181   "bodacious and bold": "Single Women in TV History," *People Extra: All About Sex and the City*, June 2001.

182   "I always say": Angela Watercutter, "*Insecure*'s Issa Rae Knows Way More About Female Comedies Than You," Wired.com, October 17, 2016.

186   "all of her finery": Patricia Field, interview by Bonnie Datt, Archive of American Television, October 18, 2011, New York, NY.

187   "The more heightened that gown was": Ibid.

188   "That is the way": Ibid.

190   "In real life, Carrie and Big wouldn't": Jake Nevins, "Candace Bushnell: 'In Real Life, Carrie and Big Wouldn't Have Ended Up Together,'" *Guardian*, July 3, 2017.

10
Ever Thine, Ever Mine, Ever Ours

191 thirty thousand to four hundred thousand: John Stossel, "He's Just Not That into You," ABC News, October 22, 2004.

191 "evil genius": Rick Marin, "For Women Who Count on Men to Be Jerks," *New York Times*, October 17, 2004.

192 "'Busy' is another word": Greg Behrendt and Liz Tuccillo, *He's Just Not That into You* (New York: Simon Spotlight Entertainment, 2004), 34.

192 "Men are never too busy": Ibid., 30.

192 "Let's start with": Ibid., 145.

195 "I'm just not that into them": Maureen Dowd, "Courting the Finicky Women," *New York Times*, October 15, 2004.

196 "icon of the decade": Naomi Wolf, "Carrie Bradshaw: Icons of the Decade," *Guardian*, December 21, 2009.

197 encapsulating all of these changes: Jesse Oxfeld, "Yesterday, an Oppressed Minority, Today, an Old Maid," *Observer*, June 27, 2013.

197 unmarried women outnumbered: Mark Mather and Diana Lavery, "In U.S., Proportion Married at Lowest Recorded Levels," Population Reference Bureau, 2010.

197 "After I suffered through": Ryan Roschke, "How Sex and the City Helped Me Through My First Big Breakup," *PopSugar*, February 10, 2016.

198 once again mentioned the supposed rift: Mara Reinstein, "Is There a Sex and the City Feud?" *Us Weekly*, March 15, 2004.

198 *Newsweek* reported: Ibid.

198 Parker mentioned Davis and Nixon: Ibid.

198 At that year's Golden Globes: Ibid.

198 HBO confirmed: Joey Bartolomeo, "The Sex and the City Movie Drama," *Us Weekly*, June 14, 2004.

198 "Kim and the girls": Ibid.

198 *Variety* reported: Ibid.

198 Davis was "pleading": "Kristin Davis in a Sex Film," *Times of India*, November 19, 2006.

198 "I ain't got no rich husband": Whyte, "Kim Cattrall Talks to Kenneth Whyte."

199 "You know your counterpart's": Ibid.

199 "I had a clear, emotional reaction": A. J. Frutkin, "Nets Look to Sex," *Mediaweek*, September 17, 2007.

199 "It's interesting": Ibid.

200 green light in July 2007: Reuters, "'Sex and the City' Headed to Movie Theaters," July 5, 2007.

200 "Don't you feel": Whyte, "Kim Cattrall Talks to Kenneth Whyte."

200 racks full of wedding dresses: Field, "Fashion Icons."

202 "It is difficult to locate": Mandy Len Catron, *How to Fall in Love with Anyone* (New York: Simon & Schuster, 2017), 167.

202 $26 million on its opening night: Michael Cieply and Bill Carter, "'Sex and the City' Leads Weekend Box Office," *New York Times*, June 2, 2008.

203 $56 million in its first weekend: Ibid.

203 biggest opening ever: Ibid.

203 Analysts were surprised: Ibid.

203 "the best American movie about women": Mick LaSalle, "Movie Review: 'Sex' Improves with Age," *San Francisco Chronicle*, May 29, 2008.

204 declined to allow: Nicholas McGeehan, "Sex and the City 2 in Abu Dhabi? Carrie, This Is Wrong," *Guardian*, May 18, 2010.

204 "Twenty minutes in": Mick LaSalle, "Review: 'Sex and the City 2,'" *San Francisco Chronicle*, May 28, 2010.

204 "as cheesy as a bad designer knockoff": Thelma Adams, "Review: 'Sex and the City 2,'" *Us Weekly*, May 26, 2010.

204 "squealing audience stampede": Kate Stables, "Sex and the City 2," *Sight & Sound*, August 2010.

204 "not-very-convincing rumination": Brian Lowry, "Review: 'Sex and the City 2,'" *Variety*, May 23, 2010.

205 "With his Cosmopolitan-style approach": Claudia Puig, "Tasteless 'Sex and the City 2' Stumbles Badly," *USA Today*, May 27, 2010.

205 "I understand, I actually get it": Yohana Desta, "Sarah Jessica Parker Totally Gets Why Fans Hate *Sex and the City 2*," VanityFair.com, May 21, 2017.

205 "more mature": Jessica Finn, "They're Back! 'Sex and the City' Cast Officially Signed on to Film Third Movie," *Radar Online*, December 22, 2016.

207 "Creating a field": David Rooney, "Review: 'Rabbit Hole,'" *Variety*, February 2, 2006.

207 announced her engagement: Katherine Thomson, "Cynthia Nixon Engaged to Christine Marinoni," *Huffington Post*, June 17, 2009.

207 "We could go to Canada": "Cynthia Nixon Welcomes a Son with Partner Christine Marinoni," *Los Angeles Times*, February 8, 2011.

207 That October she spoke: "'Obama, I Know You Are Listening': Gay Rights Activists March in D.C.," CNN.com, October 12, 2009.

207 Nixon married Marinoni: Tim Nudd, "Cynthia Nixon and Christine Marinoni Get Married," People.com, May 28, 2012.

207 King presented Nixon: Sara Werner, "Cynthia Nixon and Joy Behar Honored at the 21st Annual GLAAD Media Awards in New York," GLAAD.org, March 13, 2010.

208 "Ironically, since Carrie is still a virgin": Tim Goodman, "The Carrie Diaries: TV Review," *Hollywood Reporter*, January 14, 2013.

208 "The problem is that": Matt Zoller Seitz, "Seitz on *The Carrie Diaries*: Everything About This *Sex and the City* Prequel Feels Wrong," *New York*, January 14, 2013.

209 "The condescension is palpable": Emily Nussbaum, "Difficult Women," *New Yorker*, July 29, 2013.

210 "What I find so unusual": Starlee Kine, "The Best Sitcom of the Past 30 Years, Round One: *Sex and the City* vs. *30 Rock*," *Vulture*, March 6, 2013.

210 "I watch *Sex and the City*": Alexandra Klausner, "Carrie Dragshaw Is NYC's New 'Sex and the City' Fashion Icon," *New York Post*, May 2, 2017.

212 "This is not Carrie in the suburbs": Susan Dominus, "Sarah Jessica Parker, Leaving Carrie Behind with HBO's 'Divorce,'" *New York Times*, September 22, 2016.

Interview List

STEVE ABRAMS, via phone, September 26, 2016.

JULIE ARMSTRONG, via email, July 4, 2017.

ANDREA BARTZ, via email, August 22, 2017.

GREG BEHRENDT, via phone, October 5, 2016.

JEN BERGSTROM, via phone, May 23, 2017.

JENNY BICKS, via phone, September 19, 2016.

GEORGETTE BLAU, in New York, September 19, 2016.

CANDACE BUSHNELL, in New York, January 25, 2017.

VERONICA CHAMBERS, via email, August 22, 2017.

CINDY CHUPACK, via phone, December 1, 2016.

ALLEN COULTER, via phone, October 9, 2016.

DOUGLAS CUOMO, via phone, September 28, 2016.

KRISTIN DAVIS, via phone, February 15, 2017.

DAVID EIGENBERG, via phone, February 7, 2017.

JULIE EISEN, via email, July 12, 2017.

Interview List

MICHAEL ENGLER, via phone, September 1, 2016.

DENNIS ERDMAN, via phone, September 28, 2016.

BARBARA GARRICK, in New York, August 31, 2016.

MICHAEL GREEN, via phone, November 3, 2016.

AMY B. HARRIS, via phone, August 2, 2017.

MICHAEL PATRICK KING, via phone, February 8, 2017.

ALISON MACLEAN, via phone, September 26, 2016.

MOISES MENDEZ, via email, July 14, 2017.

ADAM NEAL, via email, July 13, 2017.

SARAH JESSICA PARKER, in New York City, February 10, 2017.

JULIE ROTTENBERG and ELISA ZURITSKY, in Brooklyn, September 28, 2016.

ELIZABETH SCHAP, via email, July 13, 2017.

SUSAN SEIDELMAN, via phone, September 26, 2016.

MICHAEL SPILLER, via phone, August 31, 2016.

DARREN STAR, via phone, March 10, 2017.

CAROLYN STRAUSS, via phone, May 24, 2017.

JAMIE TARSES, via phone, June 15, 2017.

About the Author

Jennifer Keishin Armstrong is the author of the *New York Times* bestseller *Seinfeldia: How the Show About Nothing Changed Everything* and *Mary and Lou and Rhoda and Ted*, a history of *The Mary Tyler Moore Show*. She was on staff at *Entertainment Weekly* for a decade and now writes for BBC Culture, *Dame*, *Vulture*, *Billboard*, and others.